About the Author

"Bob Bone is both widely traveled and keenly observant, someone who knew the Hawaiian islands when they were unspoiled, and was a friend to Hunter Thompson on the Proud Highway when he was maniacal - in short, a reliable witness."
— **Paul Theroux, premier travel writer and novelist, author of** *The Great Railway Bazaar*

"Bob Bone was one hell of a reporter-photographer when we worked together so long ago on the (San Juan) *Star*. Now he's summing up his life and he's got a mountain of great stuff to sum up. *Arriba! Roberto*."
— **William J. Kennedy, author of** *Ironweed* **and other books**

"During my 19 years as travel editor of the *St. Petersburg Times*, I was fortunate to have a go-to guy if I needed readable, authoritative, articles on Hawaii and the Pacific: Bob Bone. And I feel certain that all of my editing colleagues also recognized that byline as the specialist on the islands. Bob earned our respect, even our appreciation, with his fine writing."
— **Robert N. Jenkins**

"Bob Bone has been a truly professional travel author virtually for time immemorial. During my time as travel editor of the Chicago Sun-Times in 1982-1994, he was a highly reliable source of lively and accurate stories from around the world."
— **Jack Schnedler, retired, a Lowell Thomas Travel Journalist of the Year laureate**

"Bob's insightful and sensitive approach to travel writing during his lifetime comes across in this bio that covers some of America's more fascinating sociological and technological changes."
— **Jeff Miller, author and former editor,** *Encompass* **magazine**

"Robert W. Bone was a frank and diligent source when I was researching my biography of Hunter S. Thompson. Bob's long career turns out to be as varied, adventurous and fascinating as his friend's." — **E. Jean Carroll, author, relationship expert, and advice columnist for *Elle* and other publications**

"Bob Bone played a vital role in the golden age of newspaper-section travel journalism. His memoir recreates for us those heady times." — **Lee Foster, author of *Northern California Travel* as well as many other books, and a recipient of eight SATW Lowell Thomas Awards**

"While surfing the media I usually look for three clues to the readability of a story: the publication, the writer's byline and the headline. I've learned over the years that when I spot Bob Bone's byline, it's a safe bet the story is worth reading. I need mull my interest no further." — **Bob Schulman, Travel Editor, *WatchBoom.com***

"There is definitely something wrong with Bob Bone. Here's a guy living in Hawaii, and he wants to—loves to—travel to places where they sometimes actually have to wear jackets, if not snow suits. It was my pleasure in 16 years as travel editor at the *Chicago Tribune* to read and run his delightfully skewered stories on places where the weather might not have been perfect but the experiences through his eyes and words were perfectly wonderful." — **Randy Curwen**

"While some journey for relaxation, Bob Bone has always had something else in mind: sharing the joy of travel with others and helping them find their own adventures, discovering new horizons in unlikely places." — **Larry Bleiberg, former travel editor of the *Dallas Morning News***

"When we needed first-rate coverage on Hawaii, Bob Bone was our go-to guy." — **Al Borcover, retired travel editor, *Chicago Tribune***

For Libby Smith Aloha, Bob 8-1-2014

FIRE BONE!

A Maverick Guide to a Life in Journalism

Robert W. Bone

Peripety Press U.S.A.
WALNUT CREEK, CALIFORNIA

Peripety Press U.S.A.
1901 Skycrest Dr., Ste. 4
Walnut Creek, CA 94595
www.peripetypress.com

Ordering Information:
Quantity sales. Special discounts are available on quantity purchases by corporations, associations, and others. For details, contact the "Special Sales Department" at the address above.

FIRE BONE! A Maverick Guide to a Life in Journalism
Robert W. Bone. — 1st ed.
ISBN 978-0-9905091-0-3
Library of Congress Control Number: 2014942894

For my immediate family,
Sara, Christina, David, Gracie, Harley and Robert.

Also dedicated to the memory of my parents and grandparents,
and to that of three special friends,
Howard Rausch, Mal Browne, and Hunter Thompson,
all of whom didn't survive nearly long enough.

About the Title

Throughout six decades of my professional life,
I've never been fired from a job.
Perhaps there were some who would like to have
seen that come to pass.
But only one tried to do it.
"Fire Bone!" the big boss ordered.
Yet it didn't happen.

This book would not have been possible without the contributions, insights and assistance of the following:

Nita Alspach, Amy Apel, Norbert Baer, Tony Bartlett, Peggy Bendel, Vera Benedek, Bruce Benson, George Beres, David Bridge, Muriel Buriff, Ian Cameron, E. Jean Carroll, Richard Carroll, Rick Carroll, Richard Clark, Patricia Coil, Ulla Colgrass, Georgia M. Coxe, Randy Curwen, Timothy deMeza, William B. deMeza Jr., Sheila Donnelly, Eleanor Egan, Elizabeth Evans, Jesse Fahnders, E. Jerome Felty, Lee Foster, Anne Harpham, Candy Harrington, Virginia Hynes, Donald Hinkle, Penny Hinkle, Jerry Hodgson, Robert Hollis, Robert Jenkins, Russ Johnson, Bob Jones, Nadine Kam, Sally Kaptein, Mary Helen Kaser, Edward Kennedy, William J. Kennedy, Stefan Ketele II, Terese Kreuzer, John Kroll, Spencer Leifheit, Dorothy Loeffler, Christine Loomis, James Loomis, Peter Mandel, Linda McCrerey, Jeff Miller, Carol Mulvehill, Dan Myers, Gale Myers, Lee Nelson, Darlen Obertance, Jules Older, Carolyn Pappas, Mary Poole, Ann Schaller, Bob Schulman, Ruth Schwartz, Richard Short, Paulo Silva Jr., Lisa Sonne, Roberta Sotonoff, Shirley Streshinsky, John Strobel, Paul Theroux, David Tong, Victor Waldrop, Paul Weisser, Baba White, Bill Williamson, Stan Wawer, Sondi Wright, Walter Wright, David Yamada, Orah Young, and Ron Youngblood. And with equally grateful appreciation to the inevitable forgotten person.

TABLE OF CONTENTS

FIRE BONE!

A Maverick Guide to a Life in Journalism

PROLOGUE

LIKE ANY WRITER WITH A LONG CAREER, I've come across some of the world's more interesting characters. A few became good friends.

Perhaps the most fascinating was Hunter, who first appeared to me as an eccentric fellow reporter on the Middletown (N.Y.) *Daily Record* in 1958. This was Hunter S. Thompson, destined to become widely known as the inventor of the "gonzo" personal approach to literature and journalism.

For better or for worse, Hunter eventually became an inspiration to scores of younger writers, some of whom are still attempting to copy his techniques.

Hunter killed himself in 2005. His outdoor Colorado funeral was built to his personal instructions. It was a spectacular affair, enveloped in noise, fire and smoke. It included a contingent of his Hollywood buddies along with other hangers-on attracted to greatness. I was invited, but didn't go. Hunter wouldn't be there.

Our close association formed when we were equally unknown to the world at large. In the 1950s and '60s Hunter and I shared adventures in New York, Puerto Rico, and Brazil.

For a time I was in love with Sandra Conklin, who later became Hunter's first wife. In late 1961 and early 1962, Sandy and I lived together in Greenwich Village. Hunter was in Louisville, preparing to begin his travels in South America on meager funds, gathering material for his literary objectives.

1

There would be no place for a gentle soul like Sandy on his precarious trip. And on the second floor rear left flat at 107 Thompson Street in Greenwich Village, I was acutely aware that Sandy was definitely "Hunter's girl."

I was 30 and a junior editor at *Popular Photography* magazine, and I happily returned each evening to the three-room apartment, usually to find a waiting meal and pleasant conversation. It was a safe address, located across the street from the mother of a local underworld figure. The goodfellas, playing bocce or hanging out on the corner, enforced peace and quiet when needed.

There Sandy and I made beer and enjoyed each other's company without the aid of sex or television. She slept in my bedroom; I slept in the living room; the sound of bubbling beer continued day and night in a large jug atop the refrigerator in the kitchen between us. That's all there was, but it was enough.

Except for once. On our last night together she came into the living room without a word and laid down beside me. We went to sleep with my arm wrapped around her.

Each five-gallon batch of our home brew was known as a "baby," and we kept detailed records of the process. We got as far as "Baby Five," I think, before my love was spirited away.

PART 1

1932 to 1957

The last time I was the center of attention.
Standing (left) Aunt Dick and Grandma (right). Others unknown.

1
Pekin & Gary

"LOOK AT THAT BACKBONE! Now that's what I call a good, strong back!"

That was reportedly said by my grandfather at my debut on the 15th of September 1932, at a maternity hospital in Gary, Indiana.

My interests in travel, photography, writing, and music began early. I was raised in three cities, two of them at the same time: Gary, Indiana, and Pekin, Illinois. My grandparents lived in Gary, and my father was the art instructor at Pekin Community High School.

A blue-collar town on the Illinois River, Pekin is almost a suburb of the better-known Peoria, and many Pekinites built a successful lifetime career in Peoria's large Caterpillar tractor factory. Others worked in Pekin's smoky Corn Products plant alongside the river south of town, turning out the basic glutens and starches to be converted into syrups, corn oils, and breakfast foods.

Pekin's claim to fame was as the home of the colorful U. S. Senator Everett Dirksen, the flamboyant foghorned-voiced orator who *Harper's* magazine dubbed "the wizard of ooze." The senator represented Illinois for 35 years in Washington and also found time to cut inspirational record albums, once even winning a Grammy. My father knew him, and I often ran across his nephew, though Tommy Dirksen was a couple of years my senior.

As a member of what *Time* magazine dubbed the Silent Generation, I was too young for the Greatest Generation and too old for the Baby Boomers. But like most arbitrary labels, though, this one made no sense. I was far from silent, and neither were others of a similar age.

The 1930s were those desperate times that called for desperate measures. My parents' method of coping with the Great Depression was inspired. At the beginning of each school year my father rented a furnished house or apartment in Pekin for only nine months. Then we moved out again in June, saving three months' rent. Our home on any subsequent school year was apt to be at a different address from the previous one. Sometimes we would return to a place we had lived in two or three years before.

At Christmas, Easter, and throughout the summer, I was with my grandparents. There was no air conditioning to mask the summer sounds of Gary. On warm July nights I went to sleep near the window at my grandparents' house at 637 Virginia Street, listening to the whistles and chug-a-chuffs of far-away steam engines, speculating on where these trains came from and where they were going. I also wondered where Mother and Daddy were, too, catching on only gradually that they were in New York taking advanced classes at Columbia University.

I had my Gary friends, like Lannie Prescott, and my Pekin friends, like Pat Joe Tobin. The only time Lannie and Pat Joe ever met was in my dreams. Mine was truly a bifurcated world.

The constant changes of residence – short periods in Gary and changing addresses in Pekin – set me up for a lifetime of seeing the new as the norm. I learned to like waking up and being surprised by my surroundings. After nearly a lifetime of professional travel, I still do.

My mother's name was Georgia Juanita Clapp, and her nuclear family lived in an economically depressed area in southern Illinois. She often told me that she had a difficult life before meeting my father, leaving me to speculate on the details.

I do know she worked hard to get an education, mostly in opposition to her family's wishes. I recall only once being introduced to her parents, along with a sister and a brother. Her father's first name was Pearl, and I can only imagine what effect that might have had.

She also had dropped her first name in favor of her second, and by the time I came along, most called her "Nita." Few knew of her childhood struggles, and my father's family quickly became my mother's family.

My paternal grandfather, William Bone, affectionately called her "Piffle," and she called him "Dad." And speaking of nicknames, my father often called me "Epaminondas." I never knew why he came up with that multisyllabic moniker, but somehow it pleased me, perhaps because it was always accompanied by a warm smile. (At school, of course, I was often known by some of my classmates as "Bonehead" and similar phrases.)

While I loved my parents, I also resented some things. Both were prize-winning contract bridge players, and when they came home from a session, they were more interested in deconstructing the evening than in talking with me.

"Then the damn fool trumped my ace!" I can still hear that in my mother's voice. My father was more subdued, often punctuating his comments with a short simple laugh.

Mother also spent considerable time practicing the flute, resolutely refusing to stop playing when her little boy wanted her attention and affection. Or so it seemed to me. I avoided flutes and bridge the rest of my life, and gave no credence to my mother's later contention that I should at least learn bridge in order to become a social success.

Still, there were nice touches in our relationship. In her efforts to get me to eat my oatmeal, Mother would draw into it a map of Winnie the Pooh Land, and I might choose to chew my way from Pooh Corner to Christopher Robin's house. Her inspired technique was later described by Shirley Streshinsky in the book *Oats!* (Celestial Arts, 1996).

Both my parents were smokers – especially my mother, who often kept a cigarette going all through a meal. That was acceptable in those days. So I guess I was a second-hand smoker long before I ever lit my own.

During World War II, they had a small cigarette-rolling device, and I mastered filling it with tobacco and attaching the special papers. I took some pride in turning out dozens of professional-looking cigarettes when bridge-playing company was expected that evening.

My primary schools switched frequently because of those dizzily changing Pekin addresses. When we lived at 1301 Market Street, I attended first grade with my first love – Miss Higgins – at Garfield

School. Later, while we were in residence at 503 Willow Street, I was at Lincoln School, where the sixth grade was guided by the imposing, full-figured Mrs. Lohnes.

Her nephew was also in my class. Once, when Mrs. Lohnes was out of the room, Billy Lohnes did a side-splitting imitation of his aunt with two volleyballs tucked up under his shirt, upon which he rested his forearm, just as she did. That may be when I became intrigued with women's breasts.

Seventh and eighth grades were at the Pekin's Washington Junior High School, where bald Mr. Abernathy, a shop teacher, had long ago lost some fingers on an electric saw blade. He had a habit of surprising misbehaving or sleepy-headed students from behind with a "nodder" – a sudden scrape on the scalp with those tough, unfeeling stubs.

I was sick a lot in grade school, a fact attributed to the fact that I had barely survived a severe bout of pneumonia when I was three, before sulfa drugs or antibiotics were known. Mother often kept me home from class, and my education was supplemented by radio soap operas and books, the latter including the inspiring travel accounts by Richard Halliburton. I also liked the American History books for children by Sadyebeth and Anson Lowitz – the *Pilgrim's Party* and several others.

Comic books were generally prohibited by my parents. My grandparents, however, easily caved on the stricture, so I read *Superman*, *Captain Marvel*, etc., during those Gary summers.

Because I wasn't good at sports, I eventually decided they were pretty much a waste of time. When teams were chosen up in gym class, I was always the last one picked:

"OK, come on, Bone," they said.

My father and I often went to the library together, where I picked out gems like the "Oz" books, by L. Frank Baum. I also read Greek mythology plus Mark Twain's adventures of Tom Sawyer and Huckleberry Finn in the original versions. In those years they were not controversial. A chapter in the latter entitled "Peter and the Pain Killer" once had me in stitches.

During these home periods my mother taught me some French. I could sing simple songs like *Frère Jacques* and something about a shepherdess that went: *Il y a était une bergère, et ron, ron, ron, petit pi patapon.* I think some of this was before I could even read *any* language, even English.

Mother did not have a Gallic background, but she had been a straight "A" student in French at the University of Illinois.

Grandpa bought me a jigsaw puzzle that was a map of the United States, with the pieces cut out along state lines. Ever since that day, I have mostly been able to tell the states by their shapes and locations – although with only a 50 percent accuracy with New Hampshire and Vermont – two similar-sized and adjoining small states printed on a single piece of the puzzle. (In those days future states Alaska and Hawaii, of course, were not included.)

One thing was out of the question under our peripatetic living conditions – a family dog. Instead, we became cat people. My first cat was Petey, perhaps named after Twain's "Peter and the Pain Killer." Petey was given permanently to Shepherd's grocery when we made one of those summer moves to Gary. Petey and I had a special greeting. If I held my hand a little above his head, he would stand up tall on his hindquarters to be petted. For several years thereafter, I would occasionally return to the same small store even when we no longer lived in that neighborhood just to see if Petey still remembered to greet me in this fashion. He always did.

The second cat was Lillian Russell, and I don't remember what happened to her. My mother claimed Lillian had a certain show-biz personality and took more than a passing interest in the neighborhood toms.

The third and final cat was Topsy, a long-haired black female named after a character in *Uncle Tom's Cabin*, and she was my dependable, long-time companion when things became more unstable – almost as good as a nanny.

In Gary, Grandpa was a President Roosevelt hater during the Depression and the war. The fact that he religiously read Colonel McCormick's *Chicago Tribune*, which then fostered a very conservative point of view, probably had something to do with it.

Fifty years after the Attack on Pearl Harbor, on Saturday, December 7, 1991, and writing from my home in Honolulu, I scored a front page bylined Pearl Harbor anniversary story in the Tribune's "main sheet" – the very first page of the front section. How I wished my grandfather could have lived to see that.

I only remember my grandfather singing one song. He bounced me on his knee to the rhythm and sang:

I went to the animal fair; the birds and the beasts were there;
The old baboon, by the light of the moon, was combing his auburn hair.
The monkey he was drunk; he fell off the elephant's trunk:
The elephant sneezed, and fell on its knees;
And what became of the monk (the monk the monk the monk)?

Grandma, however, sang hymns and Christmas carols. She was a devout Methodist and sometimes took me to church or Sunday school in Gary. Grandpa would never go.

"If I went to church, Bobby, the roof would fall in!" he declared.

So I guessed he stayed home to protect the heads of Grandma and me.

He also had some special habits. When he shaved, he used a straight razor at his workbench down in the basement. And if I got too close, he took the brush and deftly placed a dab of shaving cream on my nose. I laughed and loved it.

G&G's Gary basement also boasted an old-fashioned, wind-up, non-electric Victrola, and dozens of my father's and my uncles' old 78-rpm records. So I learned a lot of unusual pop tunes of the 1920s like the "Blue Hoosier Blues," the "Charleston," the rather racy "I Used to Work in Chicago," and various vocals by Eddie Cantor and Al Jolson. (I still have a few of these disks.)

Will and Gertie Bone placed a lot of pride on my young shoulders. Although their art-teacher son, Robert Ordway Bone, was one of three brothers, he was the only one of the trio who had any offspring. That singular individual was I, Robert William. So I was fated to be the only Bone child in my generation, and the only hope that the family name and bloodline might someday be carried into the future.

My son David bore that same responsibility, until finally his own son put in an appearance. Harley Bone, a commercial artist in his 20s and still a bachelor, now has that heavy weight on his shoulders. If he ever stops to think about it.

Uncle Russell, who was married to Aunt Ruth, was an executive with the Anchor Hocking glass company somewhere in New Jersey. Everyone considered Ruth and Russell the most well-off members of the family – and also the most distant, in miles and in temperament, mixing more with the upper classes than we were accustomed to doing.

The third brother was Uncle Jay, a history teacher who lived with his fun-loving, former flapper Aunt Donna in Fremont, Ohio. He had a very prominent mark on his forehead. As a child, he was kicked by a horse, leaving a large and deep dent above the eyebrow.

Somehow, Uncle Jay's dented forehead always fascinated me, and if I drew him, the dent was always in the picture in exaggerated proportions.

"Who's that?" my mother asked.

"It's Uncle Jay!" I replied. "See the dent?"

Later, in the 1970s, Uncle Jay became an executive at the Quickcut knife factory in Fremont. He and others made it big when they renamed the Quickcut knives Ginsu (a Japanese-sounding word which actually doesn't mean a thing) and promoted them in national TV infomercials with a Samurai motif. They're still sold today.

The summer of 1939 was quite different from earlier summers. I was now six – almost seven. Instead of depositing me as usual in Gary, my parents took me to Manhattan. There my father finally received his Master's degree at Columbia Teachers College.

For three hot months we lived in Apartment 512, a furnished railroad flat in Bancroft Hall, 509 West 121st Street between Broadway and Amsterdam Avenue. There I enjoyed running the building's self-operated elevator, both for myself and for any grown-up who might come along.

Once I got stuck alone in that elevator for an uncomfortable length of time, until it finally disgorged me in the basement. What did I know? Elevators didn't exist in Pekin or Gary – well, at least not to my knowledge.

Thirteen years after that, I operated an elevator professionally for a time at the Hillcastle Apartment Hotel in Oakland, California. And still later, I got stuck for an hour in another one in Rio de Janeiro. Experiences with elevators and escalators seemed to have special meaning throughout much of my life – actually and symbolically.

That hot summer in 1939, my parents and I attended the New York World's Fair. Among other wonders, I was among a few privileged six-year-olds in the country who saw working television, a feature only available at the fair.

The theme of the exhibition was "The World of Tomorrow" and I'm still waiting to see all those family auto-gyros flying commuters to and from their jobs and landing on the roofs of Art Deco high-rise office buildings.

The fair took place while war was beginning in Europe, which cast a rather sour note for my parents and the other grown-ups attending. Everybody felt sorry for the personnel manning the Czechoslovakian and Polish pavilions after their countries were invaded.

I felt little of that, and concentrated on fun activities at the fair and the city in general, like the three of us climbing up inside the Statue of Liberty, until we peered out at New York Harbor from the windows in the crown.

We also explored the decks of the ill-fated French luxury liner *Normandie*. A short time after we left New York that magnificent ship mysteriously burned – allegedly sabotaged – and was partly sunk at its mooring. It remained a New York landmark while lying on its side at Pier 88 throughout the war years.

I remembered the Normandie again in 1957, when I sailed from the same or nearby dock on my own young adult adventure to Europe. And this would eventually lead me to work at a different world fair. I also sailed from about the same pier a dozen years after that with my wife and daughter in an uncertain career move to Spain.

I went to summer school in New York, too, with sophisticated, smart-aleck Manhattan kids, and ultimately starred in a classroom production of *Ferdinand the Bull*. Yes, I played Ferdinand himself, who renounced a violent career in the ring in favor of just sitting under a cork tree in Spain, smelling the flowers. *Ferdinand* was already one of my favorite books, and I felt especially honored to portray the peace-loving protagonist. And with my limited sports aptitude, I was ideally cast for the role.

One year later, in 1940, my parents bought a new Chevrolet sedan, and we took off from Pekin on a road trip to the West. There I learned about motels and Burma Shave signs, and once we stayed in a tourist court composed entirely of individual family teepees.

It was also an eye-opener when I saw a leathery-faced cow poke in a ten-gallon hat changing a tire in New Mexico. Prior to that, this young buckaroo assumed that cowboys only rode horses. I took his picture and later pasted it in my photo album. We also visited Carlsbad Caverns, never suspecting that a similar large cave might also someday play an important role in my professional activities.

Like many others in the US, my parents were listening to a broadcast of the New York Philharmonic on December 7, 1941, when it was interrupted with the announcement that Pearl Harbor had been attacked. I remember picking up the Pekin *Times* from our front porch at 503 Willow Street the following morning, reading the headlines, and asking my mother what it all meant.

For the next four years I followed the military campaigns in Europe and the Pacific in the newspaper, in *Life* magazine, and on the radio, as long as it didn't conflict with favorites like the *Lone Ranger, Captain Midnight*, or *Little Orphan Annie*.

My early World War II knowledge came back to me a generation later when I traveled to and wrote about places in the world where some of that action had taken place.

No one would dare to take my mother's seat on the ferry.

2
The Battle of Peleliu

THE BATTLE OF PELELIU BEGAN on my 12th birthday, September 15, 1944. The following is a travel article I wrote in 1997 about visiting the island of Peleliu. It was printed in the *Chicago Tribune,* *The Boston Globe*, and the Cleveland *Plain-Dealer.*

We fought our way up a difficult jungle rise, grabbing at wet tropical foliage that seemed to grab back at us, slapping at bare legs and faces as we tried to move forward.

The day was forebodingly dark. It had been raining off and on, and now it was on again. But Tangie Hesus, our diminutive yet indefatigable Palauan guide, urged our little group onward, explaining there would be shelter ahead.

Our uphill struggle was nothing compared to the travails of Americans and Japanese a half-century earlier. We were exploring the South Pacific island of Peleliu, the scene of one of the bloodiest and perhaps most useless battles of World War II.

The tiny island of Peleliu is today one of the states of Palau, an independent nation of islands in the Caroline group. Palau is largely unknown to Americans today, except to avid scuba divers. For them, it offers some of the clearest and cleanest waters and the richest collection of colorful ocean fish in the world.

But the atmosphere at Peleliu, a 20-minute light plane ride from Palau's capital of Koror, is different. Here, thousands died violently or miserably between September 15 and November 25, 1944. Estimates put the toll at nearly 2,000 American soldiers and Marines plus 11,000 of the island's Japanese defenders.

15

As we grappled our own way up the hill, I thought about stories I had read: Allied commanders, flushed with recent victories, thought Peleliu would be a two-day cakewalk. They also thought the island would be flat.

Advance intelligence had failed to discover that it was full of rugged hills and ridges into which the Japanese had bored an elaborate system of virtually impenetrable caves and tunnels. At this stage in the war, they were no longer trying to beat back Allied forces on the beaches. Instead, they now relied on heavy firepower from camouflaged and well-protected interior positions.

Moreover, President Roosevelt and Prime Minister Churchill had just met and already decided that the assault on the Philippines was to begin immediately, and further island conquests en route were unnecessary. But the wheels of fate were already in motion. The Peleliu operation was not turned back.

Thunder was echoing off the hills. The rain came down harder, and I remembered reading that GIs had come across similar weather a few days into the invasion. Then I moved over a muddy rise and suddenly found myself staring into the mouth of one of the meanest, greenest, heavy gun barrels I had ever seen, its rifling still apparent after more than 50 years. Except for the moss on its metal surface, it looked ready to fire.

With the accompanying thunder, lightning, and the torrential downpour, the sight was one of the most startling experiences I had had since we began exploring the island. Sure enough, we found shelter behind the gun, which was mounted at the mouth of one of the thousands of caves still present on the island.

We explored a few tunnels, and after the rain let up, we made our way back past the old cannon and down the hill to return to Tangie's van. He took us to other remnants of war — ruins of burned-out blockhouses, wrecks of tanks and planes, the painfully sharp coral-strewn invasion beaches, and to various lonely shrines erected by both Americans and Japanese in the years following the war.

We also went to a one-room museum where he had gathered a collection of war's detritus — hand grenades, bayonets, Coke and *sake* bottles, and some poignant reminders of the personal nature of war.

There was an optimistic letter from an American private on Peleliu to his sister, telling her he was in fine health and "not to worry about me," four days before he was killed. And from the other side there was a Japanese flag with hand-scrawled characters on it. Tangie translated it for us: "We're just a bunch of boys who know we're going to die, and we miss our mothers."

As we returned to the airfield, Tangie apologized because the bad weather had kept us from some of the more elaborate caves and tunnels. These included one that had housed more than 1,000 Japanese, until they were finally killed by a new and more powerful flamethrower that had just entered into the war.

We were glad we came, and the rain certainly suited the mood of the place. But we were also glad to leave Peleliu and fly back to Koror and the cheerful and sunny Palau of today.

3
Blue Ribbon Year

MY FATHER REPORTED FOR DUTY as soon as war was declared. He had been in the Cavalry ROTC at the University of Illinois, but he was turned down at the recruiting office. Horse campaigns were apparently *passé*, and besides that, at 39, my father was considered over the hill.

Mother wrote Grandma and Grandpa, saying she was satisfied with our situation. Her men were too old and too young to go to war. However Dad was haunted for years by memories of former students who never returned alive to Pekin.

During the war years, along with Pekin friends like Jesse Fahnders and Spencer Leifheit, I was heavily involved in Boy Scouts, collecting newspapers and scrap metal for the war effort. We also learned First Aid techniques and manned an aerial lookout of sorts.

From bubble gum cards I memorized the silhouettes of various Japanese and German airplanes. If a Mitsubishi or a Messerschmitt ever flew over central Illinois on the way to bomb the Caterpillar or the Corn Products factories, by golly, I would have immediately sounded the alarm and become a hero.

Anyway, I did win a blue ribbon at school for my great-looking okra, raised in my Victory Garden behind our rented house at 503 Willow.

I took up the trumpet, and later the baritone horn, and thought that I might someday have some sort of musical career – if we won the war, that is. I was sure Adolf Hitler or General Tojo would not like my kind of music.

My parents were classical music fans. Each weekday morning began with the voice of the man my mother called "Uncle Normy." At seven o'clock, Norman Ross hosted the "Four Hundred Hour" on Chicago station WLS. It was the only radio program I ever heard of that was sponsored by a train, the Chicago and Northwestern Railroad – the C&NW.

Uncle Normy's theme was a few bars of Tchaikovsky's *Sleeping Beauty Waltz*. And today if I happen to hear that on the radio, I still feel it must be time to quickly get dressed, brush my teeth, eat breakfast, and get ready for school.

They bought me my first record album, a set of 78 rpm disks called *The Whale Who Wanted to Sing at the Met*. The story was narrated and sung by Nelson Eddy, and featured a partial performance of *Pagliacci*.

At age 12, I built a crystal radio set, after that a one-tube receiver, and I also strung a private telegraph line between my bedroom and Bill Doty's next door. (Ever after, my mother would laugh at the term "variable condenser," a common radio device for tuning in different stations.) I was well into Morse code as well as photography. I sometimes took 15 cents to the drug store to buy a single-use flash bulb, which I used judiciously. Daddy also showed me how to make contact prints using negatives in a printing frame.

But my primary accomplishment that year was to travel all by myself for a long trip on Uncle Normy's bright yellow C&NW train on the way to visit my Gary grandparents.

The end of the line was the old LaSalle Street Station in Chicago. (I was later told it was the one destroyed making the film *Silver Streak*). I managed to get off the train, obey the traffic lights, pass under that wonderful clock that was suspended overhead on the corner of Marshall Field's, cross busy Michigan Avenue and then board the electric South Shore Line, which took me on to Grandma and Grandpa in Gary.

G&G then made a rare long-distance phone call to Pekin. My family was proud of my solo accomplishment – and so was I. I've always felt that that affirmation of my self-confidence was important for a future lifetime of extensive travels.

My grandparents didn't own a car, but they often took me on the bus to the beach near Gary. There on those dramatic sand dunes on the southern shore of Lake Michigan we could sometimes see across the water to Chicago. G&G told me it was "The Loop," and for a time I thought that any group of tall buildings anywhere was called a Loop.

They also took me several times on the South Shore Line to Chicago. Once I explored a one-man midget Japanese submarine put on display for a War Bond rally on Michigan Avenue. As a relatively small person, I could easily crawl right through the thing.

Much later in life, I lived in Kailua, Hawaii, near where that very same sub was originally beached and captured.

On other occasions in Chicago, I absorbed stimulating experiences like the Field Museum of Natural History and the Museum of Science and Industry. In the latter, I loved taking the special elevator down to the coal mine, one floor below.

But best of all were the Brookfield and Lincoln Park zoos.

I was in awe of the irascible 550-pound gorilla, "Bushman," the most popular exhibit at the Lincoln Park Zoo for years. Bushman was notorious for occasionally throwing his poop at the spectators — although, of course, he never would do that to me.

Several decades later, when visiting Chicago as a grown-up travel writer, I was somewhat startled to see that Bushman was still on view —stuffed, mounted, and now forever poop free staring out at the world with a piercing gaze behind glass at the Field Museum. I think he's still there.

ALL QUIET. A 15-year-old Bowling Green, O., camera fan, Robert W. Bone, sub mitted this photo. He suggested the title "Business Slow."

This sleeping boss was my first published photograph.
(Photo by Bob Bone)

4
Ohio on the Horizon

DURING THE WAR YEARS, when gas was rationed, my father usually rode his bicycle to his teaching job at Pekin Community High School. When I reached high school age, we often rode our bikes together to school. But I once detected some reluctance on his part after I decided to paint my bike.

With mock concern, he told Mother he might damage his reputation as an artist, by riding side by side with his son, whose bike was decked out now in sloppily rendered patterns of flaming orange and bright green.

"Orange and green – how did you possibly come up with that combination?" he asked.

World War II ended while I was at Camp Wokanda in Illinois with my Boy Scout troop. I was glad to be going home early, since I didn't take well to sleeping in tents and getting dirt in my food. Despite my Scout training, I remained both in ability and in rank a Tenderfoot.

In my freshman year at PCHS, I went on my first date, with shy classmate Nancy McCord from across the street. We walked to the roller rink downtown, and then held hands while skating together. This new technique provided an added thrill to the activity.

A half-century later I was surprised to learn that Nancy had never married. Someone missed a good skater, and a good bet.

In high school, I failed Typing, of all things – perhaps something to do with not setting up a business letter correctly at my final exam –

the only "F" final grade in my school career. I was embarrassed and humiliated. Second semester I retook it and passed with a "B."

Unknown to me, after the war was over both my Gary retreats and even my days in Pekin would soon come to an end. The first hint of this sea change in my life was when my grandfather retired from his wartime job as a foreman in the Gary steel mills. Almost immediately he moved with my grandmother to Bowling Green, Ohio.

That was a town I had often heard the family discuss, though I didn't realize until later that it actually was the Bone family's ancestral home. My great grandparents had homesteaded in B.G. (as we called it) after emigrating to the U.S. from England.

Grandma's sister, my great aunt, had lived there all along. Emily Ordway was a beloved retired schoolteacher, and the last to bear one of the town's most respected surnames. (Ordway Avenue in B.G. was named for my great-grandfather, Amherst Ordway, who served long ago on the City Council.)

Legions of Bowling Green grade school students remembered "Miss Ordway" fondly. But she was always known in our family for reasons historically unclear as "Dick." Aunt Dick's handwriting was amazingly small and precise, and to me, she was most famous for getting at least twice as much legible information on the back of a picture post card as anyone else. She also spoke in an unusually high voice, almost a falsetto.

Another childhood memory was the time Aunt Dick attacked the toaster with a table knife in an attempt to retrieve a recalcitrant piece of bread. Sparks flew all over the dining room and Aunt Dick ended up almost upside down. She was all right, but was literally floored.

Electricity in Gary often was problematical. Probably due to the demand of the nearby steel mills, it was DC in those days – direct current, whereas most of the country, including Pekin, was AC – alternating current. To me, it meant that any time I received a Christmas present that involved electricity, like a model train, I probably couldn't play with it until we returned to Pekin.

Then there was the time in Gary that Grandma was struck by lightning. She was holding on to a water faucet in the kitchen when a bolt struck the house, and enough of the charge came up the pipe to propel her halfway across the kitchen. But like her sister she was tough, and none the worse for wear.

In Bowling Green, Ohio, the rambling two-story house at 312 South Main Street was built in the early nineteenth century by my great-grandfather, Amherst Ordway, but was later partitioned into two parts. In 1946, after their move from Gary, my grandparents took up residence on one side and the upstairs. Aunt Dick lived alone in the smaller portion all at ground level. Her front parlor always looked like a museum display or a stage set depicting an earlier time. A couple of the lights were converted oil lamps. (I have one of those today.)

In front of the house was a large rock that my grandfather painted white shortly after moving there. On it he inscribed in black letters "George Washington never slept here." That was Grandpa's brand of humor.

He was a big fan of the wit and wisdom of Will Rogers, and my parents later noted that he was born the same day as Rogers's birth and died on the anniversary of his death. I remember thinking that was spooky and probably significant in some way.

So my Gary days were now finished, and my Pekin days were numbered. For the summer of '47, I was assigned to stay with Grandma, Grandpa, and Aunt Dick in Bowling Green. I had only one friend my age that summer. Dick Pfouts lived on a farm somewhere, and so I seldom saw him, except when he came into town. Otherwise Bowling Green that summer was shaping up to be a drag.

Moreover, my grandfather was becoming increasingly ill, and Grandma and Aunt Dick began to worry. Once I accidentally barged into the downstairs bathroom and discovered Grandma trying to give Grandpa an enema while he lay moaning on the floor.

I was only 15, but I decided on my own hook to write home about the situation. My mother saved the barely legible postal card:

> Mother and Daddy, Grandma doesn't know I'm writing this. She came back from the hospital crying today. Grandpa must have an operation, and she is worried sick. She wants you two to come but she doesn't want to ask you. I wish to Goodness you would come cause she says she wants you alfally bad. She hasn't got any of the family to carry part of the worry. Your loving son, Bobby. PS: PLEASE."

My parents came immediately from Pekin. After about a month, Grandpa, the tough old bird who had wrestled oil wells out west and then made heavy steel for the war effort, died of colon cancer at the age of only 68.

It was often spoken in hushed tones in the family that Grandpa just might have been the love child of "Bertie," Britain's well-known royal playboy and serial philanderer – the son of a disappointed Queen Victoria. Bertie was also known as Albert Prince of Wales and later became the more respected if tongue-tied King Edward VII.

In any case, my grandfather was born in England in 1879 to an unmarried domestic, whose name was Hannah Bone. For a time Hannah had been in service at Sandringham Castle, one of the royal residences then favored by the randy young prince.

Apparently no one ever took steps to prove or disprove that connection. In any case, the infant was adopted by his mother's brother, Abraham Bone, and his wife, Susan. The family then suddenly and mysteriously amassed enough money for all three to seek a new life far away in America – the surge of temporary wealth adding credence to the story.

On a later visit to England, my father's brother, Uncle Jay, once looked up my grandfather's birth record, which was registered in the church at King's Lynn, a village not far from the castle. It's there, but the space for the father's name has only a solid line across it.

Of course this favorite family yarn could probably be proved or disproved today by DNA analysis. But I don't think anyone on either side of the Atlantic is at all disposed to take that step.

As the expression goes: "I'm just sayin'."

Anyway, Uncle Jay, came over to B.G. from his home in Fremont and together he and Dad carried Grandpa's body at night across the back yard to the funeral home run by the next-door neighbor. In a couple of days Grandpa looked better than ever, neatly dressed in a three-piece suit and tie and lying in his casket, and wearing his Masonic ring.

I was somewhat shocked at the elaborate setup, which even included the sound of soft respiration. This aural *non sequitur* came I suppose from some mechanical device underneath the bier. I remember that the thought of Grandpa on display while apparently breathing gently and taking a nap on his back while dressed to the nines in a three-piece suit, including vest and jacket, was really *just too much*. I hated it.

On the plus side that same B.G. summer, I got my first real job, at the nearby Texaco station, also on Main Street. I learned to strip tires off their rims, repair flats, change oil, use a grease gun, set and check spark plugs, pump gas, check oil, and wipe windshields, all for the grand recompense of five bucks a week – and an occasional dime tip from a motorist. My friendly if parsimonious boss, John Frank, paid me the five out of his billfold on Saturday afternoons.

Various strange characters who sometimes came around his gas station called him "Big John." On slow days, Big John also discussed with me some interesting subjects that somehow didn't come up at home, like sex, masturbation, and the characteristics of the condoms he sold at the station. But he advocated Kleenex as the necessary accessory for adolescent self-gratification.

"Remember, you gotta have somethin' to catch it," he cautioned. I didn't say so, but I was way ahead of him on the subject. I already had a nice collection of inspiring Vargas Girls calendars hidden away at home.

With equal enthusiasm, I learned to run out on Main Street (also known as the Dixie Highway) and try to flag down large long-haul semi (tractor-trailer) trucks. I held up two or three fingers to show how many cents a gallon discount we would give the driver today if he would only pull his 18-wheel rig in to our station and let us fill up his twin 100-gallon tanks.

Big John would take a nap sometimes in his chair at the station. I took a photograph of that somnolent practice and sent the print off to the Toledo *Blade*. It was my first published photo in a newspaper, and I was darn proud of it. (I still have the clipping.) And thankfully, my boss liked it, too.

5
Last Hurrah in Pekin

FOR MY SOPHOMORE YEAR in high school, I returned to Pekin, reveling in the company of old friends for the last time. At one point I wrote the script for a school variety show act, throwing each page down Roger Sommer's laundry chute one by one to fellow actors who picked them up and rehearsed in the basement.

I also had a minor role in the major school play, *Arsenic and Old Lace*, and I vowed that the following year I would have an important part. This year I was sure my talents were underutilized. I played the dead body in the window seat.

Alas, the following year never came.

But there were Scout activities, band practices, and of course enthusiastically following high-school sports, during which I would either play in the school band or photograph the games from the sidelines – sometimes both.

It may seem strange today that our school basketball and football teams were then known and accepted by everyone throughout central Illinois for decades as the "Pekin Chinks."

Right off the bat, I can assure you that no one in our town meant any disrespect to the Chinese.

Pekin seemed about as WASP a town as they come. It's hard to believe that anyone in town had ever seen anyone of the Asian persuasion in Pekin, let alone harbor any animosity toward them.

Unlike in Gary, I never even saw any blacks there either, except perhaps for one old gentleman named Jim who lived in a shack down by the river. I was not even aware of Jews, Catholics, or Seventh Day Adventists, although there must have been some walking among us. Incredibly, I don't believe I was ever told that there were such folks.

Pekin already had played an honorable role in the defense of human rights. Back in 1841, none other than the young lawyer Abraham Lincoln had successfully argued a case in Pekin freeing a woman known as "Black Nance" who had been kept as a slave.

Local historians were fond of saying that she was the first slave that Lincoln freed.

The chosen sports team name had to do with geography and the way the town got its name in the first place. Many years before my time, when the town was founded, the wife of an early settler named it. She was of the opinion that the Chinese capital of Peking (sometimes then spelled *Pekín*, and now known as Beijing) was our town's antipode. That is, if one could bore a hole straight through the center of the earth he would come up for air again somewhere in the neighborhood of the Forbidden City.

So Pekin was named in honor of that supposed geographical anomaly. Moreover, there were various places around town that were architecturally inspired by this local Asian tradition:

Our first-run movie house, the Pekin Theater, next to the town square, was handsomely decorated inside and out as an elaborate Chinese temple.

This was where I sat through four consecutive showings of the 1944 film *Home in Indiana* before I finally caught a glimpse of my Uncle Jay, who was an extra in the film. Despite the title, some scenes were shot in Fremont, Ohio, and I told all my friends to look for my uncle with the big dent in his forehead.

Moreover, the polished floor of the high school basketball court was painted with a beautiful and elaborate Chinese dragon, a motif also repeated on posters, stationery, and other items related to the high school.

The imposing high school building, seemingly constructed some time in ancient history, had three prominent doors. One was the main entrance at the front. But engraved in stone on one side were the words "Boys Entrance," and on the opposite side "Girls Entrance." These outdated restrictions were haughtily ignored by our classes in the 1940s.

I always felt there was an egalitarian spirit to the school, as evidenced in the opening lines of its fight song:

Dear old Pekin High School, we're all the same;
Winning or losing, we're always game...

Nevertheless, we were the Chinks, and darn proud of it. Some now remember that before the beginning of a basketball game, a boy and a girl cheerleader would go to the center of the floor and bow respectfully to the cheerleaders of the opposing team. Wearing costumes topped with coolie hats, the pair of Pekin representatives was known as "Chink and Chinklet."

The football mascot cheerleader also did a costumed Chinese dance on the sidelines. Among his duties was to strike some kind of Oriental brass gong when a Pekin touchdown was scored.

In our naïve minds, all this was just innocent fun.

George Beres, a writer who was in the class just behind mine, later wrote about a cheer with a somewhat Chinese flavor. It was designed to spur on the team when it was behind and/or the game was dragging a bit:

Ahh, phooey; chop suey. Come on Pekin, hop to-ey!

This sort of thing was innocently carried on unnoticed by the wider world until the 1970s. By that time I was working at the morning newspaper in Honolulu, which closely followed things Oriental.

Stories began to be carried by the Associated Press about how a small city on the Illinois River was being challenged by some determined folks who insisted that by using the name Chinks, the school and the town itself, intentionally or not, were insulting a large and well-respected minority of the American population.

Some Pekinites expressed resentment that other sports teams continued to refer to another ethnic group, Native Americans, as Indians, Braves, Redskins, etc., and still managed to keep those names in modern times. They pointed out that most in that particular minority did not take offense and indeed had generally expressed pride in the names.

Although there is evidence that one community college on reservation land in Arizona did change its name to the Scottsdale

Fighting Artichokes. And of course the Stanford Indians became the Cardinals, among others.

I recently told this story to my good friend and fellow writer, Bob Hollis. He grew up near San Francisco, where the population has long been keenly sensitive to this kind of thing. He expressed horror at the thought of "Chinks" being vocally cheered on to victory by an otherwise polite society.

"That's really beyond the pale!" said Bob.

Anyway, it was apparently a big fight among the city fathers, some of whom honestly believed that political correctness had just gotten out of hand. I was certainly glad I was not there to witness the emotional bloodshed. But in the end, sense and sensibility won out in Pekin when the school administration declared an end to it all in about 1980. Eschewing the usual animal and bird names, Pekin chose the relatively humdrum but more politically correct team name: "Pekin Dragons," and that name has endured to this day.

The Chinese temple-like Pekin Theater was torn down a few years later. But presumably the high school did not have to immediately remove the Chinese dragon artwork from the basketball court floor. I wasn't there for the metamorphosis.

A half century later I attended the Class of 1950 reunion. The Pekin Times even ran a photo and story about me and my guidebooks and travel articles, noting this would have been my class had I remained in Pekin long enough to be graduated there.

As part of that reunion, we loyal alumni went to a football game. There Jerry Hodgson, Roger Heim, and some other erstwhile classmates, wore faded "Pekin Chinks" shirts and similar outdated regalia while in the stands. Some in genuine good humor shouted cheers such as "Yay Chinks," no doubt confusing many who after that considerable length of time had absolutely no knowledge of the good old days at Dear Old Pekin High School.

Back now to 1948. In a happy coincidence – happy at least for everyone other than me in the family – my father was suddenly hired as an assistant professor of art at Bowling Green State University. All those New York summers and the Columbia Masters degree had finally paid off.

Bowling Green, the seat of our family's history, was otherwise famous for its Heinz ketchup factory. Sometimes a summer breeze would waft the smell of spicy tomatoes over the entire community.

But it was becoming much more known as an up-and-coming college town, too. We made ready for the family's last great move — one that would house us all for the foreseeable years ahead with Grandma and Aunt Dick.

In June in that last summer in Pekin, my good friend Roger Sommer was on one of his frequent breakups with his perennial companion and our mutual classmate, Carolyn Huffman. Carolyn always seemed to me to be the ideal girl friend — good-looking, smart, unpretentious, and with great legs. (I saw her wearing gym shorts once.) I had taken many glamour-style photographs of her while hanging around with the happy couple.

In my 1948 yearbook, she wrote on her picture: "I'll look for you in Hollywood taking pictures of the stars!"

On the eve of the Bone family departure for our new life in Ohio, Carolyn and I went to the movies together. At the end of a perfect evening, I had my first genuine and pleasantly warm kiss with a woman who was not my mother.

On the way to the family's new home in B.G., my heart ached — and the emotional pain continued for at least a month. And I had only Topsy to commiserate with. (My cat took the move much better than I did, and eventually stretched out her nine lives to a ripe old age.)

I heard later that Carolyn and Roger had gotten together again, of course. And they have remained good friends to this day, even though both ended up with different spouses.

Carolyn eventually married Ike Pappas, who became a well-known CBS TV correspondent. His voice lives on forever in history — recorded in 1963 on the film of Lee Harvey Oswald's death in a Dallas police station: "He's been shot!" exclaimed Ike.

At that 50th class reunion in 2000, I spoke to Carolyn for the first time about my most pleasant-yet-agonizing memory of our date in 1948. She replied that she was sorry and embarrassed to admit it, but she didn't remember that occasion at all.

It was certainly understandable.

6

An Ohio High

THE FINAL TWO YEARS of my high school career, would be at BGSH – Bowling Green Senior High, a well-regarded institution in that university and ketchup town, 23 miles southeast of Toledo.

Again, I was in the marching band, an organization guaranteed to quickly introduce me to a group of fellow musicians. I had brought my own terribly battered and wrinkled baritone horn from Pekin. I had a habit of sitting balanced on the instrument during pauses in the outdoor marching rehearsals. This brought me to the attention of both bandleader Bill Grable and my fellow students as some kind of a nut.

Besides our regular teachers, we also were subjected to the neophyte instruction of student teachers from BGSU, to whom we often gave a hard time in one way or another. There was frequently a certain amount of flirtation, too, of course, there not being that much of an age difference between senior students and student teachers.

And there was at least one teacher-student affair that was whispered about during my two-year tenure at the school. I'd be surprised if there weren't more of those both before and after those years.

Along with my photographic activities, my musical career flourished apace, and I eventually found myself leading a dance band of sorts, named "Bob Bone and His Bee-Bop Cats." By this time, I was using a more sophisticated baritone horn, which was actually a double-belled euphonium. When I switched from the large and mellow-sounding baritone bell, to the smaller one, the instrument took on the characteristics of a valve trombone, *sans* slide.

We had a real slide trombone in the band, of course, played by Tom Alspach. The rest of the Be Bop Cats included Dickey Dean on piano, Mona Lee Middleton on drums, John Schwarz on bass, Carol Smith on clarinet, and Jack Clarke on trumpet.

Our repertoire was limited. Among the half dozen or so tunes, I remember "My Little Margie," "Girl of My Dreams," "Dinah," and Cole Porter's "De-Lovely," which could be delightfully rendered on my special two-horned instrument. We played our short program at a few after-game dances. At the end everyone applauded politely and then turned on the jukebox.

I thought at the time, and I still believe that we were the only dance band in the entire U.S. in which the leader played his solos on the double-belled euphonium.

I also liked to say during these years that I was the fifth man in a barbershop quartet. The quartet, made up of classmates, was good, winning several local prizes. John Schwarz, first tenor; Tom Alspach, second tenor (melody line); Dallas Brim, baritone; and Dick Short, bass, called themselves "The Unaccounted Four." If someone was late or couldn't show up for practice, I sometimes sat in. All agreed I was really bad. But I learned some great old songs, like "Down in Honky Tonky Town."

Along about this time, I also learned to play the ukulele – long before I ever thought I might live in Hawaii some day. And I taught myself piano, taking off from the chord patterns first learned on the uke: "Five Foot Two, Eyes of Blue" was a keyboard favorite. I also was partial to sentimental songs of a previous era:

She was more to be pitied than censored; more to be helped than despised.
She was only a lassie who ventured; on life's stormy path ill advised.
Do not scorn her with words fierce and bitter.
Don't laugh at her shame and downfall.
For a moment just stop and consider. That a man was the cause of it all!

Along with some of my friends, I think I was known as a "cut up." When Albert Lemmerbrock lit and re-lit his Bunsen burner in physics class, it was I who was surreptitiously introducing some air pressure into the gas line at the other end of the long lab table, just enough so that Albert's fire would mysteriously be extinguished, over and over again.

Also in physics, I once brought a portable typewriter to school, saying I intended to use it to take notes. (I was ahead of my time, perhaps, and the machine was certainly not as quiet as today's laptops and tablets.) The physics teacher, known for reasons unremembered, as "Doc" Organ, would have none of it, and the machine was silenced and sent home with me at the end of that day.

Two of my good friends, classmates Dick Clark and Dallas Brim opened a small business in a tiny building downtown. They called it the Two-By-Four Novelty Shop. There we would buy such marvels as exploding matches, which were guaranteed to be noisy enough to disrupt a classroom.

One of these resulted in my being sent to the principal's office.

Dr. Parlette was an august and feared presence at BGHS, but I was determined not to be buffaloed. He began to lecture me principally about fire safety.

"Tell me, Bob. When you strike these matches, do they then go out?"

"Yes sir, Dr. Parlette, they always extinguish themselves."

The principal then begin to strike them himself, one after the other until they were used up. Each one continued to burn after the initial blast.

I spent a considerable amount of time studying quietly and doing my homework in that same office over the next several days.

My early love interests in B.G. were timid to say the least. One Halloween, after the usual high jinks, I found myself playfully wrestling in the dark with Carol Boyle on her front lawn. Suddenly she stopped resisting and just lay on her back underneath me wearing a big smile. I was suddenly dumbfounded, yet pleased. But I wasn't sure what to do. So I didn't.

For the Junior Prom, though, I escorted Ann Schaller, a cute but quite modest creature who I thought must the original "Shy Ann." A few years later I sent her a postcard from Cheyenne, Wyoming. I think she liked the joke, because she's still sending Christmas cards to me today.

I think Tom Alspach took Ann to the Senior Prom, a year later, during one of his breakups with Carol Smith (the sexy clarinet player). Carol was one of those vivacious girls we all loved. (Rather like Carolyn in Pekin.) But she eventually dumped Tom for a young banker who wasn't even from B.G. and then they moved to some obscure town in the South. That just didn't seem fair to us. Tom was initially devastated, although years later he married an amazing woman named Nita, and enjoyed the rest of his life in Yuma, Arizona.

Tom and I also once went on a double date, sort of – that is, with the same girl at the same time. Together, we took Muriel Abel to the movies. In the dark, I held one hand, and on the other side of Muriel, Tom held the other – both of us pretending that we were alone with the favored companion.

"I feel so foolish," Muriel commented. I guess I can't blame her.

In 1949, I bought my first car, a black 1936 Chevrolet sedan, but I wasn't allowed to drive it. I paid the previous owner $30 – it was either $5 a week for six weeks or $6 a week for five weeks, I can't remember which. But in any case, I didn't yet have a driver's license or insurance, so it stayed for an agonizingly long time in the back yard.

I had learned by this time that it was a neat (that's "cool" in today's parlance) thing to be able to get around town more quickly than I could on foot. I first accomplished this when my friend Jerry Felty allowed me to sit on the back of his 3-HP "Whizzer" motorbike. My mother was sure this practice was a death sentence, which probably led to the relatively early approval of the '36 Chevy as a more prudent transportation option.

Meanwhile I polished the car frequently, attached a second horn (I preferred a more robust and somewhat musical sound), and learned to use the crank to bring the vehicle to life when the old 6-volt battery wasn't quite strong enough to power the starter motor.

Finally licensed and insured, I was mobile even if I wasn't permitted to drive that car out of town. But of course I did – at first only on frequent visits to Dick Clark's place, which was on a farm a few miles out in the country. (Dick was, and still is, a great friend. But I also think that in those days I was also secretly infatuated with his sister, Barbara.)

Fate provided a more severe lesson when my old friend from Pekin, Spencer Leifheit, came to visit me in B.G.

We decided we would like to see Greenfield Village, also known today as the Henry Ford Museum. This famous outdoor-indoor complex was much farther north – near Detroit, Michigan, but we calculated we would be back home in B.G. in time for dinner.

Of course it took much longer than that and it was already dark when on the way back we stopped to consult a map somewhere in Toledo. It was there that another car plowed smack into the rear of mine at what was later estimated to be something above 50 m.p.h. Somehow Spencer saw it coming.

"Oh Jesus, Bone!"

I remember it as just a tremendously loud crash. It folded up my little old Chevy sedan into a four-door coupe. No seat belts were around in those days. Everything behind the thankfully firm bench seat became just a mass of crunched metal. I still have the 8x10 junkyard photo in my files.

Amazingly, at the hospital in Toledo, I hardly had a scratch on me, and Spencer suffered only a broken nose. In due course, my parents arrived and I remember giving my mother a big kiss – on the lips! (Only my second lip-kiss since Carolyn Huffman, as it turned out.)

On graduation from Bowling Green Senior High in 1950, I still faced some big questions. The first was where to go to college, an important project but potentially expensive. Eventually my folks and I agreed on the most practical solution: I would go to school right there in Bowling Green – and somehow arrange not to take a class from my father. As a professor's son, my academic tuition for 1950-51 would be a modest $75 per semester.

Years later, I wished I had taken an art appreciation course from my father. Among other things, Robert Ordway Bone became a co-author of a successful textbook, Art Fundamentals, which is still used in educational institutions all over the world.

I waffled back and forth between choosing music or journalism as a main course of study. Finally I decided on journalism, but I also vowed to continue playing in both the university's concert and marching bands, as well as in the ROTC band.

Music, as a career, would be virtually useless for me unless I was good enough to be a professional performer. Otherwise it would only be a practical alternative if I wanted to teach, which I definitely did not. Also taking into account my photographic bent, it had to be journalism.

It was also imperative that I would sign up for ROTC – the Reserve Officer Training Corps – which was the only way to keep from being drafted and sent to fight in the Korean War, which broke out that June.

Meanwhile, what would I do in summer between high school and BGSU? The ideal opportunity presented itself when I was accepted for summer employment at Mammoth Cave National Park in Kentucky – and as a real photographer!

Mammoth Cave, Kentucky: My first job as a professional photographer. (The apron held the money.)

7

Work & Play in Kentucky

MY EMPLOYER WAS ACTUALLY National Park Concessions, Inc., a private company that had the contract for visitor services at the park. (It still does, I believe.)

Most guys and gals around my age were hired to work in the dining room and related food service positions. But my job – along with one other guy – was to take group photographs of visitors before they entered the cave.

I think many tourists believed it had something to do with a head count or identifying them in case they became lost while underground. But it was simply to be able to sell them prints of these photos as they later emerged from their subterranean experience. Each photo included a special signboard with date, trip number, etc., as much to tell us whom to approach later as it was to tell the viewer the when and where of their tour.

The job also paid me a little more than the restaurant staff, since I would not have the benefit of tips. And I had evenings off, unlike many of my friends in the dining room. There was plenty of boy-girl action, too, some of it at a nearby drive-in movie. Of course it was all pretty tame by today's standards – or else I just wasn't privy to any more advanced assignations.

My equipment was an ancient 5x7 view camera mounted on a big wooden tripod – the kind where the photographer makes his initial adjustments on a ground glass under a black hood, and from which he emerges to put in the film holder, remove the sliding cover, and press the rubber bulb to release the shutter.

My immediate superior, an avuncular fellow who had been doing the job for years, was named Ross, who was assisted by his wife, Lillian. I liked both and admired their Kentucky drawl. Since we had to cover two separate entrances to the cave, I also had a compatriot my age, whom I believe came from nearby Bardstown. Unfortunately I lost track of Bill Logan somewhere over the years. (Bill, if you ever run across these words, I'd love to reminisce some day.)

My official boss at the park was W. Ray Scott, an especially accomplished photographer who made excellent mellow-toned prints of his black-and-white photographs. He was also a one-man PR representative for National Park Concessions in all the parks with which the company was associated.

Many years later, Ray and his wife looked up my wife and me at our home in Hawaii, bringing documents signed by the Kentucky governor that declared that we were now honorary "Kentucky Colonels." And later still I would have loved to have shown Ray my own photograph that was used on the cover of the National Park Service calendar for 2000. But he was long gone by then.

I occasionally took some kidding from the NPS cave guides for some of my photo techniques: "Be sure you can see the camera with both eyes, please!" I would shout to the visitors in the larger groups.

I felt the increased facial recognition would ultimately result in more sales — not that it made any financial difference to me since I was paid a straight 75 cents an hour, plus room and board. Thinking back now, I have the feeling that like the guides, most in the group had no idea what I was talking about.

We used a slow black-and-white orthochromatic film, meaning it was sensitive to all colors except red (like the well-known Kodak Verichrome.) Exposures were about 1/25th of a second in sunlight — a little slower or an f-stop or two larger on cloudy days.

Back in our little shack on the main pathway to the cave, we processed the film in trays by inspection instead of timing. Our safelight, believe it or not, was simply a small deep-red windowpane in the outside wall. (We could look out and see if any potential customer was approaching, too.) There was no enlarger either. We made 5x7 contact prints, and sold them for something like an even $2. (There was no confusing tax or small change involved.)

As cave employees, we summer hires were often given some extra privileges in the park, such as the occasional permission to explore portions of the cave that were not open to the general public. (Some of these required crawling through tight spaces and featured delicate crystal-like formations that could easily be damaged.) And on Saturday nights we performed in a free employee show in an open-air amphitheater.

I can't think of another summer job I could have enjoyed more.

Leaving Ohio for Blister Rust Control Camp in Idaho. L to R: Dick Clark, Dallas Brim, Jerry Felty, John Schwarz and Bob Bone.

8

BGSU, Blister Rust, & California

UNLIKE A LOT OF FOLKS, I do not look back sentimentally on my college days. No Whiffenpoof songs for me. I did not pledge a social fraternity, and was therefore determinedly known as a GDI, which stood for God Damned Independent. But I did enjoy everything concerning the band, the ROTC, and the Journalism Department. I was accepted in Kappa Alpha Mu, an honorary fraternity in photojournalism – also known, of course, as KAM.

I dated several different girls at one time or another. Occasionally there would be a dance, sometimes with name bands. On those occasions, of course, I had to split my time between my date and my photo duties. I recall photographing band leader Woody Herman, quickly developing the photos, and bringing two 8x10s back to the dance to give Herman one print and to get his autograph on another – all this while my evening's companion either waited for me or (preferably) accompanied me to the Journalism Department dark-room in the interim.

I eventually had a regular girlfriend, Pat Guthman, who had thick glasses and lots of lovely blonde hair. I wrote a song about her, scored it for the piano and the ukulele, printed out the sheet music and then pasted on an 8x10 cover photo – a major project in those pre-computer years.

My major was officially in photojournalism, which meant a little more in photography, design, etc. in addition to news writing and typography classes. Other classes that pleased me well enough were ROTC, Spanish (my mother's early French lessons helped in that one), American history and world literature. Journalism majors generally received a liberal arts education, even though their ultimate degree was, for some academic reason, a Bachelor of Science in Business Administration.

Life at home was reasonably good, too. For a long time we did not have a TV in the house, relying on newspapers, books, and conversation for entertainment.

"I am not going to turn our living room into a theater!" my mother declared on several occasions.

I began saving my money and eventually I bought a heavy second-hand TV set with a 7-inch B&W screen for $50, wrapped it up and put it under the Christmas tree as a present to the family. To ease my mother's sensitivities, my father and I soon installed it in a small room off the living room. It was the room my grandfather had died in, but after that we had moved a piano into it and called it the music room. Thereafter, my mother always knew where she could find my father when she wanted him – sitting close to the screen and usually busy adjusting the horizontal, the vertical and the contrast.

During this period, also, I managed to work on at least three different jobs – occasionally on the same day: (1) Centre Drug Store, where I sometimes served as a soda jerk, (2) a gas station (whose name I've forgotten, but no longer Big John's), and most fun of all, (3) a salesman and general clerk at the Bigelow Music Shop, across the street from the drug store. (I remember a period when I finished work at Bigelow's and then walked across the street to begin my shift at the drug store.)

Jack Bigelow, a local character who was a retired vaudeville performer, owned the music shop. He had once led an "all-girl orchestra," made up of his seven sisters and traveled all over the country in the 1920s and '30s. An accomplished jazz trumpeter, Jack was a hoot and full of stories about famous vaudeville entertainers he had known. He would sometimes laugh and tell others "Bob Bone is the best ukulele salesman I've ever seen."

Actually when a potential customer expressed some interest in that little four-string wonder, I would demonstrate how it could be fingered and strummed in three or four chords that could effectively accompany a vocal rendition of many songs, especially C&W – Country and Western numbers, e.g., "Red River Valley," and the like.

Several of my B.G. Senior High School buddies also attended BGSU at least for their freshman year, notably Dick Clark, Dallas Brim, John Schwarz, and Jerry Felty. In the spring of 1951, we began calling ourselves the Western Five or later the California Five.

That June, we embarked on an adventure that proved to be a watershed event in our young lives. We had spent long hours poring over maps while planning a trip that despite some initial adversity, eventually became a dramatically successful western adventure.

All five of us managed to be hired to work in the woods near Pierce, Idaho, on a blister rust control project. It was a summer government program to eliminate certain species of plants called ribes (pronounced "rye-bees"), which were intermediate hosts to a white pine disease. Apparently the government thought this essential to protect the Northwest lumber industry.

Beyond that, we didn't much understand the concept. We just wanted a summer in the West, away from families and what we saw as the relative humdrum of summer life in B.G.

Believe it or not, we drove some 5,000 miles in Jerry's 1941 Chevrolet club coupe – three guys in the back and two in front. We accomplished this by religiously aerating the car and switching drivers and seat positions every 100 miles or two hours, whichever came first.

Much of this trip has been described in great detail from five different viewpoints in the privately printed volume, *The Book of the BOGO Men*, published by Dick Clark in 2008. (Address available on request.)

Some highlights, however, included the time that our naïve quintet found themselves innocently looking for overnight accommodations in what turned out to be a bordello in Rock Springs, Wyoming.

"I think you all got the wrong hotel," said the woman with tired eyes, while looking at our fresh, innocent faces. "But come back again in a couple of years!"

The Idaho job turned out to be a tough one, and no doubt I thought wistfully of my previous summer working at Mammoth Cave. In Idaho, we physically pulled out certain plants by the roots from dawn to dusk in these woods while walking on strict north-south or east-west grids, no matter what the terrain beneath our feet was doing. We lived with other young guys in lumberjack tents.

At Blister Rust Camp 115, the food, at least, was great. Tent living was fine, too, including going to sleep serenaded by nearby coyotes. Everything else was, to say the least, most uncomfortable, made more miserable by our straw-boss supervisors, one of the better of whom was named Riley. Perhaps some of these bosses also hated their jobs, and some took it out on us young innocents. At first we made up songs about our troubles, accompanying them on a ukulele, guitar or harmonica.

When our B.G. gang was split up with some of us assigned to an even less desirable camp, we fought back with our version of the Hank Snow song, "I'm Movin' On."

Old man Riley was a-feelin' mean;
So he took 10 men from Camp one-fifteen, and moved them on.
They soon were gone!

In due course, some of us lower figures on the totem pole began quitting over the indignities. In our little gang of five, John and Dallas said goodbye first, after we all agreed we would re-form at some point in Oakland, California, across the bay from San Francisco. They began hitchhiking, since Jerry's car remained with him in camp.

Dick left a few days later, after demonstrating his displeasure by cutting his guide ropes dramatically in front of his immediate superior, so he was immediately fired. Jerry and I remained a little longer just so we could pick up our first pay packet, and then we took off in the Chevy for Oakland.

I was never sure why we picked Oakland, instead of San Francisco on the other side of the Bay Bridge. But perhaps one of us did some research and came across that negative review by Mark Twain that local tourism interests have been fighting ever since: "The coldest winter I ever spent was a summer in San Francisco." And Oakland, at least, also was identified as having been the boyhood home of Jack London.

We were often asked later how we managed to be able to meet up reliably in Oakland. After all, cell phones were still about 50 years in the future. So we agreed to write to each other c/o General Delivery, Oakland. Picking up these notes at the post office worked just fine.

By the time Jerry and I arrived in Oakland, we found our three predecessors doing various odd jobs – handing out leaflets, carrying advertising signs, etc. Dick had the best job, actually, as a combination bellhop and elevator operator in a mostly residential hotel called the Hillcastle Apartment Hotel. It was a first-class address generally housing respectable clients, many of them senior citizens.

We couldn't live at that high-class establishment, however. Instead, we found digs at a rather down-at-the-heels establishment a few blocks away called the Hotel Menlo. We had a special term for the desk clerk. He was a rather talkative fellow, who often doubled as the operator of the Menlo's old-fashioned, open-cage elevator.

After letting us off at our floor, he would continue to yak away in rapidly diminishing volume as we watched him disappear feet first while the cage descended on its way to the lobby. Ever after, he became known to us as "The Sinking Man."

Soon after our arrival, Dick told me that there would also be a similar position for me at the Hillcastle, except that they didn't have another uniform. That turned out not to be a problem. Dick and I were about the same size, and since we were never on duty at the same time, we simply changed clothes with each other in the utility closet. Thus the uniform managed to do double duty, even if we didn't. (Mercifully I have no memory of what we did about cleaning.)

Sixty years later, my wife and I drove by the old Hillcastle and paused out front. From the car, at least, it looked rather run down. And there were enough strange characters hanging around that I decided not to get out and take a closer look. I shot a couple of photos from the car window and then drove on.

As much as I liked my elevator operator job, it soon became apparent that I wasn't earning enough money. John and Dallas had accepted jobs at the California Packing Company run by Del Monte in nearby Alameda, and eventually I joined them doing battle with millions of cans and jars of vegetables and fruit.

At one point, I was given the job of filling up metal baskets of cans, which appeared out of a hole in the wall, having been filled and formed somewhere on the floor above. When I sometimes I got behind in this activity, I could push a button that would stop the flow for a time.

But upstairs the cans were still being generated. When I pushed another button to restart the flow, they popped out faster than ever, meaning I had to double my efforts for several minutes to catch up to the flow. (A year or so later TV's *I Love Lucy* show depicted a similar though more hilarious situation on one of the episodes.)

On another occasion, I had to wheel around a cart filled with hundreds of glass jars of spiced peaches. Actually it was cart on top of a cart. At one point the top cart rolled off the bottom cart and everything crashed onto the cement floor creating a pile of spiced peaches and broken glass. I thought I would be fired and would have to pay for the damages. But my foreman approached me with a broom and shovel instead, and handed them to me.

"Clean it up!" he ordered. And so I did.

Notwithstanding our work opportunities, we somehow found time to do some sightseeing. In San Francisco, we drove down the famous steep and twisting block of Lombard Street, visited Fisherman's Wharf, and even drove out to Ocean Beach where we dipped our feet into the water. I, at least, had visited New York City in 1939, so I announced that unlike my companions I now had been from coast to coast in this country.

I picked up a jellyfish at the beach and took it back to the hotel room, where I decided to keep it in the washbasin. I was subsequently quite surprised when I discovered that the thing could gradually just melt away, just like the Wicked Witch of the West in "The Wizard of Oz."

By this time, I had bought a used 8-mm movie camera, and some of the rest of our adventures were partly captured in images that amused us for the rest of our lives. One sequence on film was made after the rest of the gang decided to dress up and go to church. I stayed behind for some reason, but when I looked out the Menlo Hotel window to see the car drive up, I began shooting film of the guys in their suits and ties.

They spotted me and all began a duck walk, which was a spoof on me, since I have had that propensity for all my life. I thought then that it ruined the footage, but of course it ultimately became a favorite scene.

We all had a tendency to play tricks on each other. Dick once handed me his billfold on an Oakland street, and then he hung back for a moment while he pretended to adjust some of his clothing.

"Stop thief! He's got my wallet!" Dick suddenly shouted.

I think I threw it at him.

Soon enough, September approached, and we all had to return to Bowling Green for the fall semester. We piled into Jerry's club coupe again and found our way home while routing ourselves past natural wonders like Yosemite and Grand Canyon national parks.

Soon enough, our adulthood began in earnest, and some of us began peeling off into different lives. Dick Clark joined the Navy and began working on aircraft carriers, John Schwarz joined the Army and was eventually accepted as an enlisted musician playing his French horn while marching in the West Point band. Of the California Five, Dallas Brim, Jerry Felty and I continued our full education at Bowling Green State University until graduation in 1954. Other friends like Tom Alspach, Bill Lucas, and Dick Short finished their educations elsewhere.

At BGSU I continued my life dominated by marching and concert bands, the ROTC, the Journalism Department, and my jobs at the aforementioned retail establishments in town.

One concert band performance was conducted by guest conductor Percy Grainger, the innovative composer of modern classical music. At a rehearsal, we all stopped playing in wonderment when at one point he began conducting 4/4 time with one hand and ¾ time with the other — a dizzying and seemingly impossible experience.

For the summer between my junior and senior years, two important events had to be sandwiched together. The first was ROTC summer camp.

The Army ROTC at Bowling Green was designed to prepare us for a commission in the artillery branch. We had classes in calculating azimuths, range-finding, map coordinates, and the "cannoneer's hop" with 105-mm howitzers (at least the sole non-firing one there on the campus).

We were told that young artillery second lieutenants were often used as "forward observers" in combat, meaning a potentially lonely and dangerous job far ahead of their unit, peering through binoculars while calling in and directing artillery fire. Forward observers, we learned, were a major threat to and thus prime targets for the enemy.

But at some point, it was determined that because of my poor eyesight, duck feet or something, I would not be eligible to be an officer in a "combat branch." Instead, I was headed for a commission in the Adjutant General Corps – whatever that might be.

Ergo, I would not be going with Dallas Brim, Tom Alspach, Hal Miller and the rest of my BGSU buddies to the Artillery School at Fort Sill, Oklahoma. And since there was no summer camp for Adjutant General Corps cadets, I would be sent instead to the Infantry ROTC camp at Ft. Meade, Maryland. (This later proved to have an unfortunate side effect.)

On the way to camp I drove my 1941 Hudson to Fort Meade, and decided to have a quick look at Washington, DC on the way. Driving along Pennsylvania Avenue between Lafayette Park and the White House I was surprised to see large groups of noisy people carrying protest signs. The date was June 18, 1953, the eve of the execution of Julius and Ethel Rosenberg who had been convicted of espionage for selling atomic secrets to the Soviet Union.

I seem to have repressed any memories of my Infantry camp at Fort Meade, but at the conclusion, I continued to wear my summer ROTC khaki uniform and drove up to New York City where my sailor friend, Dick Clark, piped me aboard his aircraft carrier, the USS Bennington, for a visit to his new lifestyle. We also toured the city, including the top of the Empire State Building. It was my first visit to Manhattan since my previous trip 14 years before with my parents. And I never suspected that the city would be my home for a significant amount of time in the future.

The last two months of that summer also provided a heady experience. I had been accepted as a journalism summer intern at the *Courier-Express* as a real-life big-city daily news photographer in Buffalo, New York. With my trusty Speed Graphic, I sped this way and that on assignments in Buffalo and surrounding communities, shooting everything I was assigned to shoot, from lost monkeys, various "grip and grins," along with visiting movie stars and various features with dogs or cats.

One assignment was to photograph John Wayne and Ward Bond, who were visiting Buffalo. In their hotel room Wayne talked to me in his distinctive drawl as if he were addressing a young buckaroo who was just learning to ride a horse. I told them I needed a shot that proved they were here in Buffalo.

"Well how 'bout we sit over here next to the window?" said Wayne. "You can see Buffalo out there between us."

"Fine," I said. I was late for my next assignment. I took only one shot and went on to my next job. In any case, I was more in awe of Ward Bond, a name I was more familiar with in those days in relation to his work on many radio shows, of which I was a fan. Also, he had appeared in *Home in Indiana*, along with my forehead-dented Uncle Jay, one of the "background artists."

At the newspaper I was responsible mainly to Bill Woodcock, the picture editor, who everybody called Woody. Woody's pet name for me was "Billy Bones," and that's the way I was identified in captions and photo credit lines in the *Courier-Express*. (I heard much later that when he was in his 70s, Woody ran off for a new life with a copy girl.)

One last college academic year remained at BGSU. I had my first freelance article published, which I think gave me an "A" in feature writing class. It was about my job at the drugstore and was published in a pharmacy magazine. I also had some feature stories with photos in the daily Bowling Green *Sentinel-Tribune*, the city newspaper. For a small town it was (and still is, I believe) a pretty good community paper – though my mother sometimes referred to the *Sentinel-Tribune* as the "Sentimental Trombone."

In June 1954, I was graduated with a Bachelor of Science degree in journalism, majoring in photojournalism – the first BGSU graduate with that major on his diploma.

In 1990, while living in Hawaii and turning out travel guidebooks, I received a plaque from BGSU, declaring that I was now a member of the school's "Journalism Hall of Fame." If that was to encourage me to make a donation of some kind to my alma mater, it failed. I wasn't making that kind of money.

At graduation in 1954, my father and I were photographed together, both of us wearing a cap and gown. As a university professor, he of course, wore one at every graduation ceremony.

The biggest surprise came with my commission as a second lieutenant in the Army Reserve. As expected, of course, I was the only ROTC classmate from BGSU not commissioned in the artillery. But neither was it in that mysterious and dull-sounding Adjutant General Corps. I had gone to infantry summer camp, ergo my commission was in the infantry, and that was that. Apparently my impaired vision, my duck walk, my deviated nasal septum, and whatever else were no longer impediments to my serving in a combat arm of the U.S. Army.

Pat Guthman, my fellow J-grad and love interest at the time, participated in all the graduation hoop-la. She and my mother were photographed together pinning on the two gold bars on the shoulders of my ROTC uniform. Pat brought her parents over to our place for refreshments and photographs. We never actually spoke of getting married, but I thought it was on our minds.

But at the end of it all, I suspected — and I was right — that Pat was much more interested in a tall, handsome, and muscular fellow graduate named Wayne Coil.

Well, by this time the Korean War was no longer a volatile situation, at least. I decided to get my two-year active-duty commitment out of the way immediately, and so at my request, I received orders to report to BIOS — Basic Infantry Officer School at Fort Benning, Georgia.

In due course, Pat married Wayne, and they settled down to a happy and successful marriage in Cleveland. Somehow we didn't communicate again until much later in our lives, but we have remained friends.

9
Army Daze

BIOS WAS AN EYE-OPENER, and I began to see what being in the Army was all about. We were all young officers – "shavetails" – but we went through a relatively gentle form of basic training for several weeks. The only difference was that our enlisted men instructors were relatively polite, referring to us as "gentlemen," instead of just "men."

I don't remember how it came about, but at Fort Benning, I found myself reasonably adept in writing Army-style, official-looking letters. It was partly because I was the only student officer in my immediate area who showed up at BIOS with a portable typewriter, complete with carbon paper.

From time to time I was enlisted by some fellow student who needed to request something from higher up or reply to some official correspondence, in duplicate or triplicate. I recall charging a dollar for the service.

Thinking about my having received my commission in the infantry instead of the artillery or the Adjutant General Corps, I began to suspect that for a large, complex organization, the Army was not as efficient as might be desired. On the other hand, I was in better physical condition than at any time in my life, before or since, and like many of my fellow young lieutenants, I was considering extending my military commitment and signing up to "go airborne."

As part of a campaign to augment the number of young officers in the paratroops, a large demonstration was organized at Fort

Benning. In it, a full battalion, with hundreds of parachutists together with their equipment – Jeeps, howitzers, and the like – would parachute from several airplanes and float down in a field in front of many uniformed spectators, while accompanied by live martial music from the post band.

It was indeed a spectacular event, although marred by an unfortunate mishap. One of the men jumped with a parachute that did not completely deploy. There was some air in it, but not enough. We learned later that it was called a "streamer." The lines were twisted in some way that prevented the optimum amount of air from filling the canopy.

Although not completely a dead weight, the unfortunate soldier was nevertheless passing up all his companions on his way to the ground. While the band continued to play, he thumped to a stop in front of the grandstand. The motionless man was shortly evacuated by ambulance.

I, and many of my fellow shavetails, withdrew our airborne applications shortly thereafter.

Compounding our naïveté, some of us picked up the next issue of the *Bayonet*, the camp newspaper, in an attempt to read a report of the accident and to find out the condition of the unfortunate paratrooper. But there was not a line in the publication about it. Thus I learned that the fair, objective and complete journalism I was taught at BGSU was definitely not included in the mission of the U.S. Army.

A short time later, I found myself taking my first plane ride ever. In a field exercise I was acting as a squad leader when I was unexpectedly ordered to conduct an aerial reconnaissance of the field of battle.

I immediately boarded one of those early Bell helicopters (you've seen them on *M*A*S*H*) where the pilot and one passenger appear to be riding in a large glass bubble. And indeed, from my perspective it seemed as if I was magically suspended in mid-air.

I never would have guessed that the first flight of my life would be in a helicopter. And I think I was too thrilled with the ride to notice whatever it was I was supposed to reconnoiter on the ground below.

At the end of BIOS, we all got our new assignments. A few may have been sent overseas, but it seemed that most members of our class were to report to various units scattered around the country. I was assigned to the Third Armored Division at Fort Knox, Kentucky.

Armor, of course, was one of the combat branches of the Army, along with artillery and infantry. So it looked like I was now about to have had some experience in all three, despite whatever condition it was that was to have kept me out of combat and into the Adjutant General Corps.

But when I reported at Fort Knox I discovered that instead of the highly decorated "Spearhead" tank division that had distinguished itself in the Battle of the Bulge and other wartime campaigns, the Third Armored Division had now been transformed into strictly a training unit.

I was assigned to a basic training company, processing a crop of brand-new recruits every nine weeks. I was the junior of three officers in the company, and I couldn't imagine a worse assignment. In the winter I went to work in the dark and often came back to my BOQ in the dark, exhausted, often after having demonstrated that yes, officers, too, could throw grenades and run the infiltration course, under barbed wire and live bullets.

In a departure from my usual duties, I was once in command of a convoy of three buses taking a company of men to Louisville. I rode in the first bus. But unknown to me, the second and the third buses collided with each other. I was officially responsible for this, and for a time it looked as if I were going to have to pay for the damages.

I don't remember exactly how I got out of that dilemma. Maybe the case is still making its way through channels.

I did have one memorable break during this period. After almost a year marching the troops up and down Misery Hill, supervising firing ranges, and other awful things thankfully forgotten, in April 1955, I received a three-week temporary duty assignment as an umpire for "Operation High Tide," a beach invasion exercise at Little Creek Naval Amphibious Base near Norfolk, Virginia.

Thus, I learned how good naval officers had it as compared to Infantry officers. No crawling around in the dirt for those guys. No, sir. Class A uniforms every day. And there was a beautiful officer's club serving delicious submarine (hoagie) sandwiches – something I had never experienced. After an initial training period, my only physical activity at the end of it all was to climb down the netting on the side of a ship, and then ride an invasion craft to storm the beaches of Virginia.

And as an umpire, I was not really a contestant in the exercise. I recall that during the night following the landing, umpires could build a fire to keep warm in the woods and simply declare that for the purpose of the exercise, it didn't really exist.

Returning to Fort Knox after that halcyon experience, I discovered that life could indeed be worse than my previous assignment at that post. This time I was assigned to an armor training unit, supervising troops dealing with what seemed to me to be dirty and greasy tanks virtually from dawn to dusk.

My new company commander was a first lieutenant, while I was still just a second louie – one rank below him. In my mind, he seemed a tyrant – so bad, I thought, that I suspected he would trip up eventually – and when he did I would know what to do.

Among my many extra duties, I was appointed Red Cross officer. When it came time to solicit donations from the troops, this CO told me that since his own regimental commander wanted 100% cooperation, our company would certainly comply.

"I want you to make it clear to the men, Bone, that if they don't have enough money to contribute to the Red Cross, they don't have enough money to go on pass!"

I protested that that kind of coercion was illegal and that while I would serve as the company's Red Cross officer, I would not pass on that specific command. This refusal just brought on still more extra duties for me, and a repetition that his order to me must indeed be carried out.

So drawing on my expertise at writing military-style letters at Fort Benning, I reported my CO to the IG – the Inspector General's Office. At the same time I also suggested that there must be an assignment for me at Fort Knox that would take advantage of my journalism training.

One possibility, I thought, might be the Fort Knox Public Information Office. I had met a few PIOs there briefly, including Lieutenant Gay Talese. Talese had been a copy boy for *The New York Times*, and it was thought already that he might be headed for eventual greatness. (Indeed, in later years he would become a *Times* reporter and subsequently a successful author of several books.)

I don't know exactly what happened after my IG complaint, except that someone involved in the inspector process later quoted my company commander as saying: "I don't care what you do with him. Just get the sonofabitch out of my company!"

First thing you know, with perhaps eight months remaining on my active duty requirement, I suddenly received orders to report for duty at the Training Literature and Reproduction Department of the Armor School. There at TL&R, I became the assistant editor working on military lesson plans and instruction manuals.

My new boss was a major who occupied the desk next to mine. The man was a genuine expert in the use of the English language – a grammarian who could take the most screwed-up lesson plan, often written by high ranking officers, and make it complete and clear to anyone. For the next six months I received some expert on-the-job training in a field that I mistakenly thought I already knew a lot about – or rather a field about which I mistakenly thought I already knew a lot.

Not that I agreed with the major on everything. He was definitely from an older Army – one who still believed, for example, that a commissioned officer should never carry a package. He also disapproved that even a lowly lieutenant like me would socialize with the enlisted ranks – privates, corporals, and sergeants. He did acknowledge, however, that these practices were beginning to break down now in the 1950s.

In due course, I was promoted to first lieutenant, and even received some kind of commendation for my TL&R work. My duty hours at the office were now from 8:30 to 4:30, Monday through Friday, and I wore Class A uniform every day. (No boots and fatigues except for rare occasions when I had to renew my proficiency on the rifle range.) On top of all that, a non-com or a civilian secretary often brought coffee and doughnuts to my desk in the morning.

With all that new free time, and despite my major's avuncular disapproval, I joined the Fort Knox Little Theater Group, and began to help build sets, learn speaking roles, socialize with other amateur theater buffs, and develop some friends who were civilians and enlisted men.

And there I met Peggy – the daughter of one of the highest-ranking officers on the post. It was soon apparent that besides our common love of amateur theater, we also shared a strong interest in sex.

Peggy might have been the same age or a year or so older than I. But in this field of expertise, she was imbued with the wisdom of the ages. I supposed it was a heritage of living for 20 years or so in many parts of the modern and ancient world – a "military brat," as they say. In any case, there was much for me to learn, and Peggy would teach me a lot.

"You're really very conventional, aren't you?" she smiled sweetly, and in a quote I remember vividly: "Come on. Let's try some other stuff!"

I liked her a lot, even with her clothes on. We frequently enjoyed drinking Gibsons and dining on filet mignon at the Fort Knox officer's club. And, of course the theater work gave us a common intellectual outlet.

Not that I didn't make mistakes. Once I complimented her on her appearance when she herself thought she was unattractive and dressed informally. Wow, did she get mad. I never made that mistake again – with her or any other woman.

My worst tactical error, however, took place about three weeks into the relationship. I confessed to her that although I had run the bases with college women, she had been my first home run. Sure enough, that led soon to the dreaded it's-not-you-it's-me speech.

"I'm sorry," she said. "I know that shouldn't make any difference. But I have to tell myself that the guy is…well…you know."

Been around the block a few more times, I guess she meant. And probably an impossibility, I thought.

So I had indeed made the ultimate fatal faux pas. Less than a week later Peggy chose a different companion from the Fort Knox Players. Frankly, I thought that he seemed more like a virgin than I did. But in any case, he was a nice guy, and I was a bit exhausted. He later confessed to me privately that Peggy had "saved" him from suffering through a miserable Army career.

I was ultimately satisfied with my own crash course in the military *Kama Sutra* despite its sudden cessation. I filed it away mentally in pretty much the same logical terms that I was using while editing all those lesson plans and field manuals at the TL&R Department.

I didn't like the Army very much, but as a learning experience, it was invaluable. Some of it, anyway.

As the countdown began toward the day I would again become free of the Army, I felt gradually more and more liberated.

I took a part in a live radio play on a civilian station near Fort Knox.

I visited some old Mammoth Cave friends since the national park was not far from Fort Knox, reminiscing on those carefree days of six years earlier.

I even dated a young woman in nearby Louisville for a short time, but she inadvertently repelled me when she talked of "learning how to return your love," and other phrases that I thought just too saccharine for words.

The best experience during these final Army days was when a millionaire flew me to New York City for the weekend.

In an issue of *Editor and Publisher* magazine I had learned that a Manhattan plutocrat wanted to establish a new daily newspaper in a small town in competition with an old established daily, probably in upstate New York. This was J. M. Kaplan, sometimes known as the Welch Grape Juice King, but who was also famous for various philanthropic and inspirational enterprises in New York.

The idea was based on recent technical improvements in the off-set printing process meaning that a new daily newspaper could be established and produced more rapidly and cheaply than previously. But this was not the main attraction for me.

Because the printing was done without using the traditional "hot type" letterpress method, photographs could be reproduced in much higher quality – about a 110-line screen, close to the glossy magazine reproduction in magazines like *Life* and *Newsweek*. Virtually all other daily papers had letterpress systems and could only use photos engraved with about a 65-line screen, a much lower resolution – i.e., fewer and larger dots in each photo.

I applied for a job on this non-existent futuristic publication. To my surprise I received a letter, some advance expenses, and a plane ticket for a quick flight from Louisville to Manhattan for a Saturday night interview.

J. M. Kaplan's office was in the Empire State Building, and I took a taxi from LaGuardia Airport to see him. But instead of the great man himself, I was interviewed by an aide, Harry S. Milligan.

Harry pointed out that this new newspaper would use many more and often larger photographs, including a two-page center fold feature picture spread in every issue, seven days a week. The reporters would all also need to be photographers – something simply not allowed on most daily papers that were hampered by union contracts. The Newspaper Guild almost universally prohibited photographers from acting as reporters and reporters from taking photographs. This would be a non-union newspaper.

For me, trained as much as a photographer as a reporter, it would be the ideal dream job. I also liked very much doing "layout" – designing the centerfold and other feature picture pages.

At the end of the interview, Harry told me I could have the job. In fact he added that I could probably design and equip the photo needs, including the darkroom, to my specifications. There was only one problem. I would be out of the Army in April and the plans for the paper might not come to fruition for several months.

I didn't care. I told him I would find something to keep me busy in the meantime.

Lieutenant Bone, Officer of the Day, Fort Knox, Kentucky, 1955.

10
Buffalo & Middletown

RETURNING TO MY PARENTS' home in Bowling Green, I had a good idea just what to do. I called up "Sky King," the managing editor of the Buffalo *Courier-Express*, where I had been a summer intern while in college. I told him that this Army vet was ready to come back to work at the paper again, this time as a full-time photographer.

Actually his name was *Cy* King, but I always mentally pictured him as the flamboyant cowboy aviator of radio-TV fame.

So again I shuffled off to Buffalo and again I joined the cadre of photographers in the photo department, photographing loose monkeys, visiting movie stars, and the occasional accident or fire.

Most of the photo staff was much older than I. Closer to my age, though, was Bob Scott, a Canadian citizen married to an American. "Scottie" often was sent on assignment in Canada, whose border crossing was near Buffalo at Niagara Falls. So he learned to pronounce "Buffalo" with a loud and distinctly American accent in order to forestall time-consuming questions and a possible interview every time he was asked his residence when re-crossing the border to return to the office.

But most of the best photo assignments went to chief photog Frank Schifferle or to a long-time veteran photographer named Iggy Sorgi. Iggy, who might have been described as Buffalo's answer to Alfred Eisenstaedt, took a liking to me and at some point, Iggy proudly presented me with an 11x14 personally autographed copy of his most famous photograph.

Iggy's prize photo, taken in Buffalo in 1942 with an old Graflex with a 1/1000th of a second focal-plane shutter, was a technically perfect image of a woman who jumped from a high floor in a Buffalo hotel. Iggy's camera captured her in mid-air in her last second of life just before she hit the sidewalk.

From time to time over the years I have displayed interesting autographs and photographs on the walls of my various residences. But somehow, I could never bring myself to do it with that depressing image. Incidentally, when Iggy died at 83 in 1995, that famous photo was even mentioned in his obituary.

The best thing that happened to me in Buffalo in 1956 was that I met a lovely woman named Virginia Falcone. Ginny was a nurse, and ever since that day, I have been especially attracted to nurses, most of whom seem to possess a special ingrained empathy for and genuine interest in people they meet.

I even managed to get her picture into the *Courier-Express*, testing some drinking water or something. (I still have the clipping somewhere.) Every time we went out together, I took her photo. Then fellow-photog Bob Scott, took an excellent portrait of us together, too, which I then thought would probably be the one saved for our children and grandchildren. For the first time, I was truly falling in love.

Ginny was a Roman Catholic, and she convinced me to go to church with her a few times. She told me about things I never thought about. I remember the concept of Limbo, which I had never heard of. But she wasn't able to tell me the difference between Limbo and Purgatory – at least not to my satisfaction. I remember thinking that either or both were probably like being in an elevator stuck between two floors, a sense of being absolutely nowhere – something I was already familiar with. As an unbaptized agnostic, that's where I was no doubt headed.

I also kidded her about church members routinely praying for the conversion of Russia. To me that was an exercise in futility. (Years later I noted that they finally gave up on that – several years before the 1991 collapse of the Soviet Union. Too bad, perhaps. I thought the Catholics, with all those prayers, might otherwise have been able to take some of the credit for that.)

In June, 1956, about the time I was first going to propose to Ginny, I got the highly anticipated call from the aforementioned Harry Milligan, henchman to Kaplan, the Welch Grape Juice king. The new newspaper launch would be in Middletown, New York in Orange County, about 60 miles from New York City. And it was about to go full steam ahead. Would I like to come to work immediately and take charge of setting up the photo facilities?

Cy King seemed hurt when I told him I was leaving the *Courier-Express*, and he quizzed me for several minutes in his office, asking me for all the reasons. Of course I had to say it wasn't him, it was me!

Again, I was looking forward to the thrill of the new – an affliction that has guided me or dogged me for better or for worse up to then and for many years thereafter.

And on the bright side, I still looked forward to seeing Ginny, at least on the weekends, since Middletown was only about a five-hour determined lover's drive south of Buffalo via the New York State Thruway.

My new career in Middletown was in most ways a dream job, even more thrilling than my summer at Mammoth Cave. I spared no expense in setting up the photo and darkroom facilities. I bought one Speed Graphic, but I knew the trend was going to smaller format cameras, so I also bought three twin-lens reflexes, which would be easier for the average reporter to handle.

These cameras took 12 photos on a roll, 2½ inches square, relieving the photographer from having to decide between horizontal or vertical We had each reporter shoot a self-portrait at the end of an assignment so that the darkroom would know to whom the photos were to go. Generally the reporter then turned in a contact sheet along with his story.

After about a week of dry runs, the first official issue of the Middletown *Daily Record* came off the presses on July 30, 1956 in a tabloid format. In the subsequent weeks and months, it made a wide-ranging impression, not only on Middletown, but also on the business and technical cadres of newspapers all over the country. It was hailed as the first large scale offset printing process for daily newspapers in the U.S. We had visiting delegations dropping in almost daily from all over the country.

Eventually I complained that my work in the darkroom, etc., was cutting into my opportunities to write stories, take pictures, and design feature picture pages. So they hired a darkroom man, an enthusiastic older fellow named Ben Wiggins. We became good friends and excellent colleagues. I miss Ben to this day, and regret having lost track of him over the years.

With Ben's help, I developed an initially difficult process that we called pre-screening – an important technique then, but certainly now out-of-date. In some cases, photos could be printed in our darkroom to the exact dimensions they would be used in the newspaper, but projected through a screen in order to put the needed dots onto the image. This technique was also a definite time saver, a special benefit when on deadline.

It was a challenge at first because the dots all needed to be totally black – not gray. The ultimate and desired amount of grayness was an illusion indicated by dots that were smaller than the larger ones, which formed darker parts of the image. If the print had true gray dots instead of black ones, it might look correct to the eye but not work on the ultimate printed page. We finally found we needed to use extremely high-contrast enlarging paper to do the job.

Of course these kinds of problems no longer exist on modern daily papers most of which now generally use fine-screen images on offset presses. But the Middletown *Daily Record* was the first, and I was proud to have been an important part of it.

Along with other reporters on the newspaper, I soon developed an *esprit de corps* that resulted in enthusiastic competition with the long-established Middletown *Times-Herald*.

That paper had had an interesting history itself. It was owned by Ralph Ingersoll, who was previously a respected figure in the publications world in New York City, including the early incarnations of magazines such as *The New Yorker*. He was most famous as the founder of the idealistic but short-lived no-advertising newspaper, *PM,* in New York City in the 1940s.

But without competition in Middletown, the *Times-Herald* coverage of local news was uninspiring. Soon after the *Record* was founded, the *Times-Herald* hired fresh blood, and its coverage began to improve considerably. It was often said in those days that Middletown and Orange County, which had one mediocre newspaper for many years, suddenly found they had two really good ones.

Our first managing editor, Bill DeMeza, was a hard-working veteran of several newspapers, and he immediately won the affection of the staff. Some of his actions were dramatic:

When smoking was common in newspaper offices, occasionally a small fire might erupt in a wastebasket full of paper. One such began to flare up one evening near Bill's desk while he was busy on deadline. Without missing a beat, and without even removing his copy pencil from his hand, Bill quickly picked up another basket, and shoved it into the first one. End of story, fire out, and I'll never forget that technique.

There often was a lot of pent-up energy among the staff of the paper in the early days. One evening, after the last flat was sent to the pressroom, another editor, Bill Loftus, started a water balloon fight to release all the tension. We all loved it – except perhaps one David Bernstein, who thankfully wasn't there to see it.

Bernstein held the title of "publisher," and he maintained his control supposedly from an office near J. M. Kaplan at grape juice headquarters in the Empire State Building in Manhattan. Occasionally, however, Bernstein would drive 60 miles north to Middletown to exercise a little personal control.

During World War II, he had served as a PIO (public information officer) to General Douglas McArthur in the Philippines, and so he thought he knew a lot about journalism. He also seemed to have inherited something of the general's storied demeanor.

One day, Bernstein's Cadillac pulled up in our parking lot beside the paper and he discovered that the trunk of my car was left open, revealing several items of photographic equipment. He was livid with the thought that the camera, flash, film holders, and other company property were in danger of being stolen. He was right, of course. Somehow I had carelessly overlooked the open trunk, and on being informed of the situation I ran out and took care of it. (Actually the only camera in view turned out to be my personal property.)

When he got back to New York later that day, he took a pad of light blue paper, each sheet of which was pre-printed "From the desk of David Bernstein" at the top. On it he scrawled a two-word message and mailed it to editor Bill DeMeza:

"Fire Bone!"

When Bill received it, he pulled up some discarded yellow wire service copy, tore it into a small piece, put it in his typewriter and typed on the back:

"From the wastebasket of Bill DeMeza:

"Bone stays!"

I also survived a second legendary "firing" at the *Record*. When the paper hired a new advertising manager whose name also happened to be "Kaplan," Assistant Editor Bill Loftus (of water balloon fame) suggested I go see "Mr. Kaplan" in the office.

I, of course, thought that the almost legendary J. M. Kaplan, the great grape juice financier whom none of us had ever seen, had finally come down from the heights of the Empire State Building to check on his Middletown domain.

Irv Kaplan was actually a fatherly -looking fellow with a Stalin-type mustache, and absolutely no relation to J. M. In any other situation, I would have found him an immediately amusing and good-natured fellow. He proceeded to question me about my experience, motivation, and other things while I nervously tried to come up with the right kinds of answers. At the end of it all, my inquisitor suggested that perhaps I should be looking for work elsewhere.

Of course, it was all just a grand joke, and for years afterwards, fellow ex-reporters and editors would ask me to tell them the story of how I was once "fired" by the advertising manager of the *Record*.

The only person who remained un-amused, however, was my Buffalo girlfriend Ginny, who was visiting me in Middletown at the time. It was a long time before she forgave those who had perpetrated the joke.

And as far as I know, the real J. M. Kaplan never did visit the Middletown *Daily Record*, unless he did so later or while I was on a leave of absence. He died in 1988 at the age of 95 – long after selling his interests in Middletown.

Bill DeMeza, who had refused to fire me, was later instrumental in furthering my international journalism career.

Part II

1957-1971

Ben Wiggins and Bob Bone work on a picture feature layout for the Middletown Daily Record.

11

All at Sea, in More Ways Than One

I CONTINUED TO SEE GINNY THROUGHOUT my first year at the *Record*. We stayed together in Buffalo, Middletown, and in visits to Manhattan, which we both loved. We couldn't afford to go to Broadway shows, etc., but I always mentally associated our romance with *My Fair Lady*, especially the song "On the Street Where You Live," which was then popular.

We didn't know anybody in New York in 1957, and we stayed several times at the Hotel Paris, on 97th Street, a wonderful 1920s-style building a few steps from Riverside Drive, and a stone's throw or two from where I had briefly lived with my parents 20 years earlier.

After a year working for the *Record*, two disappointments presented themselves. I bought an engagement ring for Ginny, and then discovered that she really wasn't ready for that step, although she did wear it for a day during a final Buffalo visit.

Her family was against it, and then in a double disappointment, I discovered that mine was also. Ginny was a good Catholic and I, like my family was an agnostic Protestant. I was raised in an atmosphere of tolerance, however, and I was surprised and deeply disappointed that my own parents, especially my mother, were not keen about having a Catholic daughter-in-law and, I suppose, Catholic grandchildren.

My mother constructed and sent me a sort of sentimental scrapbook, with several photographs, old letters, and the like outlining something of our family history. Unsaid, I suppose, was the thought that I would be letting the family and our ancestors down if I were to default in some way to the Catholic religion.

Perhaps I should have fought back at all these impediments, but for better or worse, I didn't. I sold the ring back to an unamused jewelry storeowner in Middletown for a fraction of the price I paid.

My next idea was flying lessons. I could finance that under the G.I. Bill if the newspaper would sign off on the idea. That idea was killed too, this time by David Bernstein again. The publisher thought that if I got into an accident, the newspaper would be financially responsible.

By that time, I knew a big change was needed. I decided that I would quit the *Record* and go to Europe. My old mentor Harry Milligan convinced me not to cut my ties with the paper but to seek a leave of absence instead. It was immediately granted.

So I promised to return to the paper in a year. Yet, it was a promise that I wasn't sure I would keep.

I'd saved some money to start a new life with Ginny, and now applied that toward an adventure beginning in the United Kingdom. I didn't really have enough to cover all contingencies. But what the hell, I wanted to go.

In the 1950s, only the rich flew from New York to Europe, and then only on slow propeller flights. In any case, I was sure it would be much more fun to travel by ship. There were a number of choices of vessels out of New York. After very little research, I booked Tourist (third) Class passage on the Cunard Line's RMS *Scythia,* which offered a nine-day-long voyage from New York City to Liverpool, England.

Illogically named for an ancient civilization bordering the Black Sea, the *Scythia* was then the oldest ship in Cunard's fleet of a dozen liners. Launched in 1920, it was converted to a troop ship during World War II. When the war ended in 1945, it was briefly famous in Canada when it transported a large number of war brides of Canadian soldiers from Liverpool to Halifax.

The *Scythia* boasted a single funnel and two tall masts, one forward and one aft, design features carried over from a previous age.

For all I knew, it could still have raised a couple of sails to use in an emergency.

I boarded the *Scythia* in September 1957, and found my bunk somewhere below the water line. Well, I'm not sure about that, but there was definitely no window or porthole on our deck. It was as dark in the daytime as it was at night.

I shared the cabin with three other guys. The bathroom was somewhere down the passageway. I didn't care. I had a bunk and all meals included for the next nine days on the ocean. What was not to love?

This was not a cruise ship. In the '50s, passenger ships were line voyages, hence the term "ocean liner" – designed to take folks from one place to another. Like many vessels of the era, the *Scythia* offered three classes of travel: First Class, Cabin Class, and Tourist Class. One of the best things about Tourist Class, from my point of view, was that all dining was conducted on long tables where the passengers couldn't help getting to know one another while passing the salt.

And speaking of salt, on day one, I picked up the "shaker" to salt my spinach and inadvertently smothered it. I had never seen a British-style single-hole salt container before. This experience was symbolic of the kind of exotic stuff I was soon going to learn on my first trip outside the U.S.A.

Tourist Class on the Scythia that trip consisted largely of quick-witted young people. These were British who were going home after a summer visiting the U.S., and Americans, some of whom were on their way to study abroad for a semester or two. I didn't fall into either of those categories.

I was not exactly sure just why I was on board.

Our dining room, lounge, and a small section of open deck were at the stern. Nevertheless, a congenial multicultural group of us soon formed, and we began calling ourselves the "Blunt End Kids." We called the First Class area up near the bow the "sharp end." In theory, the sharp-enders had the run of the ship, but we never saw any tuxedo-clad dandies down our way.

Cabin Class passengers, however, who occupied the middle area of the ship were allowed to invade the Tourist Class area, and indeed there was one Cabin couple who often attached themselves to our active group. But the rest of us were kept strictly to our own modest quarters and the open deck aft.

At night we had an orchestra of sorts, consisting of four gray-haired men on violin, piano, drums, and saxophone. They favored us with tunes that included Marty Robbins' "A White Sport Coat and a Pink Carnation," and Bob Russell's "You Came a Long Way from Saint Louie."

I learned to dance the *schottische* on the *Scythia*. I also learned that it was fun to run up the carpeted stairways between the decks in rhythm with the downward pitch of the ship as it plowed through heavy North Atlantic swells – a light-footed experience. The Blunt End Kids didn't rate an elevator.

Stabilizers hadn't been invented yet, either, but we didn't roll much anyway. But I remember being surprised that the ship creaked, and the sound was particularly noticeable after dark. Then a crew-member told me that all ships creaked, and soon enough, it became a welcome, comforting sound, especially at night – and it always has been. (After more than 50 cruises today, I still love it.)

In any case, our lungs were full of the bracing sea air, and our young legs were strong. In my general exuberance one midnight, and unknown to anyone else on board, I climbed to the top of the mast and looked down on what seemed to be a toy boat bobbing about in the midst of a great, dark sea. I could have fallen to my death, the smoke from the funnel could have changed direction and over-whelmed me. So I'll never do it again. But I'll also never forget the thrill.

Almost immediately after boarding I began paying special at-tention to Orah Moyal, an attractive woman of 20 who exhibited a type of sophistication that I had not previously experienced. She had spent the summer in San Francisco, and she spoke often of a man named Sol she had met there. Orah had come to love the city, and I shared with her the experiences there with my Ohio buddies in San Francisco and Oakland six years earlier.

Orah and I were soon spending most of our waking hours together. I couldn't imagine what she could see in me other than just a naïve young American with a short haircut. Anyway, I thought that I might be falling a little bit in love again. Anyway, it was a feeling that went a long way toward curing my disappointment with Ginny.

Orah Iliana Moyal (I loved saying her full name out loud) was British, but born in Israel. She and her family had been refugees from Nazi Germany in World War II. She spent some time in Paris and was fluent in French. And she was really into art appreciation – the French Impressionists, mostly. I thought she had the most delightful voice, with an accent very different from other Britons.

By the time we landed in Liverpool, we made a promise to each other to meet again soon in London, after she visited her mother and grandmother in Manchester.

12
At Home in London

ON THE TRAIN FROM LIVERPOOL to London, I ordered roast beef with Yorkshire pudding – and liked it a lot. New country – new food, I thought.

But not every subsequent culinary experience was as inspiring. I recall that there was a chain of shops selling what they called the "Wimpy," based on a popular hamburger-loving character then in the Popeye comic strip.

The Wimpy was a disaster, as far as I was concerned. I couldn't even finish the one I bought. (I understand they still exist, and per-haps have improved a lot, but on subsequent visits to Britain, I never had the nerve to try one again.)

My first digs in the city were a rented room in a private home. It included breakfast, too. Ever after I developed a habit of always eating a big breakfast in foreign countries because you never knew what you could afford or what strange stuff might be on your plate the rest of the day.

"Cold, hard and dry," I learned was the British preferred form of toast. But when I was confronted with a soft-boiled egg in a shell standing upright in a small pedestal, I didn't quite know what to do with it. The lady of the house, surprised to see that I was completely unschooled in egg cuppery, showed me how to gently crack the shell open at the top, slice off the upper bit and then take the tiny spoon to scoop out the insides.

That landlady also had lots of opinions on people she'd met that I, at first, did not entirely comprehend.

"You know, I've always *liked* Americans really," she admitted. "As long as you don't get two or more of them together!"

Soon enough, I couldn't wait to get out of that place.

I saw little of London before I met John Frey, from Dayton, another American about my age. He was an architectural student who had just bought a brand-new left-hand drive (that is, the American configuration) Ford Anglia that he was later going to export to the U.S. Meanwhile, he was going to drive it throughout England to experience, take notes, and photograph every cathedral he could find. John said he was going to stay at youth hostels along the way and that I could come along with him because he wanted the company.

John was single-minded in his academic pursuit. We saw cathedral after cathedral but almost nothing else. I remember driving by Stonehenge, glimpsed only at a distance from the moving car. I wanted to see it, but it was not on John's list. And we were late for touring the next cathedral at Canterbury before dark – or something.

Furthermore, it was a frightening time for me whenever he wanted to pass a large commercial lorry. All roads were two lanes, and of course we drove in the left one like everyone else. But I was sitting in the position the driver normally would sit in England. I could usually see when there was no room to pass before he could. My comments were often limited to "No! Get back, Frey! Get back!"

In those days at least, young drivers with new and expensive cars were generally not welcome at youth hostels. We usually parked down the road, slipped on backpacks and then walked to the door of the hostel just as if we had been hiking all day with not a bead of sweat on our brows.

After about three weeks of inspecting trefoils, gables, and flying buttresses, we returned to London. Frey took his Anglia on to the Continent, driving on the right again, and where he no longer needed a screaming companion in the passenger seat to tell him when it might not be safe to pass. We never met again.

I went first to the American Express office to pick up mail, which is what Americans did in those days, whether they were official clients of American Express or not. Remembering my previous success using the Oakland post office for rendezvousing with my buddies in 1951, I had told Orah to write me c/o American Express in London, and we would find each other.

Orah's letter was waiting for me, and I had a short time to find us a place to stay. I came up with a small room in a hotel in Kensington, which we kept for a few days.

As happy as we were to see each other, Orah insisted that from here on we must now maintain separate quarters, and so we found two non-connecting rooms in the slightly better but also small Hotel Alexa nearby at 73 Lexham Gardens. It was a stone's throw from Earl's Court, a busy commercial intersection with a convenient Underground Station.

From there we could get "the tube" to almost any place we might want to explore in London, and we spent a lot of time together happily learning our way around the city. Orah was looking for work during this period, and finally came up with a tiny nearby restaurant down some outdoor steps and below street level in nearby Hogarth Place, called Ann's Kitchen.

So now, as the Prophet said, there were spaces in our togetherness. I began reading some of the books Orah recommended, including naturally enough, Leon Uris' *Exodus,* about the founding of Israel.

And early during this period occurred the most depressing and initially embarrassing experience thus far in my young life. At first, I couldn't even tell Orah about it.

I was having lunch alone in a Lyon's Tea Shop, a chain restaurant then about as ubiquitous in London as McDonald's is in the U.S. today. Seated near me was an attractive woman, about my age, who struck up a conversation.

"You're really an American?" she asked. "I've never met an American before!"

She then asked me if I had an American passport.

"I've never seen an American passport. Would you show it to me?"

As it happened, I was indeed carrying the thing with me (why, I will never know) and so I let her take a look. She studied it for a moment, and then suddenly she made a dash for the ladies room with my official documentation – AND NEVER CAME OUT!

At my request some minutes later, a woman employee went in to have a look. There was nobody there. And a window was open.

Well, I thought I knew what to do. I knew where the American Embassy was, and that very day I trudged rather sheepishly past that imposing statue of FDR in the front garden and entered the large building to report the unfortunate occurrence to the consular offices.

After filling out a couple of forms, I was quickly granted an audience with the most upset first lieutenant I'd ever seen – on a par or even more so than with my old CO in the tank training company at Fort Knox.

The more he talked, the angrier he got. What the hell was wrong with me, he wanted to know. Did I know I was a disgrace to America, bumming around England like this? And how will I feel when I run out of money and I have to appeal to the embassy to send me home? This guy went on and on. I'll never forget that day, and from time to time over the years, I have had occasion to remember the tongue-lashing I received.

I had been a first lieutenant myself a couple of years earlier. Nevertheless, I felt the sting, even if I could not bring myself to believe that I was bringing quite that much disgrace on myself and my native land as he claimed.

The last thing he declared was that I should also report the theft to the local authorities. And with a certain amount of trepidation, I went home and phoned the police, with my voice quavering considerably.

"Well now, Mr. Bone. I wouldn't worry very much about this matter, if I were you," said the slow and reassuring voice. "These things usually have a way of working themselves out."

The officer was virtually patting me on the head over the telephone. It was hard to believe that I had experienced such a contrast between my mean and heartless countryman at the embassy and this avuncular British police officer on the phone.

Less than a week later I received a phone call from another policeman, with a similar even-tempered voice:

"Ah, hello, Mr. Bone. I wonder if at your convenience you could pop 'round and see us here at the Tottenham Court Police Station?" he asked.

"I believe we have your passport here."

Of course I complied immediately. Initially they were just going to have me sign a receipt and let me go on my way. But there I gently protested, saying the event had disturbed me greatly and could I please have a little more information?

"Well, we picked up a young woman on a drug charge, and in the process we discovered that she was in possession of an American passport. I don't think she knew exactly what she was going to do with it. We surmise that she thought somehow that it might be worth some money."

I thanked the officer profusely. I didn't bother to inform the American Embassy, however, and for all I know it might still be an open case at the State Department, just like my bus accident in Louisville. But I did speak to that gung-ho intolerant lieutenant again – or perhaps his counterpart – in Moscow about nine years later. Stay tuned for that one.

My Grandma used to say, "In the end, everything works out for the best." That's been pretty much my experience, too. As long as you keep your health and your wits about you, you'll get along somehow.

Dago Morris, the car with underperforming
offside and nearside lights.

13

On Fleet Street

MEAGER AS IT WAS, I was not entirely without income. I had begun mailing a few articles and photographs of my experience on the *Scythia* and some wide-eyed impressions of London back to the Middletown *Daily Record*. They were running them and even paying me for them. Apparently I was now a "local angle," being that mine was at least a recognizable byline because of my previous staff work there. And the Bowling Green *Sentinel Tribune* was also buying the same stories.

At age 25, I was now a foreign correspondent.

As for my getting a real job, I was told several times to forget about it. Foreigners in England would have to be granted a work permit – a virtual impossibility, everyone agreed. So sometimes Orah and I pooled our resources just to share a meal or two.

Up to this point, I confess I was not paying as much attention as usual to current world and U.S. affairs. I do remember one day in early October seeing one of those special news agents' hand-made placards, written more or less like headlines, that warned: "Red Moon over London."

This marked the beginning of the U.S. vs. U.S.S.R. space race. The Soviets had beaten the Americans to the punch by launching Sputnik, the first successful artificial earth satellite. I didn't know that this was going to be important to me three months later.

Along with one check from the *Record*, I received a note from Bill DeMeza, the managing editor who had saved my bacon by defying publisher David Bernstein. Bill gave me the name of an editor he had known in Rome and whom he thought I might like to look up on Fleet Street.

Fleet Street, of course, was not just the name of a street. It was considered the nexus of British journalism, and where several daily newspapers were headquartered. The man Bill mentioned was a photo editor with United Press. He turned out to be a perpetually intense and worried-looking gentleman with a pronounced limp named Leo Stoecker.

To my intense surprise, Leo offered me a job!

The photo department of United Press in London during the 1950s was also registered under the name Planet News Limited. There were a half-dozen or so staff photographers, three or four darkroom technicians, and I became one of about four "editors" – photo deskmen who alternated between three eight-hour shifts – daytime, evening, and overnight.

Our mission at Planet and UP-London was three-fold: (1) to service all the British papers with local and world-wide photographic coverage, (2) to service all the UP bureaus and newspaper clients on the European continent with photo coverage that either originated in our London headquarters or came in from the U.S., and (3) to a somewhat lesser degree to service the UP headquarters in New York with photo coverage from London, as required or requested. I believe the Continental UP bureaus generally fed their photo coverage directly to New York.

It was a complex operation, since not everything was supposed to go everywhere, and there were constant requests from the bureaus and clients for photographs, either existing ones or photos to be especially assigned.

These complications were exacerbated by the fact that there were several different types of wire photo machines in use – different standards depending on who in which country was going to be receiving the photographs over phone lines. The darkroom men often had to make prints of different dimensions to wrap around different-sized cylinders in order to be able to transmit them over phone lines to the receivers in far-away cities. We deskmen were both photo traffic cops and caption writers, too.

There were also messages to be sent, everything usually typed in triplicate so the copies could go to different transmitting points in the building – always typed without "the" or "an" in special transmission-speak. Some messages went "overhead," racking up charges based on word or message length. (For example, "Exlondon" meant "from London." "ProNewYork" was "for New York." And for some unknown reason, "Rox" meant Associated Press – the competition. I can no longer remember all of the codes we used.

And the British government was persuaded to let me do this job since I would be the only American in the office (not counting Leo), and supposedly imbued with special knowledge of the American photo market, etc.

Also, unlike my fellow deskmen, I would be paid with checks for U.S. dollars instead of British pounds, so apparently I would not be a drain on the local economy – another point in my favor. I converted my checks to pounds, shillings, and pence at American Express.

Yes, the U.K. was not then on the decimal system. There were 12 pennies (or pence) to the shilling, 20 shillings to the pound. And there were coins like the half-crown, which was worth two shillings and sixpence.

The job was often difficult and hectic, but I was ecstatic. I liked my fellow workers, and I was now able to remain in London for an indefinite period. I became familiar with the names of famous British and European newspapers and magazines. I also soaked up all the unique or unusual experiences of mid-century British life – like drinking warm beer and learning to eat peas squashed on the back of my fork. These were all weird and wonderful things.

And with my new status as an employee, Orah and I could now continue to explore the city for months ahead. And so I bought a car.

A vehicle that made it through the Blitz, it was a 1938 Morris, two years newer than my first car in B.G. I can't remember the exact price, but it was cheap enough, and I quickly learned to swing around the Piccadilly Circus roundabout with expert abandon. (At that time, it was still a complete circle.) The car had all sorts of strange quirks, the details of which I've forgotten. I remember the turn indicators were like little yellow ears that unfolded from the sides of the car and then popped back in again.

One ongoing difficulty was the little lights mounted on the fenders. In the U.S. we called them parking lights. Several times a friendly bobby would stop me and say something like "Sir, your *offside* light is off." Or sometimes it was "Sir, your *nearside* light is out." I would thank him immediately and promise to take care of it "directly."

My only problem was I never really learned my nearside from my offside. And besides, when I got the car home again, both lights would be working just fine.

Orah loved our car. She named it "Dago," inspired by the number plate, which was DKO 201. I put a Middletown *Daily Record* "press" sign just inside the windscreen, and a UP (United Press) decal on one of the wing windows. We took several photos of ourselves with Dago. It seemed like our handicapped adopted child – one who didn't know his nearside from his offside.

I should point out to Americans who visit Britain today that London in the winter of '57-58 looked and smelled different then. Buses and taxis were all run by diesel engines, giving them a certain aroma and a special sound. Today when I catch a whiff of diesel fuel on a cold damp morning, or hear a certain putter-putter sound, I am reminded of London in the middle of the last century.

Burning coal and wood at home or in industry was permitted, and the faces of public buildings were dirty and grimy. Moreover, the city was often dark with air pollution and it was almost impossible to see the sun at least during the winter months.

Interestingly, there were Londoners who declared that they liked it that way, and complained years later when things began to get cleaned up.

I maintain that during the winter when I held that job with UP, the sun was out just once when I was actually off work. And that was the day that Orah and I chose to explore Hampstead Heath, a large tract of hilly parkland in North London.

We occasionally held hands as we let ourselves get lost on the many trails of the heath. We also sang and told jokes. Orah sang "You'd Be So Easy to Love" and then she told that awful joke about a strange animal called the Rarey who, when being pushed over the cliff, protested: "It's a long way to tip a Rarey!"

Orah's singing of that old Cole Porter standard seemed to sum up our situation. I had been coming to the conclusion that despite our current affinity for one another, when it came to Orah's future life partner, it was going to be someone who shared her heritage and her same depths of interest in life. Ultimately she was surely going to marry a Jew.

If I were to propose to her, it would have ruined our friendship in the same way that my taking that road with Ginny did. It sometimes looked as if I were always going to be attracted only to Catholics and Jews, and that was going to be my downfall, at least with my own Midwestern family.

Meanwhile, back in the U.S., the space race was continuing, and an element of that was going to affect my next big adventure.

When my country finally managed to launch its first successful satellite, January 31, 1958, it was the middle of the night in London. At UP Photos/Planet News Ltd., only Willy, a darkroom man, and myself were on duty. Suddenly and with no fanfare, a rather ordinary-looking photograph of a rocket launch arrived on a single machine in the darkroom, and Willy brought it over to me.

Luckily, I immediately recognized the news and political significance and told Willie there was going to be no napping for the next few hours. It was, of course, the successful launch of Explorer I, the satellite that finally put the U.S. back into the space race with the Soviet Union. The UP bureaus and clients in England and all over Europe would want that photo immediately.

Willy began duplicating the image for all the different sizes and other technical requirements for the several transmission systems. I wrote captions and cables. And then together we began taking those prints and fastening them to all the different rotating drums and sending them by wire to all the British papers as well as to dozens of addresses all over Europe, sometimes waking up editors and bureau chiefs. I don't remember the specifics, but I know we got all of this done in jig time. No one had anything to complain about, and we were pretty proud of ourselves.

At the end of my shift in the early morning, Leo Stoecker arrived at the office and told us off:

"You should have called for help," the boss declared. He did not say anything about a job well done. It seemed to me that he might have wanted to share some of the credit for the operation. So there was apparently at least a little bit of my old tank company CO in Leo.

As grateful as I was to Leo for giving me a job a few months earlier, I felt quite hurt for both myself and Willie, and I began thinking hard about leaving.

And I knew just where I wanted to go. The upcoming Expo '58 – the Brussels World Fair.

At first, I appealed to anyone who would listen, suggesting that I could do a first-rate job with writing and/or photography for UP at the fair which was due to open April 17. After all, I had fair experience, having explored at age six that 1939 exposition in New York. And the Brussels one would be the first World Fair to be held anywhere since then – the first since the end of World War II.

Long story short, I got nowhere. I even went over to the London Associated Press office and talked to an editor there. He was sympathetic, even admiring my enthusiasm, and predicted that I would succeed in my journalism career. But he would not hire me and send me to the fair.

Partly because of my fond childhood memories of the New York World's Fair, I became obsessed with the desire to become involved in some way with this one almost next door in Belgium – so much so that I began taking French classes in preparation for the move.

Learning French in England was a hoot – or *zut alor*, perhaps.

The instructor, Monsieur Fournier, from France, had a night class of about 20, most of whom were hampered terribly by their native tongue – several different versions of English, any of which were much further from French than my American version. This seemed especially true for the women students, some of them apparently transferred from the Eliza Doolittle school of English. Thus, I attained the "teacher's pet" status that I had never known when I was in school.

It was not that I remembered much of the French my mother had taught me as a child. It was more because I was much closer to being able to pronounce pure vowels, especially the "o" that the teacher so much wanted to hear.

"O" in "London Speak" seemed to be mostly rendered as a triple diphthong. That is, it was often formed by running together "eh," "oh," and "oo." As an American, my "o" was normally formed by a simpler diphthong, "oh" and "oo." But I easily learned to drop the "oo" and pronounce the pure "oh" that the teacher wanted, and he held me up as an example to the class.

In the back of my mind, I thought of the song from *My Fair Lady*, called "Why Can't the English Teach Their Children How to Speak?"

Professor Higgins: "It's 'Aaoooww' and 'Garn' that keep her in her place; not her wretched clothes and dirty face!"

Anyway, M. Fournier took an interest in me, and when he heard that I wanted to go to Belgium, he even wrote down some differences in Belgian French from the version spoken in France.

When I came back to Kensington after class, Orah laughed and said she feared that I would never learn enough French in a short time to get along on the Continent. Of course, I secretly hoped that Orah would ask me not to go at all. But instead of that, she said that she might be able to visit me in Belgium for a short time before she and her mother moved to the U.S.

That was the first I knew that she and Suzie were planning to go to the States at all, and I took some comfort in that, even though it was to be San Francisco instead of the East Coast. I liked Suzie a lot, too, and we got along well together. Orah and I had gone up to her home in the Manchester suburb of Wilmslow for Christmas.

Suzie often called me "Bao-bab" after the name of the trees in the story of the Little Prince (*Le Petit Prince* by Antoine de Saint-Exupery). Indeed, I would have liked very much to have had her for a mother-in-law.

In contrast, Orah's name for me was mostly "Bobby." Although it was usually uttered in affectionate tones, I always felt that it was at least subliminally meant to indicate that she didn't take our relationship quite as seriously as I did.

When the time approached for making the decision to leave for Belgium, one of my colleagues at UP informed me that he had heard that the translator in the Brussels UP office was thinking of taking in a boarder during the fair months. Arrangements were made, and then it was definite. I was going to Expo '58, and I had a place to live.

But first I would have to get rid of Dago Morris – the car with the erratic offside and nearside lights – that admittedly was not worth much. I procrastinated to the point where one of my photo editor colleagues, Ken Runyun, offered to try selling it for me after I left.

On April Fool's Day, I took the boat train to Belgium – thrilled at the thought of a new adventure in Europe, but still wondering if I might be making a big mistake – still wondering if that angry lieutenant at the consulate might be proven right.

The Atomium, symbol of the 1958 World Fair in Brussels.
(Photo by Bob Bone)

14
Meet You at the Fair

SO EVEN THOUGH I QUIT my United Press job in London, my first contact in Brussels was the UP office. There I met a friendly reception, both from Jock Anderson, the Scot who was the bureau chief, and from Stefan Ketele, my new landlord, and ever afterwards known by myself and others as Steve.

Steve was officially a translator, but actually he was a fully competent reporter. I guessed immediately that his title as translator was just a ploy by UP not to pay him as much as he was really worth.

Belgium is more or less sandwiched between the Netherlands on the north and France in the south. Its history is complicated, but I soon caught on that the country was created in the nineteenth century by combining Flanders, whose residents spoke Flemish (on paper, at least, the same language as Dutch), and Wallonia, a French-speaking area in the south. Brussels, the capital, is approximately in the middle.

As in Canada and a few other countries, everything even remotely official – money, documents, traffic signs – had to be slavishly printed in two languages by law.

Steve was proudly Flemish, but just like Hercule Poirot (uh, well, presumably), and other educated Belgians, Steve spoke both French and Flemish fluently. Beyond that, his English was also almost perfect, although he had never visited an English-speaking country. And I remember he could get along reasonably in Spanish, Italian, German, and perhaps another language or two beyond that.

We hit it off immediately, and he drove me to his house in Dilbeek, an attractive suburb of Brussels, where I met his wife, Terêze, and two young sons, Stefan, six, and Alex, four – known thereafter as Stefka and Alexka. There I was assigned a room of my own, with a nearby window framing a park with a charming little "castle" complete with a moat and swans. The building was actually Dilbeek's city hall.

Today Stefan Ketele is the Brussels station manager of TAP, the Portuguese national airline, and Alex is an internationally known metals sculptor.

One of the first letters I received in Brussels was one from Ken Runyun in London. Dago the car had finally broken down for good. He moved it to his back garden and his wife had planted flowers in it.

I didn't care at all. I was simply thrilled with my new home on the Continent.

My rent included breakfast, and on my first morning in Dilbeek, I told Steve and Terêze that although I expected to be a journalist, I thought I should first demonstrate some financial responsibility by trying to get a real job.

This was about a week before the fair opened, and I had learned that the American pavilion was hiring local personnel, including perhaps some expat Americans who might be hanging around. I showed up to a cattle call and almost immediately was hired – as a soda jerk!

Yep, my job was to work in the soda fountain display produced by the Brass Rail chain at the dramatically designed American pavilion, dispensing ice cream sodas, sundaes, and other frozen delights popular in my home country. This was in a section of a building that was then making history as the world's largest freestanding structure. My European soda fountain customers, by and large, had never seen or tasted Yankee versions of ice cream flavors and syrups, all of which was flown from the States to the fair.

For me it was a flashback to a marketable talent I had when I was in high school back in Bowling Green, Ohio. Now at almost 26 I couldn't help wondering if, after four years of college, two years as an Army officer, and another year as a competent reporter-photographer-editor, I had really progressed in ability and talent from the age of 18.

Anyway, after two weeks of building sodas and sundaes, I turned in my scoop and broke away from a sure thing to return to more serious – if only modestly successful – freelance writing and photography. By that time, I had secured a permanent pass to the fair, so I routinely took the tram daily to see what I could find at the Expo.

Whenever anyone important showed up at the fair, I was there. I witnessed one of the last speeches ex-president Herbert Hoover ever gave. (Hoover was especially popular in Belgium because of the relief efforts he ran after World War I.) Then land-and-water speed king Donald Campbell and other sports figures were blinded by my flash and subjected to my sometimes inept non-sports-fan questioning.

I covered various royal and political personages as they made the rounds admiring the displays, etc. Not being much up on European society and politics, I didn't know the exact identities of many of the queens, dukes, and titled folks I was photographing until I returned to the UP office and Jock or Steve helped me identify the subjects of my photos.

But one fair experience stands out above all others.

The centerpiece of Expo '58, the "First Fair of the Atomic Age," was the gleaming 335-foot tall steel structure called the Atomium. It was a giant rendition of a single molecule of iron consisting of eight spheres representing atoms and connected by tubes containing displays and escalators, etc. It was supposed to be Brussels' answer to the Eiffel Tower and other iconic structures in other world capitals. After a week or two, I knew the Atomium and its innards fairly well.

Meanwhile, on the other side of the Atlantic, a Cuban revolution led by Fidel Castro was gaining ground in its efforts to defeat the regime of dictator Fulgencio Batista. Castro's battle flag, a red-and-black banner emblazoned with the date, "26 de Julio," was just beginning to become well-known.

One day in July, a lone Cuban, a short fellow whom I thought might be Castro's brother, walked into the UP office in Belgium, and explained to bureau chief Jock Anderson that he would like coverage of a forthcoming event, when he would fly this flag high up on the Atomium, thus giving a PR boost to the Cuban struggle for freedom on the world's stage.

His only problem was that he needed some assistance accomplishing the effort.

Jock told him that no staff member could have anything to do with helping him set up such a politically sensitive project, but he knew somebody who might be able to help – a youthful American freelancer who knew his way around the Expo.

So I got the assignment.

Working with my college Spanish, and Raúl's bad French, I explained that there was physically no way that his banner could be displayed at the very top of the topmost ball in the Atomium. But it could conceivably be attached to one of the braces connected to the cross tubing between two of the giant atoms.

That was acceptable, but I should choose the highest location possible. So I arranged with him to meet immediately after the fair opened in the morning, when there would be only a few people on the various platforms and escalators of the Atomium.

Somehow we did it, tying the banner to a high railing, and then racing pell-mell and skipping steps down the escalators to the ground to a position I had staked out in advance. The flag fluttered in the wind for a few minutes, and I managed to grab two or three shots, at least one of them acceptably sharp, before two uniformed guards emerged from one of the chromium balls and took the banner down.

But it was enough. I had the photo and I wrote a short story for United Press to go with it. The revolutionary left happy, and I think I made about $100 – worth a lot more in those days, when I could buy a plate of spaghetti with meat sauce for the equivalent of about a quarter.

I didn't think too much about it at the time, but in later years I think I was probably lucky on several different levels, since I never had any problems as a result of my flag-raising efforts.

But I also have taken comfort in the thought that if I ever got in trouble in Cuba after Castro took power, I could appeal for mercy on the grounds that "Hey – remember I was your advance man at the Brussels World Fair in 1958!"

During this time, by the way, UP bought INS (the International News Service) and changed its name to United Press International, and there were jokes about UP becoming UPIA.

"UPIA, UPIO!" Steve sang in a version recalling a verse in the popular song "Ghost Riders in the Sky."

I also had the special experience of meeting Aline Mosby, UPI's star (and perhaps only) female international correspondent. She was then just 36 and already one of UPI's ace reporters, and had just started working out of its London bureau.

On introducing me, Jock said in respectful tones that Aline had actually been "around the world." Not many reporters of either sex could say that in the pre-jet age of 1958. Aline told us that the Russian delegation to the fair had just invited her to visit and write about the Soviet Union. Indeed, she did that the following year.

In the process of compiling this book, I ran across Aline's video account of interviewing Lee Harvey Oswald on that Moscow trip, long before he shot President Kennedy. Until she retired in 1984, she was one of the most respected women journalists in the U.S.

But it was more significant to me when I ran across Ernest Weatherall at the fair. I knew Ernie when he was running a small weekly paper in Goshen, N.Y. (near Middletown). But now he had managed to join the European edition of *Stars and Stripes*, which was then published out of Darmstadt, Germany.

Ernie talked me into coming back with him to see the operation for a couple of days. Before returning to Brussels, I expressed an interest in working on the publication perhaps after the fair was finished in the fall.

Ten years later I visited Steve and Terêze again in Dilbeek. Steve handed me an unopened letter that had been sent to me from Germany shortly after I left Belgium in 1958. On opening it, I saw that it was an invitation to return to Darmstadt that year for an official interview with Stars and Stripes.

I remembered Frost's "the road not taken." Or perhaps it should be Walt Whitman's lines: "Of all sad words of tongue or pen, the saddest are these: 'It might have been.'"

Over the years, though, I have had several occasions to remember these lines for this and other reasons.

By the time August rolled around, I was almost beginning to think of myself as an established resident of Dilbeek, Brussels, Belgium. I was by then a firm friend of Steve and Terêze. When they went out in the evening I would stay to look after Stefka and Alexka. And although it wasn't exactly in our original contract, I began taking almost all my evening meals with the family.

The first English Stefka ever learned was calling me at the bottom of the stairs to come for breakfast or dinner: "Eet ees ready!"

I was also continuing my occasional articles and photos for the Middletown *Daily Record*. I learned that an exchange student from Orange County, N.Y. was living with a family in the Netherlands, so I made a quick trip there to interview him and take enough photos to do a *Record* picture page on his life with his Dutch host family.

But the climax of my summer experience was when Orah announced (or agreed – I can't remember which) that she would come to visit me for about a week that could include at least a few days in Paris. At around the same time, I was beginning to get some letters from the *Record* asking when I was going to return to my job in Middletown, Orange County, New York.

15
We Almost Had Paris

ORAH GOT ALONG FAMOUSLY with Steve and Terêze. I gave her an insider's tour of the fair, telling her about my encounters with some of the world's famous people whom I had never heard of. She slept in my room while I bunked in with the boys. Everyone had a good laugh when Orah pulled on the toilet flush chain and it collapsed in her hand. I took a photo of her grinning and still holding the handle.

Taking me aside, Steve suggested that I take Orah on a visit to Brugges, known then and now as the most romantic town in the country. It was a good idea.

Many today who might never have known about Brugges, enjoyed a 2008 British heist film, entitled *In Brugges*. In 1958, however, it did not have to contend with crowds of visitors now that it has been named a UNESCO World Heritage Site.

The ancient center of the city is laced with canals, and it has been called the "Venice of the North." The brick streets meander through a town that traces its beginnings to the 12th Century. Medieval churches, buildings and quiet squares invite leisurely exploration. Orah and I wandered nearly through it all, pausing now and then so I could make a photograph, usually including Orah in various artistic poses.

As evening approached, we soon realized that we were in danger of missing the last train.

"Let's say to hell with it," suggested Orah. Smitten by my lovely companion and the equally inviting surroundings, I easily agreed. We found an outdoor restaurant and enjoyed a leisurely meal.

I anticipated a stay in a Brugges hotel, but that wasn't in the cards. Instead, it was Orah's idea to see if we could hitchhike back to Brussels. It took much longer than anticipated. Finally a car full of Finns picked us up around midnight, and dawn's early light found us at the main railroad station in Brussels. We slept soundly on the train bound for Paris.

Paris was certainly Orah's town. We saw everything we could see with hardly spending a *sou*, walking through the Tuileries and even taking the Metro to Montmartre. I photographed Orah in the Louvre and everywhere else. I was sure that it was going to be the last that I ever saw of her before she moved to San Francisco and eventually married a nice Jewish boy.

We had a tiny room in a small hotel just off the Place Denfert-Rochereau on the Left Bank. That's the one with the massive statue of a lion in the center.

Yes, we had a good time and we even pretended it was something more than that. But it was really a beautiful conclusion, and not in any sense a beginning. Actually, I think we both thought that we might never see each other again.

Happily enough, that was not the case. And at least we remain friends to this day.

I had one more day in Paris after Orah left, and decided to take the elevator up the Eiffel Tower, one thing we managed skip on our explorations of the city. Following that, I wandered for a while nearby in the park-like Champ de Mars.

A car pulled up on the little road near me and the driver leaned out the window and spoke:

"Excuse me," he said. "Do you speak English?" I walked over and answered in the affirmative when he continued: "And do you also speak French?"

I explained that my French was pretty poor, but he continued, saying he didn't speak a word of it and that he had a problem that maybe I could help him with. He needed to find an address. Could I possibly accompany him?

Sure, why not. I certainly needed something to occupy my mind, which was still charged with unrequited emotion. Then he explained that he was a pilot for Air Canada and that he had in the trunk of his car several bolts of smuggled fine cloth material that was spoken for by a buyer at a certain address. But since he was about to go on duty, he didn't know what to do with the stuff.

Up ahead of us was a casually strolling Frenchman, arms folded behind him. He looked much like actor Maurice Chevalier, and my new pilot friend pulled over and asked me to translate for him. As bad as my French was, Maurice seemed to understand me perfectly. (That should have been an immediate warning.)

Maurice joined us in the car, and thereafter we followed a long trail around the city, wasting an hour trying to find the mysterious address. But gradually with my weak translations, we discovered that Maurice would like to buy the cloth himself – as soon as his wife arrived from out of town with the money.

But that was going to be too late. The pilot had to fly away before that time. Their inspired "solution" was to have me put up the dough until the arrival of Maurice's wife, at which time I would receive a handsome commission for helping them out.

What a laugh! I barely had train fare back to Brussels. They suggested that perhaps I could sell my camera – another joke since it wasn't worth that much. Suddenly the two men who couldn't speak to each other began arguing heatedly.

"Just let me out right here. *À bientôt, je n'espère pas!*" I sputtered on recognizing a Metro station from which I could find my way out of the situation. Before anybody could say anything more, I opened the door and propelled myself into the busy street.

I had never been in a situation like that before, but I recognized a nefarious plan when I saw one – even if belatedly. Later still, I learned that I had been the intended victim of the classic "pigeon drop" scheme.

When all was said and done, though, the interlude provided a welcome distraction just when needed.

Later, back in the bosom of my adopted family in Dilbeek, I began to consider what I would do now as the freelancing opportunities at Expo 58 seemed to be winding down. I had heard that expats like me could get along by renting deck chairs on the Riviera. Since I had heard nothing more from *Stars and Stripes*, that almost seemed like a viable plan.

Surprise of surprises. Out of the blue I received this telegram:

IF YOU'RE READY RETURN MIDDLETOWN
IMMEDIATELY WILL ADVANCE AIR TICKET AND
DOLLARS 50 TRAVELING EXPENSES. WE WANT YOUR
REPLY COLLECT. DAVID BERNSTEIN.

Wow! David Bernstein – the publisher who once wrote "Fire
Bone!" on his personal "From the desk of David Bernstein" notepad.

A little more correspondence made it clear that they wanted me to
leave the world's fair and come to Middletown in time to cover the
Orange County (NY) Fair. The pot was sweetened a little when they
declared that I would receive a raise, which would certainly help pay
back that airfare.

I agreed, except that I would fly home from Rome instead of
Brussels.

I had made friends with a nice guy about my age, a Canadian
named John Capraru from Toronto. I think he was one of my fellow
workers at the soda fountain. He, too, wanted to travel to Rome,
making a few stops along the way. We bought the cheapest train
tickets we could find, said goodbye to Steve and Terêze, and headed
for the station.

We made several stops along the way, notably in Lucerne, then
Pisa (where we climbed to the top of the Leaning Tower), and
Venice, which in 1958 seemed to be the quietest large city in the
world. We even made friends with an Italian family on the train, got
off with them and enjoyed a terrific home-cooked meal somewhere
in a small town along the Italian Riviera.

It seemed as if everywhere we went, we kept hearing the new
Italian song about flying – "*Volare.*" Officially, *Nel blu di pinto di blu.*
(And that song seemed to follow me home, becoming popular in the
U.S. soon after its debut in Europe.)

After visiting ancient structures in Pisa and Venice, the train's
arrival in the super-modern Stazione Termini was startling. The
structure was once hailed as an architectural achievement of
Mussolini's Fascist government.

I had a day before my flight to New York, so I visited all the free
sights I could find. I remember walking slowly from one end of the
Foro Romano to the other, checking out the House of the Vestal
Virgins, then the Trevi Fountain and other standard sights.

I was surprised by some lettering on the wall of one narrow street: "Off limits to Allied personnel." I wondered what might have been down that lane at the end of World War II: a brothel perhaps, or just a rough bar? There was no way to be sure.

Mine was one of the last prop flights across the Atlantic, before the jets came in later in the year. After the long flight from Rome, arriving in New York was somewhat a culture shock. A bus ride took me to Middletown, and the newspaper, and soon it was almost as if I had never left. Hard to believe it was almost a year earlier. So much had happened that it seemed at least twice as long.

Orah in Paris. (Photo by Bob Bone)

Sara Bone and Howard Rausch at the ballet in Moscow.
(Photo by Bob Bone)

Malcolm Browne at a party at Hunter's cabin in Cuddebackville, NY.
(Photo by Bob Bone)

A ticklish Hunter Thompson with Tootie Seepaul in Cuddebackville.
(Photo by Bob Bone)

16
Howard, Mal
& Hunter

THE PAPER WAS LARGER AND FATTER and covered, not just Middletown, but several other adjoining counties now in our circulation area. Bill DeMeza was gone, an apparent casualty of a later run-in with David Bernstein. A few others had left, too, which was normal turnover in the newspaper business.

The managing editor now was Al Romm, who spoke gently and with a slight lisp. I soon found I liked him as much as I did Bill. Good thing, because Al recognized my value right away as a kind of local celebrity – foreign correspondent and all that. Following my coverage of the Orange County Fair, I got some plum assignments, many of them out-of-town.

One of them was to New York to do a feature on the production of a soap opera, although I can't remember the name. I watched a couple of live performances – none were taped in those days – and had a brief but fun flirtation with one of the actresses. My out-of-town situation prohibited any prolonged association, but I did believe that New York City would somehow be in my future.

It was an eye-opener for me that generally speaking, my friends from my first stint at the *Record* were not especially interested in what I'd been doing for the previous 12 months.

Over a lifetime, now, I have confirmed that people who haven't done – and who are unlikely to do – foreign travel tend to be uninterested in the experiences of those who do it.

The most significant return experience for me is that I met three new fellow *Record* staff members who became special friends of mine and stayed that way for the rest of their lives. They were Howard Rausch, Malcolm W. Browne, and Hunter S. Thompson. Although they all had my friendship, they were not especially friendly to each other. Nevertheless, all four of us seemed to me to have a certain special energy in common.

Howard was then the manager of the Port Jervis, N.Y. bureau of the *Record*. An excellent writer and clear thinker, he was also usually in an ebullient mood, helpful to the extreme, and always up for a good time. He was prematurely bald so he looked older than he was. His face seemed almost always in a perpetual smile. Howard became my standard as the complete modern man.

Mal was the true intellectual, full of fascinating and obscure facts, and always good at digging hard to get to the bottom of important and controversial stories. He seemed to thrive on danger and was determined to eventually become a war correspondent. I was sure he was headed for a Pulitzer Prize some day.

Mal was also a collector of obscure words and phrases, some of which I kept and occasionally tried to use. One was *malamaroking*, a noun, and sometimes spelled mallemaroking, described as being either an Eskimo or a Dutch word. It was defined in an earlier version of Webster's as "an orgy of seamen aboard an ice-bound whaling vessel." (Mentally, I pictured a Breugel painting filled with horny, fur-clad Eskimos.)

Another was *callipygian* – "having shapely buttocks," a word that was employed easily enough. But my favorite was German in origin: *schlimmbesserung*, defined as "the improvement that makes things worse." Ever after, I applied that term to the digital alarm clock, to which I have been prone all my life to setting the AM or the PM wrong, either for the time or the alarm. (Give me a round-face, 12-hour model any day.)

Hunter Thompson also was equipped with a better than average storehouse of adjectives and adverbs. He was visibly intolerant to the foibles of modern society and to what he saw as "hack journalism." His heroes were novelists, notably Hemmingway, Faulkner,

Fitzgerald, and Steinbeck. His enemies were usually self-important businessmen, or unaware robot-like humans, many of whom he summed up pejoratively as "Rotarians."

Strange, in the light of his future more-inclusive persona, he was in those days dismissive of drug users whom he referred to as "hop-heads," and of homosexuals, who were simply "queers."

A few years later, Mal would indeed win a Pulitzer for his Vietnam coverage for the AP and end up on the staff of The New York Times.

Howard was more self-effacing but he was destined to have a successful career as a foreign correspondent for McGraw-Hill and BusinessWeek, as a desk editor at The New York Times, and much later as the founder of his own successful technical magazine.

Hunter would invent a style of personal experience journalism he called Gonzo, and then become the darling of establishment critics, especially in the New Age west. He later supported the drug culture and the gun culture at the same time.

He also would write books that a younger generation embraced, and became a cultural icon worshiped by some, yet virtually unknown by others. I think we guessed that among us, he would be the only one to become a public figure – if he managed to survive.

We were all dedicated and prolific letter writers, and I've saved hundreds of communications from Howard, Mal, and Hunter. All three had long, stellar careers, but all three died before their time.

The *Daily Record* in 1958-59 no longer provided quite the adventure as it did in the first year of its existence. Nevertheless Al Romm gave me more interesting and wide-ranging assignments, often sending me to other cities for feature stories that would hold some special interest for readers in Orange, Ulster, and Sullivan Counties.

In my off hours, I joined the Middletown Players Club and took a good speaking part in a play called *The Chalk Garden*, somehow managing to keep it from interfering with my job.

Similar to my observations with the Fort Knox Theater group, the Middletown Players also fostered a certain amount of romance, whether covert or overt, among the members. I kept away from most of it, although I was particularly fond of Katherine Canelides, always the group's resident *ingénue*. I was very careful with Katie in those days. I think she was barely 18 during our Middletown period, although we would meet frequently a few years later in New York City.

I was socially active during this period, with much of the fun revolving around the home of a friendly older couple, Annie and Fred Schoelkopf. They lived in a large house in the tiny village of Otisville, somewhere between Middletown and Port Jervis. Fred and Annie, perhaps in their 40s, always liked to have young people hanging around.

Any weekend found groups of us bachelor and bachelorette 20-somethings sleeping over, eating pizza and other take-out, drinking Ballantine Ale, smoking up a storm, listening to favorite record albums, along with talking and arguing about local, national, and world affairs. Most were paying no attention to television in those days. I don't think Fred and Annie owned one, taking more of an interest in the vital young lives swirling around them.

A certain amount of male-female action resulted from this drinking and gentle carousing. There were no drugs – this was 1958, after all. And in my case, all of this camaraderie helped me convalesce from my romantic disappointment in Europe.

In one of many gatherings at Fred and Annie's, I recall crawling under a blanket with Joan (I honestly don't remember her last name) in the dark at perhaps 2 a.m.

"Hunter?" she awoke and asked sleepily. "No, it's Bob," I said. By that time, anyway, there was no backing down from what turned out to be a fairly quiet but a very nice time for us both.

Thompson read my expression later during breakfast.

"So. Did you pounce on Joanie?" he asked when we were alone.

"Yeah. She thought it was you," I explained. He smiled – something he didn't do a lot in those days.

And "pounce" was one of those Hunter terms, of course. We could always count on him for a different, more-colorful word or unusual turn of phrase.

On another night at Fred and Annie's, Hunter woke up laughing. He had dreamed about "cretins" in waist-high black tights and boots, pouring from subway exits into New York streets and beating everyone in sight with whips.

Don't ask me. That was just Hunter – at least at that age.

Hunter was always the dominant personality in the house. One midnight, he insisted on using Fred and Annie's phone to wake up James "Scotty" Reston, *The New York Times'* Washington correspondent at Reston's home in McLean, Virginia to complain about some story in the paper.

To everyone's surprise, Reston actually talked to him under these outlandish circumstances. They discussed the situation for at least 15 minutes and then hung up amicably. With his Kentucky accent and southern gentleman turns of phrase, Hunter could be a charmer when he wanted – even on the phone – even when he was supposedly outraged.

For those who only knew him late in life, it may be hard to imagine, but Hunter was a tall, handsome man in his 20s. Young women would melt when he began attending to them while speaking in that soft and cultured Louisville accent.

The Middletown *Daily Record,* however wasn't so tolerant.

In a story told and re-told both in Middletown and in books and articles by and about Hunter over the next half-century, he was indeed fired from the *Record* – probably just exactly what he wanted.

First of all, Hunter had been trying Al Romm's patience already before the final act. To its credit, the paper could put up with a certain degree of eccentricity with its staffers, but Hunter was warned several times not to be barefooted in the office. And once again he "forgot" to put on his shoes just when members of the Middletown City Council were given a tour of the *Record* premises.

Directly after that came the infamous "candy machine" incident. Hunter put his coin in, but the chocolate didn't come out. So this time with his shoes on, he kicked the machine and "beat the beast savagely" to use a typical Thompson phrase, until it suddenly disgorged all its contents.

The only actual eyewitness to this entire, oft-told event was Carol Black (now Carol Mulvehill), and for whom the candy machine had worked perfectly. In a recent letter to me, she recalled the episode:

"The young girls in the production department were buzzing about the cute young guy in the newsroom. It turned out to be Hunter Thompson, a new reporter. I never had a conversation with him, but I can say that I 'experienced' Hunter.

"All I wanted was a candy bar. I got my treat and moved away from the machine to make room for someone behind me. It was Hunter.

"I heard the machine click, but no candy dropped. Then the real noise began. There was punching, kicking shouting... He was having a tantrum, and I shrunk into the corner. I have no idea how long it lasted, but the noise eventually attracted others to the scene.

"Anyway, the battle was over. The candy machine lost," Carol said, "and candy was splayed all over the floor."

Hunter carefully picked up only the product he had paid for and then casually loped away, fully aware that his performance had been witnessed. By the time the powers that be came across the wreckage, the machine was almost empty. A quick check around the premises, however, revealed that many employees – especially the back-shop and pressroom – were enjoying the fruits of Hunter's passion.

Al Romm summarily dismissed the miscreant the next day, telling Hunter that he was his own worst enemy. And that, my children, is the way legends are born.

Of course Hunter did not put his tail between his legs and go back to Louisville. He had been living in New York just prior to his Middletown adventure. In fact, he had been a copy boy at *Time* magazine when Vice President Nixon's car was stoned in South America, and he liked to describe the chaos in the halls of the Time-Life Building when that story broke on deadline.

In any case, he decided he liked hanging around Orange County for a time after the firing. He rented a cheap cabin in nearby Cuddebackville, not far from Otisville, and began some serious – though ultimately unsuccessful – writing. He also bought an old black Jaguar, principally, he said, because it looked powerful, ugly, and mean. It was a vehicle that inspired "fear and loathing" at the same time.

I photographed Hunter at his typewriter in the Cuddebackville cabin while he was working on the never-to-be-published novel, *Prince Jellyfish*. The wall in front of him bore a photo of Ernest Hemmingway and was otherwise peppered with inspirational clippings and phrases designed to put him in the mood to capture the spirit of Fitzgerald – or perhaps of Jay Gatsby himself.

17
Foreign Assignments

ONE OF MY OUT-OF-TOWN assignments at the *Record* was to photograph and report on Ann Arbor, Michigan, a city that had recently turned one of its downtown streets into a pedestrian shopping mall. A similar project was then being debated in Middletown. Since Bowling Green, Ohio was not too far away, I managed to extend the trip for a few days to visit my hometown. My parents had not seen me for more than two years.

And it turned out that Orah Moyal, her brother, David, and her mother, Suzie, would be able to stop by our house for an afternoon on their way from New York to their new home in San Francisco. Although it was only going to be a few hours, I looked forward to seeing my London friends again.

Although everyone was polite, it really didn't go well. My mother didn't have much to say about Orah, but she really took offense at her mother.

"They're just not our kind of people," was all she would say later.

So here it was again – two people whom I liked a lot but who would never like each other. It seemed obvious to me that my mother felt threatened and somehow inferior. So ridiculous! I couldn't wait to return to Middletown, convinced more than ever that I had grown a lot and that in many ways my parents, or at least my mother, had just marked time.

My assignments at the *Record*, not counting the usual fires and meetings of the Kiwanis, the Rotary Club or the City Council, were generally rewarding. I recall two assigned trips to Manhattan. One was that feature on the production of a TV soap opera. And the other was a "Behind Billy Graham" photo/text feature about the extensive organization supporting the great evangelist. All these articles were accompanied by my own photos.

But the big one was a multi-part feature on migrant workers from Puerto Rico who came annually to the area to work on onion farms and other agricultural enterprises. This one also involved a week-long trip to Puerto Rico, which proved to be a fortuitous adventure.

First, my flight to San Juan coincided with a convention of the nation's police chiefs, which was attended by Middletown's own chief, Russell Adgate. The first day there I learned that the chief's wife broke her leg while swimming in the Caribbean and nearly drowned in the process. Now that may not seem earthshaking, even in 1958, but the point was that I had the story exclusively. I had to file it by long-distance radio-telephone and into a reel-to-reel tape recorder back at the office.

Our competition, the *Times Herald* could do nothing about it except to quote the *Record* story after we printed it. Scoop-de-doo!

I stayed at the YMCA in San Juan (the *Record* was not generous with daily expenses.) As I gathered material to use for the migrant workers story, I also met a gentleman who would be instrumental in the next phase of my career. William Dorvillier, an enterprising writer and editor on the island, told me he would like me to come to work for him as soon as he could solve the logistic problems with starting a new English-language newspaper in San Juan.

So it looked like it might be a Harry-Milligan-JM-Kaplan-type adventure all over again – except this time in a warm tropical paradise in the Caribbean.

But first, I had to return to Middletown.

The migrant workers series was published in multiple parts and was considered a success, leading to some improvements in this field. I now think that the *Record* missed a bet by not putting it in for some kind of award, but we were not thinking in those terms in those years.

Howard Rausch usually lived in Port Jervis, which gave him the needed contacts to cover that bureau for the *Record*, and he always was on the lookout for interesting and entertaining people he called his "characters." Next to Port Jervis across the Delaware River was Milford, Pennsylvania, and there he came to know Judith Merrill, who turned out to be a well-known author and editor of science fiction.

Neither Howard nor I were overly interested in her specialty, but we did enjoy Judy herself and her far-out cult of sci-fi and fantasy writers. They often came from great distances to stay at her place, exchange ideas, and engage in general camaraderie. One was Gordon Dickson, who taught us a science fiction song he wrote whose lyrics began something like this:

I've gone and married a Shoshonoo
How did it happen to me?
I'm sittin' here with a drink in my hand
As worried as I can be
For what'll I do with my Shoshonoo
And what'll she do to me?

Damon Knight and his first wife, Helen, were regulars at Judy's. There was also Fred Pohl, Randy Garrett, and others I can't think of at the moment. (And before you ask, I don't know if we met Isaac Asimov, whose name would not have meant much to me then.)

Around the same time, Howard and I began to squire a pair of attractive young women visiting from England. At first, Jill and Jeanie just seemed to be a perfect match for both of us, and who knows, we thought maybe it might even lead to a double wedding.

Jeanie even came home with me on a trip to Bowling Green, and surprisingly she seemed to capture my mother's heart. Mother didn't know, however, that Jeanie had some kind of a secret and unusual past, and I never quite managed to get the whole picture myself.

I do know that she had once carried a very small pistol – pretty unusual for a British woman – and that she had done some kind of undercover work in Europe. MI-6 maybe. Well, who knows?

I once asked Jeanie how she got important men to speak openly to her, and she replied by whispering in my ear in such a way that I not only heard her but felt an accompanying buzz at the same time.

In any case, both Jeanie and Jill had some obligation back home, and despite their vague plans to return to the U.S., they apparently never did – an unsolved mystery.

I was also friends around this time with Jim Pappas, the local announcer and disk jockey at WALL, the Middletown radio station. Jim's brother was the aforementioned Ike Pappas, of CBS News, husband of Carolyn Huffman, of Pekin, Illinois – the target of my first kiss. In an unlikely coincidence, Ike and Carolyn once attended a party at Jim's place in Middletown in 1958. We didn't know each other was there, and after 10 years she recognized my voice from the other end of a room full of people.

Then Malcolm Browne and I began sharing an apartment in Mulberry Street in Middletown. Years later, Mal remembered more of the seamy side of life in the area than I. Writing in his memoir, *Muddy Boots and Red Socks: a Reporter's Life* (Three Rivers Press, 1994), he described the same period in which I was happily writing, photographing, laying out picture pages, and conducting the occasional gentle seduction, in very different terms:

> Some of us on the Record had regular beats, covering the con-
> tentious politics of village school boards, town meetings and
> election campaigns. But everyone was expected to pitch in on
> murders, fatal accidents, fires and other crises, and I found that big
> cities have no monopoly on mayhem. The bucolic settings of
> Orange, Rockland and Sullivan counties, with their rolling pastures,
> wooded lakes and cozy villages, did not encourage domestic bliss,
> and when farmers murdered someone or committed suicide, the
> remains were often as sickening as any produced by war. Rural life
> also seemed to include plenty of incest, rape, child abuse and other
> crimes we tend to associate with crowded cities.

Mal wrote those lines long after his later Vietnam War experiences, a tiny portion of which I shared with him.

The *Record* sent Mal to Cuba briefly in 1959, soon after Fidel Castro's forces won their revolution. I was a little jealous, of course, since I felt I had played my own small part in the adventure by flying Castro's "26 de Julio" battle flag at the World's Fair in Brussels the year before.

And around this same time, Mal and I began sharing the same New York girlfriend, an admittedly bizarre adventure feasible only because we had different days off.

Susan lived in Manhattan, but she once came to Middletown with Mal, and she and I discovered a strong mutual attraction. For several weeks in the spring of '59, I drove to Susan's apartment on Wednesdays, returning to Middletown on Thursdays. Once when I passed him on Highway 17, I recognized Mal in his 1940 Hudson heading in the opposite direction. We never overtly made this Wednesdays-Thursdays arrangement. It just happened for a while. In fact, we never even spoke of it.

Actually, it didn't seem all that different to me than that previously mentioned evening when Tom Alspach and I took Muriel Abel to the movies in Bowling Green, each holding a different hand in the dark – each of us pretending we were the special one. Except unlike Muriel, our Susan didn't feel silly at all. And she was never with us both at the same time.

Later that year, I got the invitation I was waiting for from Bill Dorvillier in Puerto Rico. He had secured financing from the Cowles Corporation (which also owned *Look* magazine) to start the new daily English newspaper in Puerto Rico, to be called *The San Juan Star*. He was ready to hire me as soon as I could get there.

I felt a little guilty since I had only been back on the *Record* job a year. But I'd paid back my European airfare and Al Romm was terrific about it. He wrote for me the best reference letter a reporter could ever hope to receive. On Middletown Daily Record stationary, it was dated September 24, 1959:

> This is to introduce Robert W. Bone, a writer, photographer, and picture-feature layout editor.
>
> Mr. Bone completed more than three years' service with The Middletown Daily Record in these capacities. He joined the staff before the paper published its first issue in July 1956, and he helped set up our photo department and darkroom.
>
> He was granted a leave of absence to correspond and freelance in Europe for 11 months in 1957-1958. He supplied us with pictures and stories about the European scene – in England, Belgium, Holland and elsewhere – before returning to Middletown.
>
> Mr. Bone specialized in combination word-and-picture stories, on subjects ranging from a five-part series on highway programs to the life of a Puerto Rican migrant worker. He covered many hard news stories with imagination. He had the highest standards in journalistic photography and writing.

He left our staff in September 1959, in the quest for new journalistic horizons. We were sorry to see him go. He could have stayed as long as he wanted.

He is continuing to correspond for The Record, and I would appreciate any courtesy shown him when he acts as our correspondent. Beyond that, I would recommend him unequivocally to any publication that has need for a man with his exceptional talents and his fine record of achievement. – (signed) A. N. Romm, Managing Editor.

18
The San Juan Star

PUERTO RICO THEN and now has occupied a unique position in American society. It's not a state and it's not a territory. Yet all who are born on the island are automatically American citizens. For better or worse, its political status in the U.S.A. is constantly being debated.

It has two official languages, English and Spanish. In English it's formally called the Commonwealth of Puerto Rico. In Spanish it's dubbed *Estado Libre Asociado de Puerto Rico.* – an associated free state. Yet everyone agrees that strictly speaking, "associated free state" is not really a proper definition of "commonwealth." All this seems to defy the law of logic that says that "things that are equal to the same things are equal to each other."

Puerto Rico citizens cannot vote in U.S. elections. Consequently it is said that Puerto Rico has no representation in Congress. But it does have an observer in the House of Representatives, one who can speak but not vote. Consequently, citizens of the island pay no federal income taxes, but they do pay Puerto Rican income taxes.

When I moved to Puerto Rico, in October 1959, there were two principal political parties: Republican, allied with the mainland Republicans, and declared to be pro-statehood, and the Popular Democratic Party, which was pro-commonwealth. In Puerto Rico there was always one overriding political issue – the political status of the island.

There were then two revered public figures on the island – Luis Muñoz Marín, the governor, who also achieved fame as a poet. He

115

was widely known as the father of modern-day Puerto Rico. The other was Pablo Casals, certainly the most famous cellist of the 20th Century.

Just as in Middletown, I took a lot of responsibility for setting up the darkroom and photo facilities. And I laid out the occasional picture page, although the *Star* was not into that as much as the *Record.* And since it used the conventional hot-type composing and printing presses of *El Imparcial,* a Spanish daily, it also could not do photos technical justice.

Bill Dorvillier, of course, became the publisher of the *Star.* The editor-in-chief was Bill Kennedy – William J. Kennedy who later became famous as the author of *Ironweed* and several other novels. The city editor was Andy Viglucci, a devoted family man who, like Bill, was married to an island beauty. (After I left the paper, Dorvillier won a Pulitzer Prize for his editorials critical of Catholic bishops for getting involved in local politics.)

I first wanted to live in the original historic center of the city, Old San Juan. Indeed, I holed up in a tiny street-level apartment on Calle del Sol (Sun Street) that was carved out of a brick and plaster house that was at least 200 years old. I often woke up in the mornings to shouts of *"avocate, avocate"* voiced by a street vendor selling avocados, door to door.

Sol Street, however, just wasn't practical. For one thing, there was simply no place to park a car – even my car, which was a rather battered and beaten Fiat 500, the smallest vehicle that Fiat made. I soon moved to a slightly larger apartment in the close-in suburb of Santurce.

There was plenty of news to cover in Puerto Rico. For one thing, there were always government officials coming to town – either trying to sneak in, like Rep. Adam Clayton Powell, or other congressmen dramatically invading the island, holding hearings and such about the island's political status or a dozen other subjects that seemed to come up when the weather was inclement in Washington.

There was plenty of crime, dramatic auto and plane accidents, military activities, lost children, entertainment, and, of course, tourism to write about. For a time, I had the airport beat. I drove out there when the New York and Miami planes came in around noon. I often had instructions not to come into the office until I had at least one story with an airport angle under my belt.

I covered a visit by President Dwight Eisenhower, and another by Senator Hubert Humphrey, plus arriving actors like Boris Karloff and José Ferrer (who was from Puerto Rico). There were always visiting experts of one kind or another to interview and photograph. I loved the action and the activities. In some ways it was like Brussels' Expo '58 again, except that this time I was paid well and was more familiar with my subjects.

Once I had an interesting lunch with Dr. William Hitzig, Norman Cousins, and Nathan Leopold – just the four of us. Hitzig was well-known for having treated the "Hiroshima Maidens" and other victims of the atomic bomb. Norman Cousins was a prominent peace advocate and editor of the *Saturday Review*.

My story for the *Star* only mentioned those two. Nathan Leopold was forbidden by the terms of his recent parole to seek any personal publicity, so we honored his request. He was one of the two (Leopold and Loeb) convicted of murder in the infamous Chicago "perfect crime" or thrill-kill case in 1924. After his parole, he devoted the rest of his life to charitable work in Puerto Rico.

To me, it seemed that our staff had something of the same *espirit de corps* I had enjoyed on the earliest days at the *Record* – or at least those of us bachelors who worked the evening shift, and we often found ourselves still at the office after 11 p.m.

One evening at around midnight, and way past deadline, someone received a phone call in the office about some great excitement at a small village named Arroyo, deep in the most mountainous area of the island.

The caller claimed that the Virgin Mary had appeared there earlier in the evening, and virtually the whole village was now praying at the site of the apparition.

No less than four of us reporters decided we would all go chase it down immediately. I drove my tiny Fiat. Others included Paul Ryan, Ted Klemens, and Peter Anderson (the sports editor). It took nearly two hours before we found ourselves at the village. (I remember that Paul told ghost stories along the way, including one where he revealed that his aunt had once refused to enter an elevator because the operator was a skeleton, whereupon the car plunged to the bottom of the shaft.)

So we reached the center of the village at around 2 a.m. and found only a lone man keeping vigil among dozens of candles, nearly all of which had burned to extinction. A white sheet had been hung up behind the candles, and other objects of veneration were nearby.

We interviewed the man the best we could. He only spoke Spanish, and mine was not equipped with the mountain vernacular. But he confirmed the story we'd heard. Scores had seen the Virgin appear at exactly that spot. I took a photograph of the scene, and we all headed back to our homes in San Juan just about when dawn was breaking.

The next afternoon I decided to develop the film before writing a short story about our excursion. When the film was dry, I put it in the enlarger to make a print. As the first print began to come to life in the tray, it seemed the picture appearing bore an image that looked rather like a woman dressed in white with a crown on her head.

Wow! The Virgin Mary coming to life in my darkroom! When the print was dry, several of us, including Managing Editor Bill Kennedy and City Editor Andy Viglucci gathered around to have a look.

We concluded that the white sheet had once been folded in such a way that its vague outlines seemed to take on a human form. And there were even several small wrinkles that formed something that looked rather like a crown.

But why hadn't we seen that ourselves? Apparently it only appeared as a result of my electronic flash — just a tiny fraction of a second and so that image had escaped us, but not my camera. When all the surrounding now-dead candles were burning and shimmering earlier, the effect might have been startling.

Anyway, we did craft a carefully written story so as not to offend anyone, and even published the photograph on Page 1. Unfortunately, by the time the photo was engraved at a 65-line screen, the apparent apparition was even less visible. I thought at the time that if it had been used in the Middletown *Daily Record*, with its more detailed offset printing capabilities, it would have been much more effective.

A more conventional assignment for the *Star* was much more instructive. On December 15, 1959 the paper sent me over to St. Croix (one of the American Virgin Islands and not part of Puerto Rico). During the day, I worked on a photo feature on island tourism.

But that evening, I decided to attend a meeting of the St. Croix Democratic Club to hear an address by Paul Butler. Butler was then the national chairman of the Democratic Party, and often the subject of considerable political controversy in the country.

During Q&A at the end of the meeting, Butler, who had no idea a reporter was in attendance, made a surprise statement:

"I'll let you in on a little secret. A lot of people are trying to get me out. They are going to succeed on July 16, 1960. I'm going to retire."

So this was a genuine scoop. I phoned the paper on deadline at about 11 p.m., trying several times before I could get through, and they tore apart the front page, which had already been set in type. They dug up a headshot of Butler and ran my story with it. Managing Editor Bill Kennedy was highly pleased.

But an eye-opening lesson for me occurred after I also sent that story the next day to the Middletown *Daily Record*. Somebody on the desk there who didn't know me asked UPI to check it out. Unfortunately they did that simply by calling Butler's office in Washington. They denied the story, so it never appeared in the *Daily Record* or anywhere else in the States.

But of course, later in the year, on July 16, Paul Butler did indeed leave his job, just as he promised the Democrat Club of St. Croix, U.S. Virgin Islands, six months earlier. Everyone else in the country was surprised – but not the readers of the *Star,* the only paper that printed the story.

Since the *Star* was a morning paper, I worked afternoons and evenings. Those of us who were bachelors on the staff had the choice of making the rounds of bars and night clubs after 11 o'clock – or going home so we could spend mornings on the beach. Often we did both.

And, of course, I continued to send freelance articles back to the Middletown *Daily Record* and a few other publications, including *Editor & Publisher* magazine.

At this stage in my life, I was far from being fluent in Spanish. Yet I knew it in theory. I could read it just fine and I had all the numbers down pat. I knew all the polite phrases. I could ask directions, order from restaurants – all the basics. But I was not as good as our truly bilingual Spanish-speaking reporters who could conduct intensive interviews with politicians, policemen, doctors, etc.

Yet, I tried to fit in as a multi-cultural citizen as much as I could. At one point, I even wrote a song in Spanish. Well, sort of. Anyway it began this way, to the tune of Ella Fitzgerald's "Blues in the Night" (From Natches to Mobile… etc.)

Parada de guaguas; y bomba de aguas;
No parque su carro… Aqui!

(Hints: *guagua* in Puerto Rican Spanish slang is a "bus." "*Bomba de aguas*" is water bomb or fire plug.) I got a lot of laughs out of this little ditty.

Soon after arriving in Puerto Rico, I wrote Hunter Thompson suggesting that this tropical environment would be a comfortable place for him to live while working on his novel. He then began a correspondence with my managing editor, Bill Kennedy, pointing out in typical Hunter flamboyant phrasing why Bill should hire him for a job on the paper. Kennedy never hired him, but after Thompson showed up on the island anyway, they began a friendship that lasted for years.

Hunter and I spent considerable time together in Puerto Rico during my off hours. He scrapped *Prince Jellyfish* and began writing a new book based on his life in Puerto Rico called *The Rum Diary*. Although I asked him several times, Hunter would never let me read any of it, and the book was turned down by several publishers over the years.

Many years later, long after Thompson had won success and fame with other books, and after considerable rewriting, *The Rum Diary* finally saw the light of day. I discovered only then that one of the characters in the book, "Bob Sala," was an amalgamation of two reporters at the *Star* – me and Pete Sala.

The real Sala hated living in Puerto Rico, and I remember him stating often through his teeth about his obsession: "I gotta get off the rock!"

More than my apparent participation in the book's activities, however, was the role played by my car, the midget Fiat 500, with its fully retractable roof. (It was not really a conventional convertible since the sides always stayed up.)

Some of the real adventures with that car were not covered in Hunter's book, and should have been. One event that stands out was the time I tried to pass an overloaded truck that was brimming over with sugar cane.

Hunter rode in front. Two young women were in the back. And as usual the top was off the Fiat. Just as I began to pass the truck it hit a bump in the road, causing a deluge of sugar cane to pour directly into the car, into our hair and onto our laps.

No harm done, but to the tune of screams from everyone, I pulled off to the side and we divested ourselves of the stalks. The truck continued on, and I doubt the driver ever knew he'd lost the stuff.

The Fiat also had an annoying habit. The hood never would fasten down completely, allowing moving air to pour in under it. Every now and then, probably again after a bump in the road, the hood would suddenly lift up and crash back against the windshield, blocking the driver (usually me) from seeing the road ahead.

But, of course, with the roof off I could stand up and drive while looking over the top of the combination hood and windshield. Of course I only did that long enough to pull over to the side and stop, get out, and again fasten the hood down approximately in its proper position.

You can see Johnny Depp manage that stand-up driving technique in the movie made from the book, *The Rum Diary*.

And another trick, this one documented by a photograph, occurred when I once parked the car in an impossibly narrow space between two other vehicles when I was going to work at the *Star* office.

I couldn't open the doors, so I threw the roof off. Then, taking my jacket, notebook and camera bag, I jumped out over the back of the vehicle. Unknown to me until later, another photographer grabbed a shot while I was in mid-air. He presented a print to me later. It is now a favorite souvenir. (See cover.)

When *The Rum Diary* was made into a movie in 2011, six years after Hunter's death, I felt that the producers of the film should have hired me as a consultant. But I didn't offer to do it and they didn't contact me either.

While Hunter was first writing *The Rum Diary*, he was living far out in the country in a modest bungalow in the coastal village of Loiza Aldea, beyond the reach of paved roads, and purportedly the center of some voodoo activities on the island. It seemed a depressing place – or it was, anyway, until Sandy Conklin showed up to take care of Hunter. She brightened the place considerably, and I found myself rather envious of his a casual, beachside lifestyle with a beautiful, sarong-clad woman at his side.

Eventually, however, Hunter and Sandy decided to leave and try a stint in Bermuda. I took their picture as their DC-3 waited in the background – looking something like a more upbeat ending to *Casablanca*. (The picture has been published several times in articles and books by and about Hunter.)

About this time, though, I was dropping the club scene to spend some time with a girlfriend of my own. Sue Schmidt, of Cincinnati and New York, who was on the island to do some writing. At one point, I took a week of vacation, and Sue and I made a flying trip, island hopping down the chain of the Lower Antilles, stopping at various sleepy islands until we reached the French island of Martinique.

Martinique especially seemed like another world. I could speak some French again. The capital, Fort-de-France, was a romantic place, where we slept under a mosquito net.

We rented a car and then spent several hours exploring the island, including evidence of the major eruption of Mont Pelee. The 1902 disaster wiped out the previous capital of St. Pierre, killing 30,000 people. In the local museum we made friends with the curator, a wizened old scientist wearing a pith helmet who was probably about as old then as I am now – but looked older.

A couple of years later, Martinique turned out to be relatively profitable when I sold quite a few photos taken on that trip to the French government tourist office in New York. It certainly helped that the man acting as PR for the office, Joe Petrocik, had been a fellow soda fountain worker at the Brussels World's Fair.

Martinique was exotic enough, but our most startling experience was going to the movies on one of the other islands. This was either on Antigua or St. Kitts. The theater looked something like a cement blockhouse. We bought tickets through a hole in the wall – a couple of bricks had been removed – and we were told we could only sit in the balcony. It was soon apparent why.

Upstairs was the only place in the theater where there were conventional theater seats. Down below us the local population filed in to sit on several long benches. We soon discovered that the audience believed in talking all through the film – except when they were shouting.

Along each end of the movie screen, however, there was room for a sign with capital letters spelled out vertically on both sides. These letters appeared only when somebody, perhaps in the projection booth, began erratically flashing the lighted words over and over again spelling out: SILENCE PLEASE! SILENCE PLEASE!

It was only minimally effective.

Not long after this trip, Sue returned to New York, having first suggested that I should begin thinking about doing the same thing.

Anyway it was a good 12 months in Puerto Rico. I had great assignments. I liked my bosses and fellow reporters. I even learned to perform the limbo. But I had never lived and worked in Manhattan, and now I badly wanted to do just that.

19
New York, New York

BY THE TIME I GOT TO THE CITY, Sue Schmidt had temporarily gone to visit her family in Cincinnati, so I immediately began to see Susan again. There was no competition from Mal this time. He had moved to Baltimore to work for the AP. I suspected that Susan had other men in her life, though. I never asked and she didn't say.

A brief visit back to Orange County resulted in a pleasant afternoon with Helen, Damon Knight's ex-wife. But Helen was not interested in moving to Manhattan, so that put her in the same category as women who lived in Brooklyn or the Bronx – GU: Geographically Undesirable.

I was walking west on East 34th Street one morning and coming toward me in the opposite direction was David LePage, who had been a fellow reporter on the Middletown *Daily Record*. Dave said he had just been at a job interview with a magazine for which he believed I was more qualified.

I already knew something about *Popular Photography*, having read it occasionally as far back as high school. It now was considered the leading magazine for amateur photographers in the country. With Dave's blessing, I went to an interview by Managing Editor John Durniak, an earlier graduate of BGSU, and almost immediately I was hired as the junior editor on the publication.

In later years, John would become the highly respected picture editor both of *Time* magazine and *The New York Times*. But in 1960, he seemed just a big kid himself, enthusiastically running the photo magazine as his personal toy.

Popular Photography was just one of a group of hobby and special interest magazines overseen by the Ziff-Davis Corporation. All were headquartered in the One Park Avenue Building. Entrepreneur Bill Ziff Jr. had his own office at this prestigious address, which occupied the block between 33rd and 34th Streets on Park Avenue. Ziff had recently taken over the reins after the death of his father who had developed the parent company into the country's most successful enterprise of that type. Bill Ziff was only two years older than I.

So I felt I had hit the big time almost as soon as I arrived in town.

The titular head of *Pop Photo* was Bruce Downes, who had a large corner office. But I seldom saw him. He always seemed to be away judging contests, traveling in Europe or somewhere else researching and writing several of his many photo books. He was distinguished looking, white-haired, white mustache, dressed stylishly and always in demand for special events.

Bruce did hold final approval over major elements of the magazine. But John actually ran things with a staff of about a dozen, counting about four clerical workers, and a strange man named Bob Sterrett, who worked in the combination mail room/darkroom in the building's basement.

Sterrett seemed always a bundle of nerves, but I was fascinated by the fact that he had posed for the creation of the well-known statue of George M. Cohan, which stands in Times Square.

For a time I decided to save money and get some exercise to boot by riding a bicycle to work from Greenwich Village. I would take the bike up the freight elevator and park it in Bruce's empty office. But the first time he unexpectedly returned, he put a stop to that nonsense. Good thing, because I was taking my life in my hands on those streets, anyway, and had had a number of close calls in traffic.

The man with real artistic appreciation of good photography was Charles Reynolds, who supplemented his editor's salary by performing magic semi-professionally. (Years later Charlie became a respected full-time magician.) Then there was the magazine's art director who also knew his stuff. He was gay in the days when that alternate lifestyle was beginning to be accepted, at least in New York City. One of the female editorial assistants set out to seduce him and eventually succeeded. They became friends for life, although she eventually married someone else, had a child, and later divorced.

Some staff members were less like artists and more like technicians, writing reviews of new cameras and photo equipment, although much of that, too, was farmed out to columnists and regular freelancers.

The man with the best job was Les Barry, the travel editor, who was often, indeed, traveling. I vowed to have a job like that some day. Les was among the earliest members of the Society of American Travel Writers. I was quite envious of him in those days. (We met again years later when we both were members of SATW.)

My initial tasks at Pop Photo were to handle the Letters column, deal with freelance articles that came in "over the transom," and edit copy submitted by regular columnists. Especially difficult was dealing with a man named David B. Eisendrath, who wrote a column called Color Clinic, and who seemed to specialize in obfuscatory prose more than he did in Kodachrome or Ektachrome.

Serious amateurs who worked in color were a minority in the 1960s. Most of our readers confined their efforts to black-and-white. When David died in 1988, *The New York Times* said he was "admired for conveying often abstruse subject matter understandably." Frankly, I'd like to take credit for some of that.

Coming up with interesting articles for each monthly issue of Pop Photo was no mean task. I often was assigned to ghost write pieces based on my interviews with professional photographers. "How I Photograph Snow" by Axel Grosser was a typical example. (I wrote it; he got the byline.)

John Durniak would often come up with catchy headlines, which he wanted turned into stories. One morning he bounced into the office shouting "Hidden Darkrooms. Hidden Darkrooms!" Spying me, he said it again, adding "Bone. I want you to write that article!"

With no more direction than that title, I came up with a plan. Working with Harvey Shaman, one of our regular freelance photographers, we built several fake arrangements depicting photo darkrooms that could be temporarily created out of bathrooms, basements, foot lockers, closets, etc. – things that could be set up and then neatly put away again in some manner.

These set-ups were never actually used as darkrooms, of course. They were built like stage sets, photographed, and then dismantled.

They developed neither film nor prints – unless some reader followed our lead and actually constructed one. It was hard to imagine that someone did that.

On another occasion Harvey and I were given free rein to photograph for several days in the Metropolitan Museum of Art for a single story. Most of the resulting images published were Harvey's, but I enjoyed the experience and eventually had several salon quality prints of my own of various museum objects, including sculptures, suits of armor, and other kinds of exhibits in that wonderful old building.

It was during this 1960-62 period that I felt I had become a New Yorker. I loved Greenwich Village, occasionally drinking at the White Horse Tavern, which was favored by Welsh poet Dylan Thomas at a still earlier time. Chumley's, a former speakeasy, was popular then – and I believe now. Many of my friends might have been described as "beatniks," although I didn't qualify for that description since I at least had a full-time job. (This was still prior to the "hippie" movement.)

The summers of 1960 and 1961 often found me at Fire Island on the weekends, as a guest of Howard Rausch, who was contributing to a beachside rental. After a stint at *The Philadelphia Inquirer*, Howard was now working at the *Wall Street Journal* and studying Russian, hoping for an assignment behind the Iron Curtain.

Also, some old friends including Hunter and Sandy showed up in town. After they moved out, their tiny apartment at 107 Thompson Street came under my control and remained that way for the next four or five years, even if I was not always in residence. It was often the scene of various dramatic events in our lives. Sometimes I shared the place with others, and other times I had all three rooms to myself.

When my science fiction friend, Judy Merril, came to New York to edit galley proofs of her books or her annual anthology, she stayed with me at 107 Thompson. I read more sci-fi there in my pajamas than I did at any other time.

For a brief period, an especially macho Danish friend, Ole Dich, shared the place with me. I liked "Lee" but he was often annoying when he had an especially amorous stewardess friend over for noisy and lengthy athletic activities. I either went out or else stayed in my bedroom, turned on the radio, and tried to read or sleep.

The apartment was located in a group of similar buildings sometimes known as the "McKinley Tenements," built in the nineteenth century to house the large population of immigrants settling in Manhattan. Number 107 was a block and a half south of Houston Street, which meant it was closer to being a part of "Little Italy," and not strictly speaking in Greenwich Village at all. There was indeed, a large population of Italian-Americans in the neighborhood.

One block over is Sullivan Street, scene of the Italian-oriented St. Anthony of Padua Festival in June. It is still popular among many long-time New Yorkers.

Those of us who were single and living in this south-of-Houston neighborhood also thought of ourselves as Villagers. Many of us 20 and 30-somethings tended to be acquainted with each other more often than did neighbors elsewhere.

There was once a city plan to extend Fifth Avenue through Washington Square, replacing Thompson Street, and calling it Fifth Avenue *South*. Thank goodness that never came to pass. But a long time after I and my beatnik contemporaries left this area for good, it was dubbed "Soho," (from SOuth of HOuston Street, and also inspired by London's Soho neighborhood). It was then largely revamped into a chic neighborhood of art galleries, trendy boutiques, coffee shops, etc.

In my day, 107 Thompson had character, and the apartment was sometimes a gathering place for many friends. But if it were unchanged in the present era, it would be called a dump – almost a slum.

Rental apartments of the type were often advertised using the term "tub in kitch," meaning the bathtub was in the kitchen. A large heavy white enameled cast-iron cover topped this fixture. Piles of dirty dishes would have to be washed before anyone could take a bath.

The kitchen was the center of the three rooms of the apartment, which left a windowless bedroom on one end and a living room on the other. In my case, the living room was next to the pair of small windows featuring an uninspired view of the fire escape and the back of another close brick building, which was actually on Sullivan Street.

Being on only the second floor of a six-story building, the flat often seemed dark. But one day I woke up to find the room flooded with light. Rubbing my eyes in disbelief, I discovered the cause: The fire escape was covered with snow!

After the snow melted, I made a project out of painting that portion of the fire escape a glossy refrigerator white, which increased the daytime *gemütlichkeit* of the place considerably – especially around noon, when the sun shone unfettered for a short time in the chasm between our building and the one behind.

Hunter and I also removed a portion of the wall between the kitchen and living room and constructed a rather nice bar or counter between them. Above it on the living room side I built bookshelves. We signed and dated the construction in some spot underneath the bar for the benefit of future generations who might someday admire this clever refurbishment.

The bedroom was also unique. The uneven walls were white, and various artistic women who visited the place from time to time felt compelled to draw images alongside the double bed, which barely fit into the windowless room. They similarly decorated the refrigerator in the kitchen.

One thing everyone seemed to agree on. There was to be no television in the apartment. One day, I did find a discarded TV set on the street and decided to bring it home. I plugged it in and turned it on. It turned out to have sound but no picture.

That was just fine. I placed some kind of material over it and a lamp on top. Once in a while I turned it on to *listen* to TV news or something that didn't need a picture to get the gist of a program. Every now and then a visitor would ask if he/she could watch the Dick Van Dyke Show, or some other nonsense.

"You can listen to it, but you can't watch it," I said. (Eventually, when more space was needed to store beer bottles, or something, we put the thing back out on the street again.)

When all the events occurred surrounding the assassination of President Kennedy in 1963, I camped out for two days across the street in a basement apartment with Bahky Haak, a former girlfriend, who had a TV with a working screen.

For a time in 1961 and 62, my kitchen also served as a sort of beer factory. This was started by Sandy Conklin and me, but was carried on with others later after Sandy moved out. The mysterious brown mixture was usually contained in a five-gallon jug standing atop the refrigerator. A small hose from the system led into a 7-Up bottle or something similar containing water. As the beer fermented, its readiness could be estimated, by counting the number of bubbles per minute in the small bottle.

If the beer was bottled too soon, there was a danger that it would explode. If it was bottled too late, it would end up being flat and tasteless. Of course mistakes were often made, and it should be noted that some of our furniture in the apartment contained bottles of homemade beer.

For example, a stack of beer cases might have a piece of plywood on it, and topped off with a tablecloth and a lamp. Visitors to the apartment sometimes were unaware of these things until a sudden explosion would occur, usually in the middle of the night, scaring the bejeezus out of an unsuspecting guest. This was especially disturbing when the bottle was one of those stored under the bed.

An added complication to our beer operation was that in order to be tolerated, the beer needed to be carefully decanted before drinking. Without shaking the bottle, we would pour it slowly along the side of and into a large pitcher, tossing away as much of the sediment as possible. This residue was highly laxative, and try as we might, we could never quite get rid of it all.

This was no problem except when the apartment was crowded during a large party and we amateur braumeisters tended to lose control of the situation. We might hear a voice shouting from the other room, "Hey, don't pour that stuff down the sink! Let *me* have it!"

I haven't yet mentioned that the toilet room for this tiny apartment, while a private one, was nevertheless located "down the hall." On party nights, there was often a line formed outside the apartment and along the corridor toward the toilet door. Some party-goers would just give up and go home – which was a good thing, since we were usually overcrowded anyway.

The beer was cheap. We estimated once that the total cost was about 10 cents a quart. Not everyone liked it, but they could go away if they wanted. Again, it was too crowded in there anyway.

My guess is that 107 Thompson Street looks very different today. I do know that some years ago, when I was just a visitor to the city, I had a look at the front door, which was always open. Now it was locked and boasted some kind of security system. I didn't see inside, but it's a sure bet that there are no longer four small apartments on a single floor, one of them favored with a "down-the-hall" toilet. My guess is only two apartments each, and probably both with pretty nice bathrooms – and with no "tub in kitch."

Nineteen sixty-one was a halcyon year for me in New York. I bloomed at *Pop Photo* and romance bloomed, too, at almost every turn on Thompson Street.

One of John Durniak's big headline ideas resulted in my byline being printed on the outside cover of the magazine: "Cameras Forbidden – by Bob Bone." This was a heavily researched piece on places around the country where photography was either not allowed, or highly restricted – usually unfairly or illegally. Following that, I was promoted a notch, giving me a raise and the title of News Editor. And I developed a new monthly column called "Newsfront."

My duties other than that remained much the same. But on the side, I began writing a regular freelance column, sending it off to London to *The British Journal of Photography,* which published it under the title of "New York Newsletter." My previous 1957-58 career on Fleet Street provided some of the impetus for that activity.

Generally speaking, I always felt that the heavy technical emphasis at *Pop Photo* tended to overwhelm the appreciation of photography as an art form. Occasionally one of the staff would throw a party at his home or apartment. If I showed up, I would discover little groups of people in heavy discussion over the reciprocity failure of a lens, the merits of fine-grain developers or some other stuff like that.

A success I was proud of was that one of my more esthetic photos was used in the magazine's coveted *Photography Annual.* This was a mid-air shot of a woman gymnast, accompanied with a detailed explanation, presumably for the education of fellow photographers:

Page 128. New York professional Bob Bone was one of about 50 photographers who were pointing their lenses at national tumbling champion Barbara Galleher one day last March. "The 25-year-old Texan," said Bone, "was performing at the International Photography Fair in New York, and was there particularly to be photographed. While watching her performance, I noticed that in one of her acts she seemed for a moment to be magically suspended – at the peak of action – in an immobile 'attention' position many feet above her trampoline. While most other photographers were lined along the longer sides of the trampoline in order to get a reasonable picture no matter which way she flipped, I took up a position at the end to get just this view. I crouched down very low and close to the trampoline in order to avoid distracting lights and other paraphernalia as well as to eliminate any point of reference in the picture. "When she hit this 'outer space' position again I released the shutter. For the strong sidelight I must thank another photographer's electronic flash. Lights in the background were bulbs strung from the ceiling of the Armory.

CAMERA: Nikkorex F with 50-mm Nikkor f/2 lens. EXPOSURE: 1/500 SEC AT F/2. FILM: Tri-X.

ROBERT W. BONE *Trampoline Champ*
125

A selfie, 1960s style. With Sara and Liz somewhere in New York.

20

The Sara Saga, Part I

ON THE SOCIAL SCENE, Sue (my Puerto Rico friend) came back from Cincinnati to New York, but then she soon got a PR job in Boston. I helped her move there and then began flying up to stay with her on several subsequent weekends. Then there was Liz, an English girl who lived in my same block but over on Sullivan Street. She found she liked spending more of her time at 107 Thompson. We used to have breakfast at a place called the Hip Bagel.

This was Greenwich Village in the '60s. I was still in my late 20s, and was not suffering from any lack of feminine companionship. Nevertheless, I melted in the presence of mystical, super-attractive Georgia, who lived near Philadelphia. And the sweetest romance I'd ever had was with Sara, a nurse from New Zealand. Sue, Susan, Liz, Georgia and Sara – any of these women could have eventually become my wife. One actually did – but not for a considerable time later.

I don't count Maxine in that list, a boisterous creature who ambushed me in early '61. In Hunter's book, *The Proud Highway,* he quoted from his Big Sur letter to Annie Schoelkopf in Otisville:

> "Maxine will pick up most of my plunder and bring it west when she returns. She will stay with Bone, and I'll be interested to see how that turns out. I can see Bone now, sitting there in the apt., drinking a bit of Tang, absent-mindedly cleaning between his toes while he reads a pamphlet on Israel – and at this very moment a great white hellbomb is heading straight for his bed, zipping across

Oklahoma with a bag of gin, muttering lewd epigrams, and armed only with the information that Bone is a dead-game sport. Ah, Robert, if you only knew…"

Among Hunter's "plunder" in the apartment was what he always called the "human skin lamp." I don't think it actually was such a thing, but it looked like it, and I was glad to see it go.

I didn't find Maxine as intimidating as Hunter said, but a little of her did go a long way, and there was a lot of her. She only stayed for about a week. In any case, it was Max who introduced me to Georgia.

The most dramatic of my love interests at that point was the affair with Georgia, from the Philadelphia "Main Line." Overwhelmed with home and social duties, family, and a rather conventional lifestyle as the wife of a commuting executive, Georgia was also the daughter of a well-known artist in the Midwest. Feeling stifled by her day-to-day life, she sent me long letters with cartoons in which she was being strangled by vacuum cleaners and other domestic devices. Georgia couldn't help longing for the more free and bohemian existence she saw in Greenwich Village.

Though I am somewhat embarrassed looking back on this now, I was a bit more reckless then. Besides, I genuinely liked this sensitive and intellectual woman who grew up in Indiana. She was my age, and had a similar background and childhood to my own.

When Georgia would occasionally show up unannounced at 107 Thompson, I couldn't help but welcome her, especially when she dressed all in black – sweater, skirt, and long socks. With an appreciative laugh, Howard once dubbed this outfit "Georgia's beatnik uniform."

Three times I took a train from Penn Station to Philadelphia and switched to the Main Line commuter railroad to make my way to her place, a modest home compared to some of the mansions in the neighborhood. I also liked her kids and even her husband, too – sort of. But then there was something not to like about him also. In any case, he left for the office early, and the kids were in school. This left Georgia and me the rest of the morning and afternoon before I again caught the train for New York.

Anyway, all this came to a sudden end when her husband found some of our correspondence. He shunted her off to a psychiatrist who soon suggested that she break it off. She wrote a poem about it, of course. Then she finally said goodbye by sending me a long tape recording, spiced with recitations of her poetry. So that was the end. And no shots were fired.

A few years later her husband indeed "dumped me for a younger woman" – to use her words.

On April 5, 1961, my friend Liz from Sullivan Street announced that on the following evening she was going to meet a friend with whom she had worked in British Columbia, Canada, and asked if I would like to come along and help entertain her.

In the Marlboro Book Shop on West 8th Street in the Village, we met up with Sara Cameron, a New Zealander, and a spark was struck. Neither Sara nor I can remember the exact sequence of events that evening, but the upshot was that the immediate attraction between Sara and me was so strong that Liz somehow just disappeared completely that evening without saying goodbye, and we didn't notice. I'm not sure either of us ever saw or heard from Liz again.

Sara, who was on vacation from her nursing job in B.C., had traveled across Canada by train and bus and then made her way down to New York. She had planned to spend one more week traveling elsewhere in the country. Instead, 107 Thompson Street worked its magic and she spent it there instead. We did emerge long enough to make one weekend trip to Philadelphia and Washington, D.C. where I showed her a bit of our nation's history. Then she returned to Canada.

Immediately thereafter, we began making more plans. She already had bookings for a ship leaving Vancouver in the summer. And it happened that the ship's next port of call was San Francisco before it sailed westward, to such exotic ports as Honolulu, Japan, Bombay, Sri Lanka, then through the Suez Canal and finally landing her in England – the long way around the planet from the U.S.

I had some vacation time coming at *Pop Photo*, so we agreed that she should fly to New York again. Then we would drive across the U.S. and I could still deposit her on the P&O ship *S.S. Himalaya*, which would sail from San Francisco on July 11.

I arranged a free car through an automobile delivery service. In those days, at least, there always seemed to be someone who wanted a car from New York to be delivered to Los Angeles. In our case, we were even paid a little money since the owner wanted only high-test gas to be used during the trip. The car was a large late-model

Oldsmobile convertible, for which we were also asked not to put the top down. Of course we violated both rules.

I wrote Hunter that we fully expected to stay with him in Big Sur, and would bring whiskey as a hospitality gift, which was more than he ever did when showing up at any of my residences. I received his typed reply on a post card:

"For god's sake don't bring Dant. Make it gin or rum. I am broke, of course, and will probably go mad trying to host four people at once. How in the hell did you & McGarr with women happen to hit me at the same time? There is something ominous about it. Sleeping quarters may be crude – food, non-existent. Proceed at your own risk."

Then he added a hand-written P.S.: "Just sold an article for $200 & spent it for whiskey & a pistol."

One of our first stops, of course, was at my parents' place in Bowling Green. This was now the fourth girlfriend I had brought home with me. Nevertheless, it went very well, although Sara was quite nervous when she was served Jello on a lettuce leaf, one of my mother's favorite salads. Anybody from a farm in New Zealand – or perhaps anyone from anywhere outside of Ohio – should be forgiven for wondering whether or not it was meant to be a dessert.

Happily we motored westward, mostly on the old Route 66 west of Chicago, and saw the Grand Canyon and a plethora of western sights. In Las Vegas, we seriously considered getting married at one of those wedding parlors and, to use my father's expression, "make an honest woman out of her."

Instead we continued onward until we delivered the Olds on schedule to the correct address in Los Angeles. Our next stop was up the California Coast to stay for a couple of days with Hunter and Sandy at Big Sur. As usual, Hunter ranted about "moss-back politicians," social injustice, human stupidity and mean editors.

Sandy was her always-sunny self. And old friends Gene and Eleanor McGarr, whom we knew in New York, were a welcome plus. Despite Hunter's warning, there was plenty of food. By this time, Sara was accustomed to meeting my "crazy friends," and somehow we all had a good time.

Gene McGarr died in 2007, but his voice lives on in various forms. One of his talents was doing "voice-over" commercials and paid announcements. I recognized him recently giving some kind of standard announcement at Los Angeles International Airport (LAX).

Last stop was San Francisco, which was again a kick for me. We visited Orah and Suzie Moyal there, two women for whom I harbored a huge amount of affection. It was the first time I had seen them for nearly four years, although we all exchanged letters often in those days. Orah was by now married to Ellsworth Young, a naval architect, and they proudly showed off their twin babies. (I was supposed to have been a godfather to one of them, but over the years somehow we all forgot about it.)

Sara used Orah's phone to call her mother in Gisborne, New Zealand. Following that, she got "time and charges" from the operator. It cost us $50 – about what we expected in that time and place.

The next morning, Sara and I toured Fisherman's Wharf and other sights in San Francisco. I delivered her to the *Himalaya*, and we handed my camera to someone to take our picture on the ship. Then my latest love sailed away – forever – or so we thought.

Hunter wrote of our visit to Big Sur in a letter to Bill Kennedy:

> Bone was here for 24 hours last week, heading for San Francisco to seek a job. It was good to see him, and we had a few good words before he left again. I've always thought that Bone was basically one of the most decent people I've ever come across. His instincts are good, and no amount of travel and sloppy sophistication can hide the fact that he's a good-hearted hick with nowhere to go.
>
> I suppose he will come to a dull end, but I hope not. When he left here he was right on the verge of marrying some girl from New Zealand, but I understand she left for London without tying him up. As of now he plans to meet her there in the fall or early winter… (from Hunter's memoir: *The Proud Highway*, Villard Books, 1997).

In much the same way as I experienced a strange occurrence immediately after I said goodbye to Orah in Paris, an equally bizarre happening came to pass after the end of this latest chapter in my love life.

My return from San Francisco to New York was a much longer one than I would have imagined. Jet travel was already well-established with the well-known air carriers. But I boarded a non-scheduled charter, Trans-Continental Airways, which offered cheap coast-to-coast four-engine propeller flights on one of those triple-tail, oft-maligned Lockheed Constellations – models that were retired a short time later.

The flight was supposed to take about 10 hours across the country. But mine took much longer due to some unscheduled drama along the way.

Soon after takeoff I became aware of a series of turns as we were flying over the Rocky Mountains. I was in an aisle seat and stopped the flight attendant to ask what was going on.

"We are not maintaining cabin pressure," she said. "So we are required to fly a DC-3 route over the Rockies."

It seemed we were flying *between* the peaks, instead of over them.

I soon discovered, however, that Trans-Continental was not going to take this impediment lying down. A male flight attendant and someone I took to be the co-pilot appeared, and one of them opened a hatch in the floor right beside my seat.

"What's going on?" I asked.

"We think there's a baggage compartment door that has not completely closed," the attendant said. "Nothing to worry about," he added as he tied a rope snugly around his waist, securing it with a half-hitch.

He then began to disappear into the hole as the first-officer kept a tight grip on the rope, while gradually letting the attendant descend into the abyss beneath the seats. I recalled our elevator friend in Oakland years before, and I wondered if this latest "sinking man" was ever going to surface again.

Of course I couldn't see what he was doing, but I imagined him tugging vainly at the baggage compartment door while the air rushed by tugging at him, too. After awhile, he did appear again safely but with his goal unachieved. We continued our flight at this lower and slower altitude.

This might have been the end of it, but eventually this supposed non-stop landed at a small airport in Iowa. Although it was never explained, it seemed obvious to me that the plane had used much more fuel as a result of its lower, slower route, and now needed a refill. We sat on the plane for what seemed an eternity, and I imagined the pilot was inside the airport, arguing over the price of aviation fuel, phoning his boss, etc.

By the time we finally landed again in New York, the elapsed time on the journey was well over the scheduled number of hours. I was late for work at *Pop Photo*, but at least I entertained some members of the staff with my tale of the experience.

"They lowered him down on a rope? My God!"

After Sara arrived in London, she began work as a private-duty nurse for an elderly woman named "Lady Camrose," and we began exchanging letters again.

One evening, I was in the company of a good friend. Ulla was a Danish reporter I had known since Middletown *Record* days, and the ex-wife of Lee, my occasional roommate with the athletic stewardess friend.

Ulla suggested that I should stop beating myself up and ask Sara to marry me. It was September 21, 1961, the same night that Hurricane Esther hit the city. Most of the damage occurred on Long Island. Nevertheless, wind-blown rain was plowing through the streets of Manhattan late at night as Ulla and I found our way to an open Western Union office and I sent my telegraphic proposal.

By airmail, a few days later, it was turned down.

Then I made a phone call. It was equally futile, angering Sara since the call was answered by her landlady at an ungodly hour due to the time difference in London. And so I began to convince myself again that after all, this was indeed just a fling – a dramatic affair that had involved a lot of fun travel and great sex. But in the final analysis, it was just one of those crazy things I might turn into a story or a song some day.

Soon enough, Sandy returned from California and moved into 107 again, and I began sleeping in the living room. She and Hunter had been evicted from their place in Big Sur. Evictions then seemed to be common in Hunter's life.

This time he headed for his childhood home in Louisville to continue work on *The Rum Diary*, leaving instructions for Sandy to go to New York, get a job, and make some money. Initially, of course, she bunked in with me at 107. As indicated at the beginning of this tale, it was wonderful but emotionally difficult at the same time.

Sandy and I channeled our enthusiasm for each other's company into making "babies" – our name for each batch of beer. One who pronounced *Baby Bonebrau* quite acceptable was John Wilcock, one of the founders of the weekly *Village Voice* and future guidebook writer. John devoted one of his columns to making home brew.

The conflicting feelings of pleasure and pain were pretty much the same as when I moved to Bowling Green after my kiss with Carolyn back in Pekin, Illinois in 1948, and after I said goodbye to Orah in Paris in 1958. I was jealous as hell of Hunter, who I felt treated Sandy badly. Still, he was my good friend, and she was in love with him.

Anyway, after helping me begin my beer manufacturing, Sandy left the apartment for the good of all concerned. And a few months later, Hunter returned to New York and began making plans to leave for South America – although not with Sandy.

21
Flying Down to Rio

ALTHOUGH THINGS WERE GOING well enough at *Pop Photo* in 1962, I began to believe that it was again time to broaden my horizons. Somehow I learned that there was an opening for a junior editor or "story producer" at *Look* magazine. After I sent in an application, I was invited to the Look Building at 488 Madison Avenue for no less than three interviews over a period of a month or two.

At that time, *Look* was one of the top magazines in the country, second only to *Life* in the large-format configuration. Some of the country's best journalistic photographers, including Phillip Harrington and Stanley Kubrick (yes, the future director), at one time or another were on the staff at *Look*. It was owned by the Cowles Corporation, another plus for my hopes, since Gardner Cowles had largely financed the launch of *The San Juan Star*. Surely my stellar career in Puerto Rico, along with my success at *Pop Photo*, would put me in good standing with *Look*.

"Your résumé seems to be rather checkered, Bob."

My interviewer at *Look* was Patricia Carbine, little known then, but destined in a few years to be one of the founding editors of *Ms. Magazine*.

Personally, I was proud of my "checkered" career – photojournalism graduate, promoted in my short Army career, good references from my newspaper work in Buffalo, Middletown, and Puerto Rico and recently promoted at *Popular Photography* magazine – and all that with some practical European experience in London and Brussels thrown in the pot.

After all, even David Bernstein, the publisher who once ordered me fired, had sent money and successfully coaxed me from Europe back to Middletown.

I made all those points in my conversation with Pat Carbine as deferentially as I could, and even brought out that super letter of recommendation from Al Romm at the *Record*, and another from Bill Dorvillier at the *Star*. Besides, everyone in the newspaper biz knew that a varied résumé like mine should not be considered a detriment. I knew I was going to make a good, well-rounded assistant editor or story producer at *Look* – probably more widely experienced than some already on the staff, I thought.

Still, I finally did not get the job, and I was devastated.

Mentally, I had already left *Pop Photo*. My instinct now was to find the first crazy, nonsensical adventure to come along and leap for that. My résumé was destined to be more checkered than ever. I soon answered an ad in the *Times,* and accepted a job offer in Brazil.

Look magazine folded for good in 1971, less than a decade later.

Hunter was by now sending me optimistic letters from South America, and he said he would soon be in Brazil himself. He was corresponding regularly for the *National Observer*, the new weekly founded by Dow Jones & Company. He told me that there was plenty to write about throughout the entire continent.

I invited Howard to take over No. 107 if I went traveling. He said yes, if it could be equipped with a shower. So we sawed away at the cabinets above the "tub in kitch," hung a curtain, fastened a hose and nozzle, and *voila!*

It was somehow obvious to me that a dose of Latin America was just what I needed. I said goodbye to *Pop Photo* and others and flew to Rio de Janeiro to accept the job: "editor in chief" of *Brazilian Business,* a monthly magazine in English published in Rio by an organization called the American Chamber of Commerce for Brazil.

It was a great title, but my sole employee was one overworked though good-natured woman in the office. Jacy Porteus, was an attractive Brazilian lady who had been divorced from the scion of a well-known family in Hawaii. My new boss worked there, too – Eileen Mackenzie, who ran the chamber office as its executive vice president.

I was so eager to accept the job that I didn't know for sure how much I would be paid until I flew down to Rio and showed up for work. Eileen had told me the salary in a phone call, which I recorded, but even then I didn't understand it. I believe it was 100 "contos" per month – a slang term for 1,000 cruzeiros. In any case, the cruzeiro was being subjected to rampant inflation, and I was told to expect at least a small raise every month to try to keep up. I never figured it all out, but it was a living wage.

In a letter, Howard, ever the optimist, pointed out to me that I was now a millionaire in cruzeiros. A millionaire in Brazil! What could possibly go wrong with that?

I knew I would probably run into Hunter again. He had begun his freelancing tour of South America by taking a smugglers' boat from Aruba to Honduras, and I was sure he would eventually show up in Rio, especially now that he knew I was there and with a real job – a similar situation to when we both were in Puerto Rico.

I was hardly prepared for the lovely setting of Rio de Janeiro. I learned that in 1808, while Brazil was under Portuguese rule, the king was so taken by its charms that he moved his entire family and the royal court from Lisbon to Rio. Many of the parks, gardens and tree-lined boulevards are credited to the farsightedness of Roberto Burle Marx, a horticulturist. He was a friend and collaborator of Oscar Niemeyer, the Brazilian architect who designed Brasilia, the inland capital, as well as some of the best modern architecture of 20th century Rio.

The growth of the city has always been hampered by things that also give it its natural beauty. Its neighborhoods wind around many granite monoliths that were thrust up in pre-historic times. In the 1960s, business-day traffic seemed virtually impossible. After-work traffic often slowed to a crawl. Hunter later dubbed this "the drinking hour," since it was much more pleasant and practical to hit a city bar at five o'clock and wait for at least an hour before hitting the tunnels and attempting to return to the beaches and pleasant atmosphere at Copacabana, Ipanema, or other residential neighborhoods.

There was also an annoying rationing of electricity. The newspapers would explain which neighborhoods would not have power on certain days. It was easy enough to keep up with which *falta* might take place for an hour in one's own neck of the city, but if you were caught in an unfamiliar location when the switch was pulled, you might be out of luck.

I spent an hour in an elevator one evening on the way to visit a young lady. When the car stopped, with lights out between floors, there was nothing to do but sit down on the floor and wait. It was not embarrassing – she guessed what had happened and apologized for not telling me the time the power cut would take place. I had missed the candle-lit portion of the dinner, but the food and the cook were kept warm, anyway.

Even with difficulties, life in Rio was still entertaining although I was not enamored of the job itself. Writing business-oriented stories simply was not my bag. Dealing with the printers was a challenge, too; galley and page proofs were always full of errors, having been set by linotype operators who knew not a word of English.

Even using the office phone was frustrating. The standard technique to making a phone call was to pick up the receiver, listen briefly to see if there was a dial tone (almost never), then laying the receiver down on the desk and picking it up every few minutes to listen again. It could take as long as a half-hour or more. And even then, you had to hope there was not a busy signal, because the next opportunity to dial might mean another half-hour wait.

One day I received a phone call in the office from José, the boss at the printers:

"*Senhor* Bobbi, you'll have to change the title on your lead story this month."

The problem was insurmountable. They simply didn't have enough W's at the plant for the headline I wanted.

Headlines were in large size, handset metal type – a kind I was familiar with from my days in the typography class at Bowling Green State University. And one could hardly blame a Brazilian printer for a lack of W's. It is a letter that is simply not used in Portuguese.

"José, just go buy some W's," said I. " We'll reimburse you later."

Of course it wasn't that simple. To buy solid type, one needed an import license, and it could take weeks for something to be shipped from the U.S. Moreover we would probably have to hire a *despachante*, a sort of "fixer" who knew all the regulations, permissions required, etc., to accomplish objectives hampered by complex government regulations.

So indeed, we did have to change the title of the piece. I can't remember just what we came up with.

Something I enjoyed at the magazine was modernizing the page layouts and designing the covers of each issue. Everything was black-and-white in those days, except that I was allowed to use a second color of my choice on the covers. There was a bit of a disturbance when I designed a cover virtually covered with 1000-cruzeiro bills, which were mainly orange. But by the time the magazine came out, the cruzeiro wasn't worth as much anyway, so somehow I got away with it.

I did little writing for the magazine, preferring to use local freelancers who knew something about business writing, and who were satisfied by relatively modest rewards. This bothered Eileen, my boss, but it was the best way in the long run. And I kept receiving compliments on the appearance of the magazine from chamber members, and I suspected they didn't read much of the publication anyway.

Most English speakers kept up with current affairs by reading the daily *Brazil Herald,* edited by Bill Williamson, a long-time Rio resident who was married to a Brazilian writer.

Not too surprisingly, Hunter showed up in Rio in a dramatic way, and my memory of his appearance has been the basis for many stories recounted in books and magazines about Hunter over about 50 years.

A good friend in Rio was an American my age who lived in Brazil most of his life. Archibald Dick had inherited a small company that built scaffolding for the use in manufacturing new buildings in and around the city. I was riding with Archie in his classic open MG convertible alongside Copacabana Beach when I suddenly recognized Hunter walking on the sidewalk.

"Stop! That's a friend of mine," I said, and Hunter came loping over to the car. He had arrived from Bolivia a few hours before, and he had a monkey with him. In fact, the animal was drunk, and had already thrown up in Hunter's jacket pocket.

Hunter laughed and explained that he had been in a bar where someone would buy him drinks as long as he could also give the monkey a drink, too.

"But this is nothing," Hunter said. "You should see the animal I've got back in my room!"

We drove to his hotel. Indeed there was something about small dog size that none of us had ever seen. Hunter's description was apt. He said that it looked like something that might be a cross between a rat and Winnie the Pooh.

Eventually, we found Brazilian friends who declared that it was (phonetically) a "qua-chee." Actually the word was *coati*, or in English, a coatimundi. Hunter said that he had rescued both animals by buying them from people who were mistreating them in Bolivia. Indeed, the *coati*, which Hunter named "Ace," had lost all the hair from its tail.

As time went on, Ace began growing his tail fur back. Moreover, we began touting him as the only *coati* that was toilet-trained, and he loved to play with soap. Indeed, he did manage to use the john and even seemed to wash his hands afterwards. Flushing, however, was beyond his pay grade.

Eventually, we gave Ace away to Lou Stein and his family. Lou was the South American correspondent for the Copley News Service.

However the monkey eventually committed suicide. We kept him in Archie's apartment for a few days, but finally he jumped off the balcony, 10 stories up. The only witness to the tragedy was the housemaid, who was vocally upset. Hunter theorized that the animal, now apparently an alcoholic, was probably suffering from the DTs.

It was great to have Hunter around, now. He told us something of his adventures making his way down the continent after first landing on a cigarette smuggler's boat in Honduras. He was selling his stuff mainly to the recently established Dow-Jones weekly newspaper called the *National Observer*. I think some of his best writing appeared in that publication.

He also made a non-conformist splash in some stories he did for the *Brazil Herald*. Editor Bill Williamson recently said he believed that one of them was one of Hunter's first "gonzo" articles – an entertaining combination of facts, exaggerations, and imagination.

That article took what might have been a ho-hum routine account of a speech by a visiting senator to a luncheon of American and Brazilian business and *civic* leaders and gave it some pizzazz. His lead graph:

U.S. Senator Herman Talmadge told Rio's American Chamber of Commerce yesterday that "We know from readin' the Bible and readin' the scriptures that neither the United States nor God can help people who cannot help themselves."

The long story continued in that vein, pointing out the senator's view that current aid programs were inadvertently helping the Communists, etc. It was probably the best read and most talked about story in the *Herald* among expats that day.

At one point, I tape-recorded an interview with Hunter about his travels elsewhere in South America. It was going well until he lit a Brazilian match whereupon the flaming match head detached from its base and flew into his clothes. (This was a common hazard in the country.) Hunter swore mightily and refused to continue with the interview. We were going to pick it up again later, but ... you know how it is.

We soon had our own little clique of English-speaking expats, all often exchanging stories of our experiences interacting with the Portuguese-speaking population. Archie, of course, was bi-lingual. At the other extreme, Hunter would speak only a few necessary words, but in Spanish – not the language of the country, but which was widely understood. Some words were indeed the same as in Portuguese.

Hunter had a few words of advice to me on the subject: "Remember, Bone, a writer should not learn too much of a foreign language," he cautioned quite seriously. I understood what he meant, but wasn't sure that I agreed with him.

In my own case, I was taking private Portuguese lessens weekly from a matronly woman who made it her mission to educate me in the culture.

From her, I learned a lot of handy expressions that were not in the textbooks. For example, a smiling glad-handed person not to be trusted was referred to as *Um amigo da onça.* – "a friend of the jaguar." (Actually, she said "tiger," but the word actually refers to a panther or jaguar. Unlike tigers from India, jaguars are indigenous to Central and South America.)

Social life for the single American male expat with limited language skills was definitely challenging. In our early days in Rio, we would spend our Friday or Saturday nights in bars like the Kilt Club, dancing with or just trying to communicate with the darker-skinned girls who hung out there. In some ways they were not all that different from girls you might pick up at a bar in Greenwich Village and take home – except that in Rio you had to pay them. (There were no pimps. Also no AIDS in those relatively carefree days.)

Hunter said that he liked the super-scratchy horsehair rug I had in my place for this kind of social activity. He said it provided "an interesting element" to the experience. I let him and his escort have the rug. I, or we, stayed in the bedroom.

Hunter suddenly broke out of this pattern when Sandy arrived in town without warning. He had forbidden her from coming down, but we both were glad when she did. Indeed, her very existence in town was a welcome fresh-air presence for me, too, even if I was only a trusted "friend of the family" – just as it had been when she similarly arrived unannounced in Puerto Rico a few years earlier.

Almost the only other dating choices for me were the higher class, lighter skin girls living at home with their families. They virtually never had their own place. These dates generally turned out to be more expensive, you had to speak passable Portuguese, and, as Archie explained, they never put out.

I tried that just once. After practicing all the polite phrases, I made a dinner date with a young lady who spoke no English. We rendezvoused at the restaurant, and – surprise – *she brought her cousin with her!* So there were then two nice young ladies with whom to converse and buy a meal for.

I had no credit cards in those days. When the bill came, I simply did not have enough for the three dinners. If the girls had any money, they never said. I explained myself as best I could to the waiter and a most unamused manager. I gave him my business card, and promised to come back the next day with the rest of the money. It was a difficult scene in every way.

Back at the office the next day, Jacy said that this was really a modern girl. I was lucky, she said, that she didn't bring her mother, aunt, or grandmother along. Anyway, it was my last date in total Portuguese.

I did have a one-shot affair with an American girl – well, sort of American, anyway. She may have had dual citizenship.

Lisa had grown up in Vila Americana. This was an interesting place I always intended to visit in order to write an article about it, but somehow never got around to it.

At the end of the American Civil War, when slavery was abolished, a group of Confederate refugees, who felt their way of life had been destroyed, moved to Brazil, where slavery was then still practiced. These families settled in an English-speaking enclave that eventually became a suburb of São Paulo, Brazil's largest city. A century later, their descendants still maintained a somewhat separate cultural identity.

Most of these families became citizens of Brazil, although they continued to speak English, if only as a second language. They also maintained their Protestant religion while surrounded by the predominantly Roman Catholic population. Today the area is called simply "Americana."

But my visit there and my continued association with Lisa was not to be. After our brief and not terribly satisfactory assignation, she apparently decided that although she called me a "beatnik," I was still going to be the love of her life. It frightened me when she pasted my picture on her bedroom mirror in the home she shared with her parents. But just as with my over-eager Louisville girlfriend years before, I felt her short-lived enthusiasm was just too much to bear.

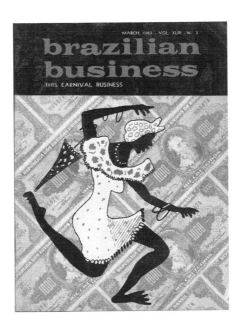

1962: Bob Bone, Hunter Thompson, and Sandy Conklin on
Copacabana Beach, Rio de Janeiro.

22
Life with the *Cariocas*

BRAZILIANS, OR AT LEAST the *cariocas* (Rio residents) by and large were very musical and quite sentimental. When the American film *West Side Story* opened in Rio, theater patrons ended up throwing bottles and other trash at the screen. The explanation I was given was that music and singing were meant for happy experiences – not for tragedy.

Had I known it, I could have been present at the birth of the *bossa nova,* which came into existence in Rio while I was living there and soon became popular in the U.S., too. The prime example, of course, was the "Girl from Ipanema" or "Garota de Ipanema," which was composed only a few blocks from my apartment at around the same time I was living there.

But I liked all Brazilian music, including, of course, the samba – which was both a musical style and a dance. I can still sing part of the winning samba song at the 1963 Rio Carnival, which evoked a lovely and fun-loving *carioca garota* breaking up with her boyfriend:

Eu agora sou feliz; eu agora vivo em paz. Me abandona por favor. Eu arranjei um novo amor, e não lhe quero mais!

"I now am happy; I now live in peace. Leave me alone please; I have found a new love; and I don't want you any more!"

Interestingly enough, Brazilians seemed to look down on the Portuguese (from Portugal) as naïve and uneducated. An example was the opening of the Hitchcock film *Psycho* in Lisbon. The Brazilians said the Portuguese managed to give away the movie's surprise ending by re-titling it: *The Boy Who Was His Mother!*

The Portuguese, in turn, generally scorn the *carioca* accent as very low-class — comparable to the Cockney accent versus proper English in Britain. A case in point was that Rio residents were prone to pronouncing their R's with what we would call an "H" sound.

When *My Fair Lady* was produced in Portugal, Eliza Doolittle was portrayed as having a typical low-class accent similar to the speech patterns of Rio. So instead of pronouncing the "The Rain in Spain stays mainly in the plain," she practiced carefully enunciating and rolling her R's just enough: *"O Rei de Roma Rumo a Madrid!"* (The King of Rome Travels to Madrid.) No doubt this interpretation of the song was not much appreciated in Brazil — especially in Rio.

Portuguese was a more difficult language to learn than it first appeared. Some words were the same as Spanish — *amigo* (friend) and *casa* (house) are examples. And we *gringo* Spanish speakers are sometimes lulled into thinking that by simply applying a few rules it is enough to understand and be understood. *Estación* (station) in Spanish becomes *estação* in Portuguese.

For example *del* and *de la*, which mean "of the" (depending on masculine or feminine tense) in Spanish, could be converted to *do* and *da*, respectively, in Portuguese. On my way to work each day my bus passed an establishment named "Casa da Borracha." No problem with *casa*, of course. And *borracha* merely meant rubber in Portuguese — a business that sells rubber goods.

But *borracha* in Spanish is different. The sign would then be determined as "House of the Drunk Woman."

Then there was simply a matter that the local population, like many people in the world, including Americans, often aren't very good at pronouncing everything precisely themselves. I sat down in a café one day and the waiter approached me with a rapid-fire question that sounded like "oh-snore-vy-tmar-goom-coys? He said it twice and I still didn't get it.

Bill Williamson said that many young people who ran words together so rapidly were from Portugal, called *portugas*, who often took jobs as waiters.

My Portuguese teacher would have said, quite correctly, *"O Senhor vai tomar alguma coisa?"* – Is the gentleman going to have something to drink?

In common with some European people, like Italians, Brazilians also seemed to use a considerable amount of sign language. "I want a cup of coffee could be conveyed with the thumb and forefinger pressed together as they might be holding a demitasse – the tiny cups that coffee was normally served in Rio. (Delicious, by the way. The best coffee I've ever tasted.)

There was also a sign for "no," which was merely the wagging of the forefinger to the left and right. And try as I might to explain that to Hunter, he always took offense when a *lotação* (small bus) driver signaled thusly when his vehicle was too full to stop to take on another passenger.

Frustrating though it might be, the wagging finger was not really scolding – just informative.

One interesting characteristic of Brazilians was their preference for taking medicine with needles rather than with pills. Near my office in downtown Rio there was a corner street vendor who sold hypodermic syringes from a display right on the street.

Sharp things like needles have always given me the shivers. I took every other route I could so that I could walk around this fellow and not see his prickly wares.

One of my good friends in Rio, Darlen Lobo (a name that would be "Darlene Wolf" in English) told me she shared an admittedly illogical tendency with other Brazilians regarding elevators. While standing on the ground floor of an office building, she would press the "down" button when she wanted to go up.

"I always thought that since the elevator is somewhere above me, I needed to press 'down' to bring the elevator down to get me," she said, quite logically. I have my own strange feelings about elevators, and so it almost seemed to make sense to me, too.

Later, Darlen moved to New York and she remained a good friend there and later in London for many years.

The food was generally good in Rio in those years – at least for everyone but Hunter, who maintained that nobody in Brazil knew how to make decent scrambled eggs. One morning he suddenly decided to do something about that.

I saw him leap over the counter at a modest café and grab a frying pan from a frightened short-order cook. While cursing loudly in English, he proceeded to teach him how to prepare delicious and fluffy *"Ovos Mexidos Hunter Thompson."*

I was much better at reading Portuguese than speaking it, and if I had failed at that, I might still be residing in Rio today. That talent eventually helped me to afford to leave the country.

My apartment – the one with Hunter's scratchy hooker rug – was actually a sub-let while its owner was in Europe. More importantly, it came equipped with a telephone, a relatively rare instrument in a private residence in Rio. Suddenly I had a chance to make some genuine Yankee dollars by stringing for NBC Radio News.

The official NBC correspondent for all of South America was the well-respected Wilson Hall. But the network constantly kept him hopping all over the continent so that he was often not in residence when some story broke in Rio.

Having the telephone was handy, but it was not good enough in technical quality for radio broadcasting. Nevertheless, I could at least get my assignments on the phone. They usually wanted a story to be ready as quickly as I could get to a studio in downtown Rio and make a hook-up.

There I often met Charles Kuralt, of CBS, waiting to use the same studio. He also attended some of the same Chamber lunches as I. Charlie, of course, was later famous for his *On the Road* TV series of reports in the U.S. – as well as for his surprise secret mistress who only was revealed to his wife and the rest of the world after his death in 1997.

My NBC radio assignment was usually to record two 50-second spots. If they used one of them it was $50. If they used both, it was $100. My objective was often to make the first spot more of a teaser so that they would take both of them. It was fun, and even more so because some of my parents' friends even heard my reports back in Bowling Green, Ohio.

With my past amateur theater work, and some local radio experience in Puerto Rico, I was in good voice for this sort of thing. But as a professional reporter, I felt guilty. Eventually I confessed to NBC, telling my New York producer, Russ Tornabene, that I was not really doing any genuine reporting.

"I just pick up *O Globo* or *Jornal do Brasil* and read them in a cab on the way down to the studio and then write a summary in English. I'm not really doing any original reporting at all."

The response I got from Russ or somebody was "Hey, you're doing just great. Keep up the good work!"

So, after all, this was just "show biz."

The best part of the deal was that I was very careful not to convert any of these dollars willy-nilly into *cruzeiros*, which were inflating at an ever-increasing rate. (I got a raise from the Chamber in the local currency every month, but often it did not quite keep up with the inflation.)

Then, after working in Brazil for almost a year, I was able to buy my plane ticket out of the country for half price by using Brazilian money that I bought at the very last minute from my dollar earnings from NBC. (It's complicated, but take it from me, it worked!)

Whereas my countrymen back home were worried about things like the Cuban Missile Crisis and the Cold War, Brazilians were consumed with the oncoming "Lobster War" with France.

Here are two 50-second spots for NBC. Morning, Feb. 28, 1963:

FRIGHTENING HEADLINES GREETED RESIDENTS OF RIO DE JANEIRO THIS MORNING AS THEY LEARNED THAT FULLY ARMED ELEMENTS OF THE BRAZILIAN NAVY WERE STEAMING NORTH TO MEET THE THREAT OF A FLEET OF FRENCH WARSHIPS REPORTEDLY ON THEIR WAY TO BRAZILIAN WATERS.

A STATEMENT ON FRANCO-BRAZILIAN RELATIONS IS EXPECTED TODAY FROM BRAZIL'S FOREIGN MINISTER, HERMES LIMA, IN THE LIGHT OF THE CURRENT TENSION OVER FISHING RIGHTS BETWEEN BRAZIL AND FRANCE.

OSTENSIBLY THE FRENCH SHIPS – INCLUDING THE JET AIRCRAFT CARRIER CLEMENCEAU – ARE NEARING NORTHEASTERN BRAZIL TO PROTECT FRENCH LOBSTER FISHING BOATS WHICH HAVE RECENTLY BEEN FORBIDDEN BY BRAZIL TO OPERATE IN ITS COASTAL WATERS.

BRAZIL'S NAVY MINISTER LEFT RIO THIS MORNING TO ATTEND A SPECIAL CABINET MEETING WHICH HAS BEEN CALLED BY PRESIDENT JOAO GOULART TO DISCUSS THE

APPARENT CRISIS. THE FOREIGN MINISTER'S STATEMENT IS EXPECTED TO FOLLOW THE CONFERENCE.

THIS IS BOB BONE, NBC NEWS, RIO DE JANEIRO

"THE WAR OF THE LOBSTER," AS BRAZILIAN HEADLINES HAVE TITLED THE CURRENT MISUNDERSTANDING BETWEEN FRANCE AND BRAZIL, HAS AS ITS BONE OF CONTENTION THE DEBATE AS TO WHETHER A LOBSTER CRAWLS ALONG THE CONTINENTAL SHELF – AND IS THEREFORE A PERMANENT FIXTURE SUCH AS CLAIMED FOR OFFSHORE OIL RIGHTS – OR DOES IT INDEED "FREELY SWIM ABOUT" (AS THE FRENCH CLAIM) WHICH MAKES IT ANYBODY'S GAME OUTSIDE OF A TWELVE-MILE TERRITORIAL WATERS LIMIT.

THE LOBSTER ISSUE, WHICH HAS BEEN BOILING UNDERNEATH THE SURFACE FOR THE PAST TWO YEARS, WAS EXPECTED TO BE DECIDED EVENTUALLY IN AN INTERNATIONAL COURT. BUT BRAZIL INSISTS THAT IN THE MEANTIME IT WILL PROTECT ITS SOVEREIGNTY BY ANY MEANS NECESSARY IF A BELLIGERENT FLEET OF FRENCH SHIPS DOES IN FACT APPEAR TO DEFEND THE ACTIVITIES OF THE FISHERMEN.

THE NAVY MINISTERY, WHICH ANNOUNCED THAT THE FIVE FRENCH WARSHIPS WERE APPROACHING, DID NOT PIN DOWN THE SOURCE OF INFORMATION EXCEPT TO SAY THAT THEY WERE SPOTTED BY THE BRAZILIAN AIR FORCE.

THIS IS BOB BONE, NBC NEWS, RIO DE JANEIRO

After saying goodbye to my Rio friends and the War of the Lobsters, I bought my ticket and arranged two interesting stopovers on my way back to New York: one in Lima, Peru and the other in Panama City.

In Lima, I followed *Time* Bureau Chief John Blashill's advice, and asked to see the "Hot Pots" museum. This turned out to be the famous Larco Museum of pre-Columbian art, much of which consisted of infinite varieties of ceramics, which depicted just about every aspect of day-to-day life more than 2000 years ago.

I was admiring these when an attendant tapped me on the shoulder:

"Quiere usted ver la sección pornográphica?"

Aha! That's what John meant. In those days, the "hot pots" were kept in a separate gallery, probably to protect some of the more explicit creations of ancient sexual acrobatics from the view of visiting school children and grandmas.

About 40 years later, I again visited the same museum, and that time it seemed that all aspects of this ancient culture are now exhibited together, although there were fewer examples of the "hot pots."

Next stop was Panama City. There, the main attraction was the U.S. territory of the Canal Zone. There was the canal itself, of course, but the interesting experience was that the zone was so clean, white, and with trimmed lawns and smoothly paved streets – U.S. military precision – in contrast to the adjoining Panamanian neighborhoods which seemed to be dirty, unregulated, and in need of repair.

I visited again four decades later, after the canal had been given back to Panama by the U.S. Then, the visual effect seemed to be the opposite. The former Canal Zone seemed to have been largely returned to the ravages of time, while the city itself had been cleaned up considerably.

23

Perennial Pelicans Persist in Panama

IN 2006 I WROTE a travel story about Panama, entitled "Return to Panama Uncovers a Birder's Delight," which was carried in the *Atlanta Constitution*, the *Pittsburgh Post-Gazette* and some other newspapers:

> PANAMA CITY, Panama – Pelicans coasted over the bay with the cool deliberation of master marksmen. When one spotted a fish, he snapped his wings into a sort of sharp-angled italicized Z and power-dived into the water. Returning to the surface with his prey, he would slide it smoothly into his gullet with a proud shake of his ample beak.
>
> I admired these deft acrobatics for an hour or two one sunny day in June 1963, in front of my hotel, the kind of marginal establishment that a nearly broke young vagabond could afford in those days. I can no longer name the hotel, but the pelican scene was firmly fixed in my memory by the time I flew home to the U.S. the following day.
>
> Returning to Panama City after more than 42 years, I again found myself overlooking the same shoreline. My previous modest accommodations were long gone. But from the balcony attached to a snazzy air-conditioned room in the Intercontinental Hotel Miramar, I saw that the pelicans had managed to remain on duty. And their aim was as good as ever.

Birds and Panama are almost synonymous. More than 500 species are said to populate the forests of this narrow country. While pelicans and flocks of slow-flying vultures are prevalent over the city, hundreds of other kinds populate the interior green jungles on the north and south sides of the Panama Canal.

One of the world's greatest engineering achievements, the canal is the *raison d'etre* of Panama. With the support of the United States, Panama was created from the rib of Colombia in the 19th century. When the massive cut was finally made, a wide, fenced-off swath of the country became the U.S. Canal Zone.

Those who lived there, who called themselves Zonians, became the proud residents of America's only overseas colony. They were often described as being "more American than the Americans."

I found Panama City fascinating in 1963. It seemed a loud, helter-skelter sort of a place but ultimately fun and an especially savory contrast to the antiseptic precincts in the American-owned Canal Zone. There, the buildings were uniformly white and set back from smoothly paved streets under cool shade trees and behind well-watered, closely cropped lawns.

Today, these aspects seem to be reversing. Panama City has become relatively clean and more conservative, dominated here and there by architecturally inspiring high-rise buildings. The former Canal Zone has belonged to Panama since Jan. 1, 2000, and except for the canal itself, the section bordering the city is not much as I remembered it.

The military-style buildings are still in evidence but generally showing their age. Instead of white, many are now painted in colors. The grass is taller and grayer, and there is generally a more unkempt look. The streets and roads are often rough and potholed, and the former tightly controlled atmosphere of a U.S. government installation no longer exists.

The cultural strains with the Zonians are now considered ancient history, and Panamanians are welcoming more Americans annually, both as tourists and retirees. Some smile and describe their capital as, "kind of like Miami – except more English is spoken."

The older parts of the city are still around: The ruins of Panamá la Vieja, the original settlement destroyed by the English pirate, Henry Morgan, in 1671. And there is Casco Viejo, whose narrow, Spanish-style streets were first formed in 1673.

Casco Viejo was favored by the French during their abortive attempt to build the first Panama Canal in the 1880s, so both Spanish and French touches can be seen.

On my recent trip, I crossed over the canal on the mile-long Bridge of the Americas to spend some time at a new coastal resort, the Intercontinental Playa Bonita. It features one of the smoothest stretches of sand for miles around. During Canal Zone days, this beach was reserved for U.S. military officers and their families.

The Playa Bonita is also an outpost for Gamboa Tours. It is an easy way to take in a visit to the canal, including the visitor center and museum alongside the Miraflores Locks. This is the first watery stair step up for ships entering the canal from the Pacific.

While Playa Bonita was a luxury beach experience, the architecturally daring Gamboa Resort provides an interior, jungle adventure, and some visitors headquarter themselves there. One morning, I joined a group led by naturalist Hector Nodiel Sanchez. We sailed on a small boat along the river and into Gatun Lake, which forms an integral part of the canal. Traffic on the water included an occasional huge, oceangoing vessel, which seemed out of place in these green, tropical forest environs.

When the lake was created, the nearby hills formed islands, and some contain landlocked colonies of jungle creatures. Hector took us to one he called Monkey Island. It was populated by families of Capuchin (white-faced) monkeys that enthusiastically welcomed our boat and the hors d'oeuvres that came with it. One of these exuberant residents landed briefly on my head while making his way toward a Snickers bar. On other islands we spotted more wildlife, including howler monkeys, a three-toed sloth, some tree iguanas and perhaps a dozen of those 500-plus varieties of birds.

After an outdoor lunch, which overlooked the Chagres River, more exotic birds and a sleepy caiman, I boarded an open-air aerial tram, which lifts visitors through the forest canopy to the summit of a hill. From the top of a 100-foot-tall observation tower there, we could see a wide area of the canal. This included the famous, or infamous, Gailard Cut, a relatively narrow slit which had given the canal builders considerable misery a century ago.

More varieties of birds were in evidence at the tower, one of which was a brightly colored toucan. The big-billed creature obligingly posed just long enough for me to make a close-up. Again, I left for home the following day, and the toucan has now joined the pelicans among my memories of Panama.

24

The Time of My *Life*

JUNE 1963 WAS NOT the ideal month to look for a job in New York City. Of course I didn't want to return to *Popular Photography*. After a quick trip to Bowling Green to see my parents, I again established myself back at 107 Thompson Street, sharing the apartment again with Howard Rausch, who was then still working on the rim (copy editing) at *The New York Times*.

I soon discovered, however, that the *New York Post* was hiring some summer replacements and – surprise – I was suddenly on the city staff in that capacity. This was the same year that Nora Ephron started working for the paper, but I never met her or any of its other famous columnists, like Max Lerner, whom I read often. Perhaps all were on vacation.

In those days, the *Post* was owned by Dorothy Schiff, and it was as far left wing then as it is far right wing today. For the rest of June and most of July, my assignments were going well enough, although some of them were pretty silly. At one point, I was sent to the courthouse to do a story on a young woman who was picked up by the cops for indecent exposure – wearing "short shorts" in public.

I was there with a gaggle of jaded big-city photographers, one of whom told me they were waiting to see which restroom the defendant might go into, at which point at least one of them would follow her in to see whether or not she used the urinal. I left that story alone.

But then City Editor John Bott sent me on the train out to Malvern on Long Island for two days to check into some suspected racial discrimination practices.

The news sources I worked with there all claimed it was a misunderstanding. I don't remember the details now, but I had the impression that I was expected to turn out a story anyway even if it was based only on rumors and misinformation. Bott said he suspected that I had political feelings that conflicted with the *Post* point of view.

If it weren't for these non-story situations, I think the Post would have offered to keep me on after the summer was over. But it didn't, and I wasn't unhappy about it at all.

In August, I was offered a job simultaneously by the *World Telegram and Sun* and by Time-Life Books, the Book Division of Time Inc. But the latter offered $10 a week less than the newspaper.

I had already visited the *World-Telegram* offices which were in Lower Manhattan in dark, dingy and dusty premises seemingly peopled only by old men wearing green eye shades – more depressing even than the city room at the *Post*. In contrast, Time-Life was uptown cater-corner from Rockefeller Center and in its own gleaming super-modern building. It seemed to be populated largely by good-looking young women wearing mini-skirts.

At one point, I stepped into a phone booth and called Beatrice Dobie, the chief researcher for the Book Division of Time, Inc. I told her of my offer from the newspaper, but said I'd much rather work for her outfit.

"Bea, I'm not asking you to outbid the *World-Telegram*. I just would like it if you could match the offer," I said.

She agreed, and suddenly a whole new career was launched. And it's worth noting now that the *World-Telegram* died pretty much unloved only three years later.

My first official job title at Time-Life Books was "researcher," and I was just one among many with that designation. I was first assigned to work on the latest project in the Time Life Science Series, a book called *The Cell*. My cubical was on the 45th floor of the building, although most of the Science Library staff was on the 32nd floor with other series in the division.

The 45th floor also seemed to be the catch-all home of several mismatched employees – not just of the book division overflow like me, but of various hangers-on employed by *Time, Life, Fortune, Sports Illustrated,* and other publications or other projects and interests of that large corporation.

Quite near me, in a rather nice windowed office, was a man who seemed to have nothing to do except work on crossword puzzles all day. I felt sure he was an example of a type I had read about in a book inspired by the *Time* and *Life* behind-the-scenes experience called *The Fun House.*

According to the author, William Brinkley, there were some editors who were eventually deemed superfluous to this paternalistic corporation, but who were never fired. Instead, they were promoted to what was informally known as the "thinking desk." Their job was to think up ideas for new articles or other projects and send out memos accordingly – memos that were never answered or acted upon.

As described by Brinkley, a thinking desk editor would remain until he couldn't stand it anymore and would finally resign. Then an announcement would be circulated to explain that so-and-so had reluctantly made up his mind either (A) to "spend more time with his family," or perhaps (B) "to return to his first love, freelance writing."

I never determined how things played out for this man. Soon enough, I was moved to the 32nd floor with the rest of the book division.

One of the aspects of the job that pleased me from the start was that Time Inc. seemed to understand the psyche of thinking, creative, and sensitive people.

For me, a good illustration of that was Elevator Bank Number Two.

I was always an enemy of New York's ubiquitous elevator music – or Muzak, as it was sometimes called.

But in Elevator Bank Two, the cars that served the editorial needs of *Time* and *Life* magazines, as well as the Book Division, were blessedly silent. For these publications it was often necessary to take the elevator to different floors while working on various projects. Somewhere and at some time in the building's history, someone in authority had apparently cottoned on to the fact that elevator music interrupted the thinking processes that were needed to get the job done for these publications.

A corollary to that is the widely held prohibition of whistling in newspaper city rooms.

In contrast, this was not the case with Elevator Bank Number One. Those cars served the offices of *Sports Illustrated*, *Fortune*, and various business offices, and they had traditional forms of elevator music. In my somewhat snobbish attitude toward both organized sports and the business world in those days, I thought that seemed logical – Elevator Bank #2 for the sensitive caring folks; Elevator Bank #1 for everybody else – including whistlers.

On the job, I soon was introduced to my immediate superior, a peripatetic picture editor who had the unfortunate name of John MacDonald – unfortunate, I thought, because so many others in the world had the same name. That included at least one well-known novelist and many others in the writing or publication business. (I always felt blessed for having a relatively unusual last name.)

But if that bothered John at all, he never showed it. He was a mass of energy, running in and out, this way and that. A veritable "White Rabbit," he always seemed to be late for something. Neither one of us was particularly knowledgeable about biology. Nevertheless he always seemed to have one good idea after another for illustrating a book about biological cells.

Working on *The Cell*, I learned a bit about the significance of DNA, for example, something new and that had not been part of my education in high school and college. In 1963 DNA had not yet figured into criminal forensics, although its potential use for that purpose was optimistically predicted in our book.

Eventually, I learned that not all of John's plans and projects had something to do with the Book Division. More on that in a moment.

For me, the term "researcher" at Time Inc. previously had the connotation as a sort of drudge job for bright young college graduates who would pencil little check marks over every word of an article, chapter, or something else to be published.

This would indicate that the researcher had dug into and somehow confirmed the source of every fact stated by the allegedly unhinged writers. It was as if *Time* or *Life* believed that if left unchecked, the writers might otherwise go off the deep end, making assumptions or just creating errors in fact out of thin air by letting their imaginations run wild. (I didn't believe it, but it sometimes seemed like that.)

Indeed, there were researchers who specialized in check marks, and all of us were expected to know how to come up with accurate information. Like other newly hired researchers, I had to take a two-week course in the large Editorial Reference Department (known as "Edit Ref") on the 16th Floor soon after being hired. There I met David Bridge taking the same course, and we helped each other out finding obscure reference material that we were assigned. (There was no Google in those days, of course.)

At one point, I made up an assignment for Dave to research: "Who's who in illiteracy in Basutoland." We laughed about that over the years whenever we happened to get in touch with each other again.

Dave, a dead ringer for actor James Garner, was assigned to the Nature Library about the same time I went to Science. We never worked directly together, but over lunch we often liked to exchange our experiences between the two divisions, often laughing about the complexities of the committee book publishing operation. Dave and I were living evidence that two friends could remain such even if they differed philosophically and politically on several subjects. He was a conservative; I was a liberal.

On *Time* magazine, I had heard that there were often two researchers on an important article, one employing normal pencil black checks and then a second *uber*-researcher making marks in colored pencil. Thus the term "red-check source" was sometimes employed to indicate that an especially reliable expert or that an entry in the *Encyclopedia Britannica* had backed up the stated facts.

My job in the book division was different, although I might occasionally have to check some captions or a copy block to go with a photo layout. As a *picture* researcher, however, I was to find photos and other illustrative material or – with editor approval – arrange to assign and supervise photo shoots that were pertinent to the subject matter. Internally, these were called "picture essays."

In the Science Library, the books were kept to a standard of eight text chapters, each of which was followed by a picture essay, related in some way to the preceding chapter, but which largely relied on the photos or other artwork to tell a separate story.

The first chapter and accompanying picture essay were often historically related. The eighth of these sometimes concerned the supposed future of the subject. Those in the middle were sometimes open to wide interpretations of the subject matter.

I got along with John MacDonald by going a little farther within these guidelines by doing part of his job – conceiving the general outlines of the needed picture essays, subject, of course, to his guidance and approval. This may have given him more time for his extracurricular activities.

There were always two or three book projects going on simultaneously but at different stages of development in the Science Library. Similarly there were other book series projects also continuing in the Book Division – some on food, some on American history, some on nature (where Dave was assigned), etc. But here in the Science Library, the subject matter – making new and often complex science subjects interesting and attractive to the subscribers to a series of mail-order books – was especially interesting, challenging and satisfying.

Officially, my immediate boss at first was the chief researcher of the Science Library, Sheila Osmundson, even though I was working under the more direct supervision of the book's picture editors. The overall picture editor of the entire Science Library was Bob Mason, a good-humored veteran of years on the magazines of *Time* and *Life*. And there was also an editor of the whole Science Library, who seemed to change from time to time.

Several of the younger researchers were a little afraid of Sheila, who seldom smiled and was often critical of her charges, constantly worried about the work that needed to be done, and whether it was done soon enough and correctly enough. Her boss, of course, was Bea Dobie, chief researcher for the entire book division – the woman I had talked out of an extra 10 dollars a week.

John MacDonald had a way of disarming Sheila:

"Sheila, you're so cute when you're mad," said John on more than one occasion.

Similarly, I was not timid either. I recall blowing up at Sheila about some procedural difficulty or impediment to getting the job done. Later, I came into her office to apologize.

"Bob, you can bawl me out any time you want," said Sheila, with a smile. It seemed almost flirtatious.

Looking back on it now, I see that in some ways our operation was much like a military organization. Normal researchers were noncoms; the chief researcher of the Science Library was analogous to a first sergeant.

Picture researchers like myself were like lieutenants working for picture editor captains. The Science Library overall editor was like a senior officer, and everybody in the library was under editors of the entire Book Division, who might be compared to colonels and generals. Promotions, demotions and replacements were possible and occurred fairly often.

Then, of course, there was "the author," a sort of civilian. He or she was a respected outside authority in the field, apparently paid handsomely, and always treated with kid gloves. His technical prose was filtered through staff writers who, with the researchers' assistance, had the special ability to make heavily technical subjects palatable to the subscriber to the series – always subject to the researchers' approval, as previously indicated.

The Book Division was fascinating work, and in some ways a paid education – especially so in the Science Library, since the subject matter was strictly up to date, and often far in advance of what any of us had learned in school and college a decade or so previously.

My next assignment was *The Mind*, and there I had the special experience of working with *Life*'s Alfred Eisenstaedt, a living legend in the building and the magazine's most famous photographer. (He was known to the general public mostly for his iconic 1945 shot of the sailor kissing a surprised nurse in Times Square celebrating the end of World War II.)

Famous or not, "Eisie" also had the reputation of being difficult to work with. For a major picture essay in *The Mind* book, we arranged that he would follow a woman sent by the courts to Manhattan State Hospital (now the Manhattan Psychiatric Center) on Wards Island in the East River. Then we would document her progress over the subsequent weeks.

The initial photos were to be taken when a bus drove up into the hospital driveway and disgorged passengers, some wearing straightjackets, and all sent there by the city courts. Eisie and I showed up several minutes before the bus was due to arrive, and already he was showing his displeasure.

"No, no no!" he declared. "Nothing's right. The angle's wrong. The light's no good. I'm not even going to take the camera out of the bag."

"Eisie, at least take the camera out of the bag," I pleaded.

"No, no, no, I'm not going to do it. Everything's wrong."

Finally I gave up and stepped back, to let chips fall as they may. A few minutes more and the yellow school bus showed up, people got off, and for a moment I couldn't see what was happening.

But when the crowd thinned, there was prizewinner Alfred Eisenstaedt, snapping away on his Leica, running this way and that to get all the best angles.

From time to time over the next couple of months, I revisited the hospital and discovered that most patients and staff had formed a bond with Eisie. He seemed to be able to go wherever he wanted, charming patients and staff members alike. I thought that it was almost as if he belonged there himself, like some doting uncle to the patients who were the subjects in his photos.

Following *The Mind*, I worked on a book called *Weather* and began acting as picture editor and was given a small windowed office on the 32nd floor with a view over the entire half of Manhattan south of 50th Street. At that time, there were no other tall buildings between my window and the Battery.

One of my good friends was Frank Kendig, a Science researcher, whose personal life took a turn for the dramatic when he was tapped to be a model for the "timelessness of love" in the *Time* book. This was not my project, but I followed some of it with interest.

Another editor decided that Frank was ideally suited to act as a model for that picture essay. They paired him up with a lithe young professional model named Marilyn, and photos were taken of them kissing in several public places while the world's activities went on around them.

At the end of one day of shooting, they began dating, and soon enough they were married. After a year or so, however, they divorced. All that kissing in streets and subways apparently had had only a short-term effect. (Much later Frank married a banker named Debbie, a much more sensible and successful union.)

My own social life proceeded apace. I made friends with many of my fellow workers, including picture researchers who were helping me carry out my vision for the various photo essays. Most of us had some utopian ideals and were dedicated to helping the subscribers digest some of the complicated scientific discoveries of the 1960s.

Many fellow workers became life-long friends, including Frank Kendig, Don Hinkle, Penny Muller (who later married Don Hinkle), Bob McLaughlin, Chuck Mikolaycak, Carole Kismaric (who later married Chuck Mikolaycak), Victor Waldrop, Norbert Baer, and others.

I also dated some of the women not only in the Science Library, but from other projects in the Book Division. One of them was Liz Evans (not to be confused with Liz Summers from Sullivan Street). As a result of my interest in Liz Evans, I learned how to ski one winter weekend up in Killington, Vermont.

Somewhere along the way, I managed to get married – not to this Liz or that Liz or one of the other bright young minds in the army of female researchers.

I was fairly consistently going with Liz the skier, when I received a long-distance phone call from British Columbia, Canada. It was Sara, my Kiwi love interest from two years previously, while I was still with *Popular Photography*. Yes, this was the one I almost married in Las Vegas in '61, the one who turned down my proposals cabled through the winds of a hurricane, and the one I angered by phoning in the night on her landlady's telephone in London.

But in 1964, Sara had again left her New Zealand home and again she was about to go to work in a Canadian hospital in British Columbia.

And I asked her to take a plane to New York instead. I met her at the airport and we went home together.

Sara in the garden at the Museum of Modern Art in New York.
(Photo by Bob Bone)

25
Mister & Missus Manhattan, 1965

AS FAR AS THE U.S. GOVERNMENT was concerned, Sara was only in the country on a visitor visa. Without even a Social Security number, she had no hope of landing any kind of normal employment, let alone anything in the medical field.

Somehow, however, she managed to find work in the British Industrial Development Office in New York, known as BIDO. Thus, for working for a foreign government she received an automatic A-2 Visa – and permission to remain in the country as long as she continued to be employed by the Brits. Her job was "archivist, first class," which she said meant "file clerk."

By this time, Ted Klemens, my friend from the *San Juan Star* days, had taken over the old place at 107 Thompson Street, and I had moved for the first time into a really decent apartment. Still in Greenwich Village, of course, it was a second-floor unit at 7 Cornelia Street. Sara was ecstatic about the new place especially because, in contrast to 107 Thompson, it had a fully equipped bathroom actually inside the unit.

This was also my first New York apartment that actually overlooked the street in front. If you know the West Village, you'll remember that Cornelia is a tranquil, one-block-long street running only between Bleecker Street and the corner where West 4th Street and Sixth Avenue intersect at an angle. After Sara moved in, it was now "our" place.

Our living room/bedroom also had a fireplace, which played a comic role a couple of times in our residency. Once we decided to see if it was still functional, and we set fire to a piece of wood to check it out. To our pleasant surprise, we discovered that when we opened the damper, it immediately drew the smoke efficiently right up the chimney.

To our ultimate dismay, however, we soon discovered to the tune of some unpleasant words from the neighbors that the smoke was exiting not through the chimney on the roof, but through the fireplaces of the apartments above. The chimney itself was apparently blocked at the very top of the building.

On another occasion, Sara and I were having an intense disagreement about something now forgotten but that must have been important at the time. To emphasize my point of view, I threw a dinner plate on the floor, and it rolled away into oblivion. After we made up, the plate had completely and magically disappeared, forming, we thought, a mystical message about the futility of such violent displays between lovers.

The plate showed up again a year or so later, hidden under the now-decorative pile of logs in the fireplace.

I remember, too, that as a symbol of our new domestic existence on Cornelia Street, I bought a small portable black-and-white television set – something that had been strictly forbidden by me and all known residents of the hallowed halls of the second-floor rear apartment at 107 Thompson.

Come to think of it, all sets were still B&W in 1964.

In any case, I got a raise and to celebrate, Sara and I took a week-long vacation to Puerto Rico in November of '64. There I introduced her to Bill Dorvillier and others still at the *Star*. All told me I should marry the girl. I got a similar message when we visited my parents in Bowling Green for Christmas (where we stayed in separate bedrooms).

That same Christmas, back in New York, we went for dinner at the apartment of Ulla and her future husband, Michael Colgrass. This was the same woman who braved the hurricane with me to find a telegraph office where I wired that unsuccessful proposal to Sara in London a couple years earlier.

This was the only time I ever saw a Christmas tree with real candles attached to the branches — a little bit of Denmark in a Manhattan apartment. (It looked mighty dangerous to me, and probably was against the law.) Much later, Ulla and Michael moved permanently to Toronto. Ulla founded a music magazine there, and Michael became famous as a classical musician, composer and editor, eventually winning a Pulitzer Prize for Music.

Outside of our fireplace misadventures, things were relatively tame at 7 Cornelia. But one notable event stands out. By this time, Ted Klemens was now employed by the New York *Daily News*. Ted, an often nervous guy, at first lived in my old place at 107 Thompson. Later he decided to move also to 7 Cornelia but up on the sixth floor, four above us.

Not long after Hunter and Sandy Thompson had a baby, the three were evicted from their place in San Francisco. They came back to New York briefly, and we organized a party at our place. The child, Juan Fitzgerald Thompson, was put to bed in our bathtub, so partygoers who needed to use the john were asked to go up to Ted's place. They could do that most easily by using the fire escape outside our window.

But a drama ensued when Ted himself decided to briefly go back up to his place. In a few minutes he quickly returned, jumping through the window and almost out of breath.

"Quick! Call the cops," he said. "There are strange people in my apartment!"

The police came almost instantly, since they had already had a report of prowlers on fire escapes. A quick investigation revealed that Ted had simply miscounted the floors, and was looking in the window from the fire escape — not realizing he was viewing a different apartment than his own.

After living together for a year, it became obvious to Sara and me that we were destined for a more permanent arrangement. Of course I had proposed two years earlier by telegram and telephone — and been turned down. I don't remember the third and final proposal, but Sara says it happened while we were walking somewhere in the Village.

"I'm not buying you a ring, you know," she said I said.

"Does that mean we're getting married?" she said she asked.

I had often read about the social anathema of diamonds – how they were mined with slave labor in Africa, the market controlled by evil people who created artificial values for the stones. I said I never wanted to have anything to do with diamonds. I suppose the memory of the ring I had bought for Ginny, back when I was a naïve young Republican might have also had something to do with it.

And we moved again, this time to a ground floor in Chelsea – a small garden apartment at 244 West 21st Street. It was rather cramped quarters in the fall and winter, but a glorious and commodious outdoor experience on warm days during spring and summer. There was so much open space out back, and at the other end of our garden was the ample recreational area for the West 20th Street Fire Station.

And we began to arrange to be married.

Meanwhile, back at Time-Life Books, *The Mind* book project was coming to an end, and I began doing picture editor work on a book called *Flight*. This one was all about the science that kept airplanes up in the air, the logistics of running airlines, and the like.

Around this time, too, I found what extra-curricular activity was keeping former picture editor John MacDonald busy. This happened when he hired me to be an actor in some documentary videos he was creating for Granada Television in the U.K. These programs were designed to give the British public some insight into aspects of American Life in the '60s.

In one, my part was to order room service in a rather mediocre hotel somewhere on 7th Avenue. What I remember most was John and his assistants were in a corner of the room manning a large motion-picture camera on a tripod. When the waiter came to lay out my meal in front of me, he showed absolutely no curiosity about that and did not seem to take notice of the production crew at all.

Some native New Yorkers are like that – taking everything in stride no matter how bizarre they might be – paying no attention to things that don't directly concern them. Sometimes that was taken to an extreme.

Howard Rausch used to tell the story of his father or grandfather who went to see a play for the first time in his life, leaving long before it was over, and then later giving his family a short review:

"There were a bunch of people mostly just sitting around talking. But it was all none of my business, so I came home."

Another of John MacDonald's British documentaries was designed to explain to the British that one way to ensure a legal divorce in the U.S. was to prove that a man or woman was being unfaithful to a spouse. For that vignette, I was to play the part of a photographer who invades a bedroom with a large Speed Graphic and flashes a photo of a couple in bed together. I think the episode was to be called "The American Way of Divorce."

This was filmed in a different ground-floor apartment. I came in stage center by leaping over a garden wall outside, quickly entering and shooting a single photograph, and then rushing out to again disappear over the wall.

One take did it all. But on my way back over the wall, I fell, injuring my knee considerably and even tearing my trousers in the process.

All this took place just about two days before Sara and I were due to meet and discuss the wedding plans with the minister who would marry us. We felt that if the reverend were to question me about my limp, perhaps he just would not understand or be sympathetic to the unsavory circumstances surrounding the injury.

As it turned out, he said not a word about my physical condition. Later, we figured that he probably thought that I was suffering from some permanent long-term disability about which it was impolite to inquire. His only befuddlement, therefore, might be to notice that on the date of the wedding, I was no longer crippled.

Sara was from New Zealand and her father had died many years before, so there was no one logical to give her away at the ceremony. Our nervous friend Ted – he of the fire escape misadventure – first accepted the role. At the last minute, however, Sara's brother, Ian Cameron, flew in unexpectedly from New Zealand to do the job. It was a delightful surprise.

We were married August 15, 1965 at the Church of the United Nations on First Avenue, across from the UN Building. Howard Rausch, my best friend, was my best man. Sara's long-time friend Robin Brown was maid of honor. In attendance also were my parents, Robert O. and Nita Bone, Aunt Donna and Uncle Jay (remember the dented forehead?), and Aunt Ruth and rich Uncle Russell, the glass executive.

Together with a few more friends, the reception was held in the garden of our small apartment on West 21st Street. The weather was terrific and it was altogether a delightful day, so we made good use of the garden. One good friend who could not show up was Malcolm W. Browne. By this time, Mal was firmly entrenched in Saigon, covering the burgeoning civil war for the Associated Press. Hunter also was otherwise engaged, although I can't remember with what.

Ian, the surprise-arrival brother, remained in New York for a year – until he married Marsha, an American girl he met on the Vermont ski slopes, and took her back to New Zealand. We all said that somehow that seemed to even the score. (Actually, they too ended up living back in the U.S. years later, and still do today.)

One dramatic result of my documentary acting career: A few members of Sara's large family in New Zealand, none of whom had ever met me, unexpectedly and quite by accident, saw my television performance in one of John MacDonald's American Life documentaries. Thankfully, it was apparently not "The American Way of Divorce."

26

Darkness in Good Guy Land

ALL PERSONS ALIVE TODAY who were residing in New York City one November 9 have a story about their experiences during the Great Northeast Blackout of 1965.

There was a second blackout in 2003, which was a very different experience. But the effect on New Yorkers in 1965 was arguably stronger – stronger even than on others in the half-dozen states when the lights went out during rush hour, just before 5:30 p.m. At that hour and during that month, the northeastern section of the U.S. is almost totally dependent on electric light.

Most New Yorkers then felt that inconveniences they had heard of that adversely affected lives in less fortunate parts of the country simply would not dare to take place in their modern metropolis. Tornados, earthquakes, floods, and massive power failures simply would not be tolerated within the Five Boroughs.

This collective hubris probably does not exist today. But in 1965 the blackout was a major shock to the psyche of a city of more than six million. Many – perhaps most – thought that such a thing could not take place in New York simply because nothing like it had ever occurred before.

As it happened, I had a grandstand view of the island of Manhattan from the 32nd floor of the Time & Life Building at 50th Street and Sixth Avenue. The normal hours of the Time-Life Book

Division, where I was a picture editor, were 9:30 to 5:30, so nearly all were still at their desks.

I first heard researcher John Hochman say, "The lights are dimming all over New York!" Then I rushed to look through the windows in a large corner area near John's desk and those of a half dozen other researchers. For a second, everything looked normal. Then a blanket of total darkness was suddenly thrown over the entire Island of Manhattan.

There was complete silence for few seconds – no talking, no clatter of electric typewriters. Then one young woman's voice, bordering on panic, repeated: "I don't like it! I don't like it!"

After a few minutes, someone found a transistor radio, and that nascent feeling of dread was compounded for some since only static was heard. Then some station far away sputtered to life, its announcers incredulously reporting nothing more enlightening than what we could see – or not see – for ourselves.

We learned much later that some in the blacked out area of 80,000 square miles, and populated by about 30 million people, could rely somewhat on a bright full moon. But here amid the looming sky-scrapers in Midtown Manhattan, the darkness seemed penetrated only by the headlights of vehicles on the streets far below. The cars were now all jockeying with each other carefully at intersections without traffic lights.

On the 32nd floor, some uneasy good humor began to return. This being the editorial offices at Time-Life after all, bottom desk drawers were opened and alcohol began making appearances as editors, writers, researchers, artists, and others began trying to take it all in stride, joking nervously while passing around paper cups of whiskey, Cokes, and whatever snacks could be found and shared.

Elevators were not working, and for the first half hour or so, everyone on our floor seemed to feel there was no good reason to take the staircases and join the chaotic scene down on the street. Gradually, some local radio stations returned to the air on emergency power, and we found we were not alone, with reports of outages coming from as far away as eastern Canada.

Amid the speculations on the causes of such a large event, there were also reports of sightings of flying saucers – UFOs. Others ap-parently thought the Soviet Union might invade at any second.

We were encouraged to see that across the Hudson River a few lights were now glowing in New Jersey. And after an hour or so, some of us gave up waiting and began the trek down to the street via the emergency stairs. That tiring descent took me almost an hour.

I couldn't then contact Sara, who was at work at BIDO, the British Industrial Development Office on Third Avenue. But almost everyone had left that office except Sara and one Englishman who had arrived only that afternoon from London. (And she learned later that some of her co-workers had become trapped and had to be rescued from stalled subways.)

The Englishman had never before set foot in the United States. Sara said he seemed to believe that perhaps this sort of thing happens frequently in strange foreign cities like New York and maybe New Delhi.

In any case, this gentleman had no idea how to make it to his hotel in this strange foreign city, and so Sara invited him to dinner, as long as he was willing to walk with her down the stairs and along the streets to our apartment on West 21st Street. About the same time, I began my own trek south from West 50th Street. I don't believe I had ever walked 30 New York blocks before, and I was surprised at how relatively painless it was.

As Sara and the Englishman made their way from the East Side to the West Side, they heard Top 40 WMCA's disk jockey Dan Daniel's ever cheerful voice coming from a radio in a bar:

"Yes, sir, the lights are still out, folks. The lights are all out all over Good Guy Land!"

"My goodness," her companion said, his fears apparently confirmed. "Where is Good Guy Land?"

Sara's brother, Ian, also showed up at our place with his own reports. He had observed a drunk efficiently directing traffic at 8th Avenue and 23rd Street, and that the drivers of all vehicles were paying strict attention and following his directions.

Since we lived on the ground floor, there was no elevator problem at home. Sara managed to cobble together a hot meal on our gas stove. We lit a candle and a little light leaked into our place, perhaps from battery-operated lights on the 20th Street firehouse from across our back garden, and maybe a little bit of that full moon.

After power was resumed in the morning, New York discovered that the city's crime statistics actually took a nosedive during the blackout. Apparently just about all New Yorkers, rapists and muggers included, had been sufficiently awed by this heretofore unthinkable and awesome event in the "Greatest City in the World."

But, of course, that was then. Fifty years ago, it was a different world.

27

Flights, & Ships, & Ceiling Wax

PERHAPS RELATED TO our 21st Street apartment's Lilliputian size in the winter – as compared to its relatively commodious dimensions with the garden in warm weather – we devoted many winter weekends to skiing in Vermont. Although in one case, this worked against us.

The skiing trips often included Howard and a new friend who came along with Howard, Bert Sweet. Bert was probably the most entertaining and good-natured professor of philosophy you'll ever meet. He taught at Rutgers University in New Jersey.

Bert often greeted us with a joke: e.g., "Bob, what's another name for a man-eating tiger?" It was useless to try to guess.

"A humanitarian!" Bert said, laughing.

Because of my work at Time-Life, I often talked with Howard about my problems illustrating scientific concepts in our books. At one point Bert chimed in, and I memorized his phase:

"I find that photography, as a depiction of reality, extremely inadequate, and perhaps suitable at times only as an art form."

Over the years I have often quoted that back to Bert, who now swears he never said it.

Sara's brother, Ian, also came skiing with us. He was well over six feet tall, and when he broke his leg in the winter of '65, it presented some challenges when he ended up in a full-length cast.

185

We had to drive his small MG coupe back from the slopes to New York with Ian sitting in the back seat, his giant, immobile leg projecting between the two front seats. It made it almost impossible for the driver to operate the gear shift.

Later, when he sat on our living room couch, he had to stretch his leg out all the way to the TV on the opposite wall, blocking all foot traffic across the room.

Although I was in effect the picture editor on *Weather*, I was disappointed to find, on publication of the book, that I was still credited as a researcher. No one was listed as the picture editor. My mentor John MacDonald now seemed to be doing his British TV documentaries full time.

For four more books, however, I did receive official Picture Editor billing. The first of these four was *Flight*, during which I learned a lot about airplanes – what makes them fly, why they seldom fall, and things like that.

The careers of my three main journalistic buddies were picking up, too. Howard Rausch left his *New York Times* copy desk job for McGraw-Hill, the publishers of several publications, including *Businessweek*. His Russian language lessons had paid off, and after a short length of time, the company sent him to Moscow.

Malcolm Browne had finally achieved star status with the Associated Press, and was reporting on the Vietnam War while heading AP's bureau in Saigon. In 1964, he shared the Pulitzer Prize for International Reporting with David Halberstam. By 1965, Mal was covering that war for ABC News, and we often saw him on our little TV.

And after some minor successes publishing freelance magazine articles, growing out of his experience with the *National Observer* in South America, Hunter was spectacularly successful in his first book, *Hells Angels: The Strange and Terrible Saga of the Outlaw Motorcycle Gangs.*

I thought it was a terrific piece of personal reporting – better than his later, sometimes drug-fueled efforts, such as *Fear and Loathing in Las Vegas,* which ironically brought him greater praise and a new fan base.

Fame is a strange thing. Hunter became popular with a readership generally younger than himself and for his more far-out "gonzo" works. (I used to accuse him of not writing for his own generation.)

And Mal, whose excellent, independent coverage of the war brought him the Pulitzer, was – and still is – more widely known as the man who took the searing photo of the burning monk suicide on a Saigon street.

In 1967 and 1968, I got the "old-time radio bug" for a while. Remembering the programs I had enjoyed as a child, I began collecting copies of vintage radio shows on seven-inch tape reels and becoming a minor expert on some radio comedies and dramas of the past. In that connection I was sometimes a guest on Archie Rothman's *Sounds of the Past* show on WRFM in New York. On one occasion, I wrote a radio script that Archie and I performed on his program.

For about a year, I had a special 16-inch turntable, the kind used in radio stations in the 1940s and '50s. On it, I could play 16-inch diameter recordings, known as ETs – electrical transcriptions. These disks were relics from the days before microgroove records were invented. Despite their large size, they actually held only 15-minutes of recorded content.

Thusly equipped, I was able to borrow or beg ETs from sources in the radio-TV world and copy the content onto 7-inch tape reels. Later I heard that many of these original recordings were simply destroyed wholesale by the stations and networks that had kept them on file for decades. I still have a few of these giant disks, although no longer the equipment on which to play them.

Speaking of radio activities, I also took part occasionally in panel discussions on current affairs on the Barry Gray Show on WABC and the Long John Nebel Show on WNBC, and soon discovered this was not really my *métier*. Nevertheless, I continued to be a fan of radio, as opposed to TV, including the dramatic reminiscences of Jean Shepherd on WOR and much of the hip content of station WBAI, New York's listener-supported radio.

Some old-timers will know what I mean when I say that I once knew all the words to the original 30-minute version of Arlo Guthrie's "Alice's Restaurant," first recorded by that station and frequently replayed there by Bob Fass.

Around this time, Sara and I began making plans to visit her large family in New Zealand – mother, two sisters, two out of three brothers (Ian, of course, was still in the U.S.), and untold numbers of older and younger relatives. We were sure it would be more difficult to make the journey after we had children. So the first question right out of the box was which direction did we want to go – round-trip to the east or to the west!

For airline routing purposes, New Zealand was considered half way around the world from New York. We soon came to the conclusion that we could make this trip completely around the world. (So take that, Aline Mosby; Sara and I could do it, too!)

I had not taken a vacation in my first two years with Time-Life. Accruing at three weeks a year, that meant I was due six weeks total. We had never taken a honeymoon, so this was going to be it. Somehow I managed to talk management out of a few more days, so we had a total of almost seven weeks to work with. Moreover, we now knew so many folks in faraway places to stay with that we might need only about 21 hotel nights out of the total of 42 days.

Sara didn't take a vacation, however. We were now officially married, so she no longer needed that "diplomatic" job at BIDO. She left the job and was fairly certain of getting another in the nursing profession after we returned from our trip.

A quick calculation, now, was that after bunking with the Cameron Clan in New Zealand for 11 days, we could then visit Mal in Saigon, Howard in Moscow, and Steve and Terêze in Brussels. We came up with the following itinerary:

Honolulu, Fiji, Auckland, Gisborne (NZ), Singapore, Saigon, Bangkok, Delhi, Moscow, Berlin, Amsterdam, Brussels, Paris, and back to New York. I packed about 30 rolls of 35-mm Kodachrome, and we began this mega-trip on Saturday, June 4, 1966 and finished it on Saturday, July 16, after a considerable number of adventures en route. (I still have the carbons of our Pan American World Airways tickets, each of which cost $1356.27.)

28
The Home Country – Past & Future

OUR FIRST TARGET WAS HONOLULU, and strange as it may seem, I was not impressed on our three-day visit. I suppose it had a lot to do with my being in a "New York" mode. Nearly every other American city seemed mentally weak by comparison. I honestly recall thinking that I was glad not to be trying to build a career in Hawaii.

Of course, years later, Sara and I lived, worked, and raised our children in Hawaii, and pretty much loved every minute of nearly 40 years in the Islands.

After Honolulu, we took a couple of days to check out two towns in Fiji – Suva and Nandi – before landing in Auckland just as the sun was coming up. Before we were allowed to leave our seats, a couple of athletic uniformed men wearing shorts quick-stepped smartly through the cabin spraying something in the air. This was designed to kill any unwanted biological bugs we may have brought with us from Fiji or some other foreign place like New York.

Sara had warned me that we would soon meet a couple of elderly ladies there in Auckland, one of whom was a relative.

"Don't be shocked, but they probably are going to offer you a whisky," she warned.

That practice is sometimes called "elevenzies" in the country, and indeed a glass of scotch was pushed into my hands. But Sara did not advise me that the first thing her aunties would do after that was to ask me to bury a dead dog in the garden.

It wasn't an easy job. July weather in New Zealand corresponds to January in the Northern Hemisphere. The ground wasn't exactly frozen, but the dirt was reluctant to give in to the small garden spade the ladies gave me for the job – disposing of a canine body I had not even known in life.

Sara explained later that to these women, I was simply a man who appeared on the scene, and that this was simply a job that any caring, considerate man was supposed to do, at least in New Zealand.

I was sexually type-cast, I suppose, and eventually my blistered hands gratefully accepted my alcoholic reward with no thought as to whether the sun was over the yardarm or not.

Later in the day, we boarded a twin-propeller DC-3 and flew on to Gisborne, Sara's hometown on the east coast of New Zealand's North Island. En route, she let me in on some further nuggets of cultural wisdom. One was a heads-up to the fact that Gisborne had a very small airport, and that the runway and tarmac shared space with some working railway tracks. We would land only when and if some train was not using the same space at the same time.

Gisborne was a fairly modern airport. Sara told me of others in the country where light planes, in order to land, had to first buzz the sheep off the grassy runways and then return to set down before the "mob" returned.

Thus with all the challenges I had absorbed, beginning with the effort of burying a dog and disheartening tales of non-exclusive runways, and my morning belt from the bottle, I arrived in a more disheveled manner than I might otherwise have presented myself. There was no train, but it seemed that practically every living relative of the family within miles met us at the airport.

To gales of good-natured laughter, Sara explained how her city-boy husband had soldiered through the dog burial during the Auckland stopover.

New Zealand in those years seemed like one large offshore farm whose products almost exclusively were shipped to the United Kingdom. Its population on two large islands numbered approximately 3 million people and 30 million sheep.

Some of Sara's "rellies" seemed to be interested mostly in sheep, cattle, corn, and wheat almost to the exclusion of anything else – except alcohol, perhaps. Their saving grace, of course, was that they were some of the friendliest, most open people to a newcomer that I had met anywhere – in the U.S., Europe, the Caribbean or South America. The atmosphere was far away from my previous experiences in London and England a decade previously. In fact, the only thing they seemed in common with the British was that they drove on the "wrong" side of the road.

So these were not simply Down Under English folk. As a matter of fact, Sara and her siblings were even part Maori, the indigenous Polynesian population of New Zealand. On the European side of the family, they were also descended from a Scottish ship captain, one of the earliest founders of the entire nation. The captain began the clan when he married a Maori princess.

So Sara's ancestors, white and brown, had pioneered all over the country, naming natural features like mountains and lakes. In truth, "Cameron" was an ubiquitous surname in the nation, although all her immediate family disclaimed connection to other Camerons in the country.

Sara had grown up on a property named *Pouparae* (Maori for "high ground"), a few miles out of town. During her childhood, it was a dairy farm, which probably explained my wife's life-long aversion to milk and "nasty, dirty old cows."

When we visited, Sara's mother Joan, along with Sara's youngest brother Eric, and youngest sister Kay, still lived in the sprawling country homestead. Sara's other sister Bette, lived nearby with her own family. Sara's older brother Alec, and his wife Rachel, lived in Gisborne. (Brother Ian, of course, was still back in New York.)

Her father, who was one-quarter Maori, and spoke the language fluently, died suddenly when she was just 13. He had been known as a tinkerer and perhaps an inventor. When he discovered that there was a gas deposit under the house, he equipped the entire place with gas lighting to supplement the electricity. The gas had long ago run out by our visit, but the fixtures remained (and I believe are still installed there today) in the old homestead.

And I, who had had so few relatives in my lifetime, felt a part of this large family almost immediately

The only downer came when 20-year-old Eric arrived suddenly after he had been speeding in his Mini Cooper. He had quickly hidden the car in the garage, and told his mother that a cop was following him – a cop who had a grudge against him.

"Quick, hide!" Mum Cameron said. "Bob, tell the man you were driving the car."

As much as hated it, I did as requested.

The officer, who wasn't much older than Eric, came in after feeling the heat on the hood of the car. He was somehow inclined not to give me a ticket, although he demonstrated his anger nonetheless.

"We're not green here, you know!" he said several times.

I didn't understand what he was talking about, but I apologized for going over the speed limit. He could have said "purple," for all the meaning it gave to me.

"We're not green, here!"

I didn't say so, but I guessed I was the "green" one – if green means dumb and gullible. I laugh about this today, but at the time I was very uncomfortable.

The eleven days in New Zealand went by quickly enough, and sometimes in an alcoholic haze. I was taken to see the place where Captain Cook landed in 1769, and also to see the local pub, where the proprietor demonstrated how he could quickly dispense beer out of a hose to a line of glasses on the bar. I took a number of photographs, but ever mindful that my film was limited and we had thousands more miles to go.

I was also interviewed – both by the local newspaper and by the local radio station – both of which expressed deep interest as to the life and duties of a picture editor with Time-Life Books in New York City.

When it was finally time to move on, one of Sara's cousins, Dick Willock, volunteered to drive us to Auckland where we would catch our ongoing plane to the Orient. One vignette on that drive stands out.

At a small café, where we stopped en route, I left a few coins on the table as a tip for the waitress.

Dick immediately scooped them up, and placed them firmly back in my hand:

"You're not going to start that nonsense in THIS country!" he declared.

29
On Our Way Again

IN ONE GIANT SWOOP Sara and I flew across the Tasman Sea, then the breadth of the country/continent of Australia, and across the Timor Sea to land in Singapore in a single day. Singapore was to be an overnight before continuing the next day to Saigon.

With a mind-set to a bit of history, however, I had booked us in the colonial-style Raffles Hotel – the home away from home of notables such as Somerset Maugham, and the site of the invention of the drink known as the Singapore Sling. The establishment dates from 1887, and later another guest, Noel Coward, may have been first inspired there to sing that only "mad dogs and Englishmen go out in the noonday sun."

We had just descended from the airplane stairs when we were met by a woman representing a travel agency we never heard of. She knew our names, and said that we would be immediately driven to a different hotel.

I protested, saying that we already had a booking at Raffles.

"I suggest that you cancel that because this accommodation is paid for," she said – the payment coming from an airline we never flew on as compensation for a delay we never had.

I immediately suspected that this had something to do with the fact that Sara and I were unusual tourists – a couple who were about to fly the following day on Air Vietnam to Saigon, a city now the capital of a country undergoing a violent civil war.

Nevertheless, a saving is a saving, and we agreed to take the free accommodations, which turned out to be in a very uninteresting neighborhood. I spent much of that evening examining our hotel room looking unsuccessfully for hidden listening devices.

The next day, we again received a complimentary ride to the airport to catch our scheduled Air Vietnam flight, which turned out to be on a French-made jet-prop airplane. Sara was the only woman on the flight. The few other passengers seemed to be high-ranking American military officers.

We landed on a pockmarked runway seemingly littered with broken airplanes. At the top of the stairs, I was pleased to see that Mal Browne had come to meet us. I raised my camera to take his picture, but immediately changed my mind as his face took on a horrified expression, and he waved his hand in a desperate expression of "no!" I guess I forgot that I was now in a sensitive war zone.

In his small, white Volkswagen, Mal drove us to the famous Caravelle Hotel, pointing out sights along the way.

"We call this McNamara's Bridge," Mal said at one point. Three years earlier a Saigon teenager was arrested and later executed for trying to mine the bridge just before Secretary of Defense Robert McNamara would be traveling across it from the airport into the city.

On a recent visit to Saigon, I discovered that the bridge and the nearby street are now named after the kid who tried to blow the bridge up. He is now considered a national hero.

30
A Warning Shot

FORTY YEARS LATER, I wrote the following travel feature, which was carried in several newspapers, including the *Atlanta Constitution*, the *Pittsburgh Post-Gazette*, and the *Honolulu Star-Bulletin*. The Pittsburgh paper headlined it "War seems distant memory in contemporary Vietnam."

SAIGON, Vietnam – The last time I visited here, somebody shot at me. And I was a tourist, for heaven's sake – not a soldier.

Thankfully, lots of things are different in these parts today. For one, Saigon is now officially Ho Chi Minh City, even if almost everyone still calls it by its original name.

Known as the "Paris of the Orient" during French colonial days, Saigon can again lay claim to that title. The conflict that Vietnamese schoolchildren now know as "the American War" has been over for three decades. Saigon and its wide, tree-shaded avenues, sidewalk cafes and snazzy shops have again become a safe and attractive destination for Americans and other international travelers.

Here in the former capital of the former South Vietnam, I recently checked in at the venerable Caravelle Hotel. It was the second time I had signed the register in almost 40 years.

In 1966, when my wife and I visited Saigon a year after we were married, the Caravelle was no taller than its 10th-floor rooftop bar. The only room we could get was a modest one a single flight up, overlooking the main intersection.

"No one wants that room," said Malcolm Browne. My friend and former newspaper colleague was a war correspondent headquartered in the city.

"It's considered within grenade-lobbing distance from the street below," he explained.

My latest room at the Caravelle was a luxuriously appointed chamber on the 16th floor of the new 24-story wing, with a view of ferry boats bustling back and forth across the busy Saigon River.

In the 1960s, Mal believed in taking his visitors out to show them the war. But because I had my bride with me, we mainly toured historic sites around the city. This included the intersection where Mal took the 1963 photo of a burning Buddhist monk, a dramatic suicide, which was published around the world.

Mal said he would like us to see the Mekong Delta, and so the four of us, including Sara and Mal's wife, Le Lieu, set off for a two-hour drive to the village of My Tho where we lunched in a small open-air restaurant with pink walls suspended over the edge of the Mekong River.

At this point, American troops were beginning to support South Vietnamese forces, although some of the fiercest battles in the war were yet to come.

Here in the Delta, though, Mal explained that it was then tacitly understood that the opposite bank of the Mekong, which we could clearly see from our table, was considered Viet Cong territory 24/7. However, all the land on this side of the river, between My Tho and Saigon, was controlled by the U.S.-supported government. Or at least it was during the daytime.

"At night it all belongs to the Viet Cong," Mal said.

On our afternoon drive back to Saigon, while driving along some rice paddies, we suddenly heard a loud whizzing sound go by in front of our windshield.

"What the heck was that?" I asked.

"You have just been sniped at!" said Mal, gritting his teeth. "Open the glove compartment!"

I didn't know that my friend had a gun in the car, but there was a .45-caliber pistol for me to hold while Mal pressed down hard on the accelerator. So I rode shotgun while our wives hunkered down in the back seat. But there was no further incident, and we arrived back in Saigon unharmed.

"I thought you told us this road belonged to the government during the day," I said later.

"Well, the VC is just like any other army," Mal replied. "There's always one guy who doesn't get the word!"

As it turned out, Mal did indeed show us the war, albeit from a safe distance. That night, we dined at Paprika, an open-air Algerian restaurant atop the Rex Hotel. The entertainment, so to speak, was a night artillery operation just outside the city.

We could see the muzzle flash from the howitzers in one neighborhood and the explosions where the rounds were landing in another area. The operation was directed by an American F4 Phantom jet, with its distinctive spooky sound, as it circled over the city.

Sara and I left the following day, as planned. But of course Mal stayed throughout the war, eventually winning a Pulitzer Prize for his coverage.

My recent trip was just as interesting and much more pleasurable. Again, I traveled out of Saigon on an excursion to the Mekong Delta, this time as part of a group conducted by Exotissimo, a Saigon-headquartered company specializing in tours throughout Indochina. Most in the bus were American travel agents.

We spent the morning and afternoon cruising the Mekong River on a tourist "junk boat," named the *Cai Be Princess*, from which we could observe villages and floating markets along the river. We received friendly waves from families and workers on boats and along the banks, and we lunched at a centuries-old Mandarin house.

It was the beginning of a weeklong tour of sites in today's Vietnam, during which we progressed from the tropical south to the cooler north. From Saigon we flew to Nha Trang, which features luxury beach resorts to rival any I have seen in Hawaii, and then continued to Da Nang, landing on the runways of the former American air base there.

We had a good look at China Beach, which once served as a large R&R facility for American servicemen. Here and throughout the country, we often saw old military construction put up either by Americans or Vietnamese.

The jewel in the central area of the country is the village of Hoi An. There we checked in at some attractive waterside garden accommodations called the Life Resort, which adjoins an outdoor market in the low-rise downtown area.

The generally slow pace of life in Hoi An is not matched by the ubiquitous tailors at work in the village. I got overnight delivery on a tailored silk suit from a shop full of smiling young women called Thu Thuy. It cost $180, and I had chosen one of the better-quality fabrics.

Also in Hoi An, our Exotissimo tour leaders sought out a poor and hard-working farm family to receive the gift of a young, female water buffalo. It is probably the most useful beast in Vietnam, for plowing, renting out to others and, of course, raising more water buffalos. Though we weren't required to do so, all of us donated something toward the $650 purchase.

From Hoi An we bused over the mountains to arrive at the ancient imperial capital of Hue. Hue has seen its share of fierce battles over the past few centuries, not the least of which was during the "Tet Offensive" between American and Vietnamese forces in 1968, two years after our first Vietnam visit.

Our own headquarters in Hue was at La Résidence, the expanded premises of the 1930 Art Deco home of the former French governors of colonial Vietnam. In Hue we visited the tombs and palaces of several former emperors, and explored the extensive ruins of the 1808 Imperial Citadel.

Also included was a Dragon Boat ride on the Perfume River ultimately docking at the famous Thien Mu Pagoda, the unofficial symbol of the city. The pagoda also houses the old Austin, which figured in the self-immolation of the Buddhist monk in Saigon, and is the background of Mal's famous photo of the event.

From Hue, we flew to Hanoi, the busy, if not totally hectic, capital of the country. A human-powered cyclo (pedicab) tour of the city provided a thrilling introduction to a traffic situation that seemed on the verge of chaotic. Much more sedate are the city's several museums, including the house of Ho Chi Minh and Hoa Lo Prison, commonly known as the "Hanoi Hilton" during the Vietnam War, and where the future senator John McCain was held.

As it turns out, there is now a genuine Hilton in Hanoi. The Hilton Opera hotel is next to the city's opera house, a scaled-down replica of *L'Opera* in Paris.

A walk from the Hilton to dinner at the Hanoi Press Club a block away was a successful experiment in keeping a steady, determined pace while legions of motorcycles whirled around our legs. The key to safety: Keep walking at a steady pace and *never* step backward!

The crowning experience in my second trip to Vietnam, however, was an overnight trip on Ha Long Bay aboard an excursion boat named the *Emeraude*, a re-creation of a similar vessel owned by a French family in the early 20th century.

Ha Long Bay, dubbed a UNESCO World Heritage Site, is populated by hundreds of steep-sided islands, many of which look like giant green gumdrops floating on still waters. Deep within its boundaries, small groups of fishing families live and work on an informal collection of boats and rafts in a sort of floating village. It was a particularly satisfyingly and relaxing end to an interesting week.

There are no noisy motorcycles in Ha Long Bay, and certainly no evidence that a war ever disturbed the tranquil existence of those who populate the peaceful waters between the gumdrop islands.

Sara and Bob Bone check out some items in
Mal Browne's Saigon apartment.

31
Returning to 1966

BEFORE LEAVING SAIGON in 1966, we enjoyed a meal at Mal and Le Lieu's apartment, trying on his helmet and inspecting some of their military hardware. (See photo on facing page.) And their little dog Niff Naff, a Chinese poodle that Mal claimed was a helicopter in a previous life, since his tail seemed to spin around more than it wagged.

Our flights continued west to Bangkok. En route we landed briefly at Phnom Penh, the capital of Cambodia. We never left the plane, thank goodness. Although the massacres of the Khmer Rouge were still to come, it was already considered a very unsettled region and one of the dominoes due to fall when communism would later overtake the region.

Sounds crazy in the light of several spectacular visits many years later, but on June 25, 1966, Bangkok was a disappointment to us – except as a sigh of relief that we had survived Saigon! And indeed that was probably enough, especially for Sara, who got little or no sleep in Vietnam.

We had dedicated ourselves to thriftiness by searching out sites and sights ourselves. I remember finding out that its currency, the baht, was worth five cents: "A nickel a tickle," laughed a BOAC stewardess.

Thailand had not yet committed itself to international tourism. Street signs and other printed material were illegible to us. The country possessed a written language that looked like wet spaghetti on a plate, and we frequently seemed on the verge of getting lost. We managed to find our way to one colorful temple, but missed seeing the Grand Palace and other sights we enjoyed on visits to the capital in later years.

New Delhi was next, and neither of us was prepared for the extreme poverty that we witnessed there. We got up in the morning to look out our low-rise hotel window to discover that the taxi drivers had spent the night sleeping in or on top of their cars.

Our main objective in India was to see the Taj Mahal, so early the following morning, we stepped carefully around more sleepers on the floor of the railway station to climb aboard the train for Agra. For this excursion, we had the company of old friends.

Before we left home, Sara was exchanging letters with Sally Kaptein, a New Zealander we had known in New York and in London. Coincidentally, Sally and her husband Ed would be moving from London to Melbourne, Australia – the opposite direction from our journey. But it turned out that we would all four be in Delhi on the same date. So we made arrangements to meet and visit the Taj Mahal together.

The Taj, of course, was indeed one of the most beautiful buildings we had ever seen. Even the grounds and outbuildings were in harmony with the structure.

As a child I had read Richard Halliburton's account of a moonlight swim in the pool reflecting the Taj. However we discovered those waters were only about a foot deep. I think you put one over on me, Richard!

Other than that, the beautiful Muslim mausoleum lived up to its reputation – as it did again when I revisited in 2001.

32
Moscow,
Nights & Days

FROM DELHI, WE FLEW NON-STOP to Moscow on a mission to visit Howard Rausch, who was now the correspondent for the McGraw-Hill publications. This was during the Cold War, of course, amidst all the potential spookiness associated with the capital of what was then the U.S.S.R. – Soviet Russia.

I thought I was pretty well prepared for Russia. For several weeks before we left home, I had practiced with Russian language records and eventually learned several key phases. I also had the Cyrillic alphabet pretty well down pat, too, and that went a long way when it came to reading various signs and headlines. Example: Туалет (л is an L in Russian). Give up? Toilet is pronounced tie-ah-let.

One of the first things Howard asked us on arrival was whether we had brought his trousers, which he had forgotten to pick up at the dry cleaners in New York. Indeed we had. And since he had traveled east to his new job, and we had met him by traveling west, he figured that between him and his pants, he, too in effect had now gone around the world!

Or something like that. You will recall that it was Howard who also laughingly came up with the fact that I was once a millionaire in Brazilian *cruzeiros*.

Anyway, we stayed with Howard for a week in Moscow, and he showed us the sights as well as he could. Red Square, Saint Basil's,

GUM department store, and all that, although we didn't join the long queue to check out Lenin's body on display in the Kremlin.

One evening we went with no reservations to one of the most popular restaurants in Moscow, featuring the noodle-rich cuisine of Uzbekistan (then the Uzbek S.S.R.) There was a long line waiting to get in, but we went to the head of the queue and Howard knocked on the door. A uniformed man opened it and Howard explained that we were foreign visitors. So we were ushered right in ahead of everyone in line.

So totally unfair. But, as Howard said, it did demonstrate to some Muscovites how corrupt things were under the communist system. Not that most of the population didn't already know it. Also we got probably the best available table in the place.

On another day, Howard decided to drive us out of the city to the village of Peredelkino, which was just barely inside the 25-mile limit from Moscow that foreigners could travel without special permission. There we hunted up the grave of Boris Pasternak, the poet and author of *Doctor Zhivago* and other works that were then not allowed to be published in Russia. I took several photos, figuring that I might be able to sell them some day. (Though I haven't, at least to date.)

The grave was in a prominent spot and surprisingly decorated by a number of flowers, apparently laid in defiance of the KGB. Howard told us a little of the dramatic funeral held there a few years before – one in which hundreds flouted the authorities by elaborately praising Pasternak and his works.

We enjoyed our Moscow visit tremendously. One day Sara went shopping with Howard's Greek housekeeper, a woman who only spoke Greek and Russian. Somehow, though, they managed to understand each other, I suppose utilizing the common interests of women shoppers everywhere. Sara even ran into someone she knew, a man who had worked with her in New York at BIDO.

"Why Sara Ann Cameron! What the hell are you doing here?"

Our only problem – and a big one – came up when it was time to leave Moscow and continue to our next stop: Berlin. In 1966, of course, that was still a divided city, with half of it serving as the capital of the DDR, and the rest a capitalist enclave surrounded by East Germany.

At approximately the same time we were due to fly from Moscow Airport, Howard was to take a different flight for a temporary assignment in Copenhagen, Denmark. But during the exit formalities, Sara and I were suddenly told in no uncertain terms that we did not have the proper documentation to exit the country!

Trapped in the U.S.S.R in 1966, during the Cold War? How bad could that be? Next stop, the Gulag, perhaps. Or so we thought.

The main stickler, apparently, was that this was a Sunday, and the offices of the police who handled this sort of thing were closed on a Sunday – amazing for an overtly godless society, I thought.

As usual, eternally optimistic Howard said that while he simply had to continue on to Copenhagen, he was sure it could be taken care of the following day.

"Just go home and call Marina," he said, handing me his apartment key. "She'll take care of it."

Marina was assigned as Howard's secretary and personal assistant, and Howard had told us earlier that he was sure it was part of her job to spy on him, too. In any case, she always knew how to do things in a bureaucratic city where it often seemed everything was hard to do.

I was familiar with this kind of thing from my days in Rio. To get anything done with the government there, you had to call a *despachante* – a sort of "fixer." In Moscow, of course, absolutely everything had to do with the government, and if Marina had that kind of talent, everything would probably work out just fine. At least that's what I told Sara.

But a big mistake turned out to be my decision to phone the consular section of the American Embassy as an extra precaution. I merely thought it might be a good idea if someone there should take our names down and be aware that we might be having a problem. An image of Francis Gary Powers flashed into my head. Powers was the American U2 pilot captured years before in the U.S.S.R. and who had only been released recently.

This, too, turned out to be somewhat hard to do.

Using a payphone at the Moscow Airport was somewhat problematic in the first place. But we managed to deposit the correct number of kopeks and got an English-speaking operator at the embassy.

"Well, Mister Bone, I'm not sure how we can help," she said. "Everyone today is out at the American *dacha*!"

The *dacha*, a sort of country cottage, is an institution for those who could afford it in Moscow – a sort of bucolic retreat out in the woods away from the rigors of the city. Somehow it never occurred to me that the American Embassy, too, would also have one.

"I believe tomorrow is your day of independence," the woman continued.

And so it was. Tomorrow would be, the Fourth of July, 1966, and I had truly forgotten. I wondered if cadres of diplomats could possibly be getting ready to light firecrackers, etc. out there amongst the pine trees.

Somehow I was eventually connected to the American *dacha,* and I spoke to an irritated official at the other end of the line, who soon expressed his extreme displeasure.

"How the hell did you get into this situation?" he demanded. I replied that I didn't know, but that I wasn't especially worried. I just wanted someone to take down our names in case something went wrong and we managed to mysteriously disappear.

"Didn't your travel agent have you fill out that police form before the trip?" I informed him then that we didn't use a travel agent.

"And you say you're flying to Berlin? That's impossible – you cannot fly to West Berlin from Moscow!" I informed him that no, we were flying to East Berlin. (The U.S. did not then have any diplomatic relations with East Germany.)

At that point, I think he lost it and I was by then being subjected to considerable invective. So I hung up on the guy while he was still talking. Thinking back on it later, I wondered if I had managed to get that same irascible lieutenant who had read the riot act to me in London nine years earlier, when I reported that my passport had been stolen.

Or maybe it was that U.S. officials abroad are always at a heightened state of uptightness.

Or maybe, too, that at the end of some dramatic scene in my life, there always had to be some kind of a special denouement: the attempted pigeon drop scheme after saying goodbye to Orah in Paris in '58, the airplane air pressure drama after leaving San Francisco and Sara in '61, and now this latest bump in the road at the end of our Moscow visit.

Remembering the calm voice of the 1957 London policeman about how everything usually works out fine in the end, I shrugged my shoulders outwardly at least and we made our way back to Howard's apartment/office on Kutuzovsky Prospekt. When Marina came to work the next day, a Monday, she laughed and said that she would take us to the proper place to straighten it all out, although it might cost some money.

She drove Howard's car to another suburban neighborhood, where we entered a palace-like building, and eventually the three of us were seated on a wooden bench in a room with a very high ceiling. Honestly, the only decoration I remember were two portraits – Lenin on one wall, and Marx on the opposite one. There we waited for about 15 minutes before Marina was admitted to an inner office, to explain the situation. In a few more minutes, she opened the door and invited us in.

There sat a very large uniformed mustachioed man behind a huge desk. He looked a lot like Zero Mostel when he played the commander of the submarine in *The Russians Are Coming, The Russians Are Coming*, a film that was released earlier that year.

Colonel Zero signed something and we signed something, and the price turned out to be the equivalent of about $10 in rubles. I didn't have the local cash, so Marina paid it and told us later she'd get it from Howard. I said that was just about the right amount to pay for the dry cleaning and long-distance delivery of his trousers.

Marina also drove us back to the airport where we boarded an ancient Soviet Ilyushin Ill-18 turboprop aircraft operated by Interflug, the East German airline.

The flight proceeded without incident, unless anyone was concerned that it took off while some were still looking for their seats – and that some seat belts were missing. We seemed to be the only ones surprised.

Our view of East Berlin in 1966. (Photo by Bob Bone)

33
Europe Again, East & West

WE DID, INDEED, LAND at Schönefeld Airport in the Eastern Zone, but those legitimately headed for West Berlin boarded a special bus. At some point, some men shouldering weapons, who I presumed were the dreaded *Stasi* I had read about, came aboard to wordlessly inspect our tickets and passports. Then we passed into West Berlin without incident. It was done efficiently according to arrangements that I'm sure were totally unknown to the consular official who had been bawling me out over the phone the day before in Moscow.

In Berlin we discovered that although World War II ended more than two decades ago, there was still some bomb damage that had not been cleared on both sides of the wall. Moreover there was the stark contrast between the freewheeling, brash, neon-lit Western Zone and the dark Eastern Zone on the other side of the Berlin Wall. In the city center, at least, neither side presented a particularly attractive picture to us in 1966.

In fact, I got the impression that all the bright festivities of rampant capitalism in West Berlin were largely a form of boasting designed to bait those living in the restricted Eastern Zone, especially after dark. It was rather like the psychological torture borne by prisoners in Alcatraz at night when they could hear happy parties and music drifting over the black waters from San Francisco.

Shortly before our trip, I read the book by Cornelius Ryan about Berlin entitled *The Last Battle,* so I knew many places I wanted to see. In line with that, we took one afternoon to proceed through the famous Checkpoint Charlie and then walk into East Berlin to experience as much as we could on foot in a few hours.

We circled the battered Reichstag, which was still in ruins, and I calculated that a certain pile of rocks had been the location of Adolf Hitler's bunker. On the way back to West Berlin, I even took a photo of the eastern side of Checkpoint Charlie, something that I knew was expressly prohibited.

But somehow I got away with it. Whew!

We flew next to Amsterdam, where I looked up Bob Geerlings, a Dutchman I had known with his wife Sandra, and their young child Frank, while living in Brazil. Geerlings was much later the protagonist of a short story by Hunter Thompson entitled "Geerlings and the War Minister's Son," which was included in Hunter's 2003 volume *Kingdom of Fear.* It was a highly exaggerated account of an incident that had occurred while Hunter and I were in Rio in 1963. (I have never been able to reconnect with Bob or Sandra since, although I have tried several times.)

From Amsterdam, we took the train to Brussels, where I was able to introduce Sara to Steve, Terêze, and their two boys, now aged 14 and 12, and relive some of our adventures at the 1958 World's Fair. Ever the do-it-yourselfer, Steve showed me how he had salvaged some material from the fair to build some features in their house and garden.

Steve also gave me the mail that had come for me eight years before, including that letter from *Stars and Stripes* in Darmstadt, suggesting that I might like to apply there for a job!

After two fine days, we boarded another train, this time for Paris, where I was able to show Sara much of the city that Orah and I had explored in 1958. This time the city seemed to be covered in flags. Inadvertently, we arrived just the day after Bastille Day, the French national holiday.

But we were in for one more treat. I read in the paper that President Charles de Gaulle would later that day welcome the king of Laos at the airport after which they would travel to the presidential palace. Looking at the map, I calculated they would be passing right in front of our hotel at Place Denfert-Rochereau on the Left Bank. (Yes, it was the same hotel where Orah and I stayed in 1966.)

Together we climbed to the roof of the hotel, I with my trusty Pentax equipped with a very heavy and large 200-mm zoom lens.

I think we only waited about 15 minutes before we heard a large number of motorcycles.

"This is it!" I said. "Get ready."

The motorcycles passed surrounded by an open car with two men in the back seat, all moving at a fast clip. One of them was His Majesty Savang Vatthana, the last king of Laos, dressed in a military uniform. Next to him was President de Gaulle, the general who was France's greatest World War II hero. Panning with the action I got off three frames on the Pentax, two of which showed their faces clearly.

"Did you see him?" I asked, Sara.

"Sure," she said. "He looked like Howard."

Actually De Gaulle and Howard did resemble each other a little, come to think of it.

This was probably King Savang's last visit to Paris. After the communists took over in Laos, he was deposed. He died mysteriously in prison not long after.

The next day we flew home to New York, anticipating that our round-the-world adventure was over.

Not quite.

Sara and I were traveling on two different passports – American and New Zealand. But returning to the States should have been no problem for her. After all, we were married and she had her green card, giving her official U.S. residence as a registered alien.

Instead, however, the immigration official at the airport had a different idea.

"Did you get advance permission from the State Department to enter the Soviet Union?" he asked Sara. If so, he needed to have proof of same.

We said we didn't know she needed proof. And after some verbal jockeying around, the official said:

"Well, it's lucky you live in New York. You can go home, but you must report to this address tomorrow and explain your circumstances." He gave her a card with an address in Lower Manhattan.

"Meanwhile, you have not been readmitted," he said.

The next day, I reported back to work at Time-Life Books and Sara took a subway to the Battery and found the required office. (We both discovered that in our absence the price of a subway token had risen from its long-time 15 cents to 20 cents.) Since she had not been readmitted to the country, she said she felt as if she were moving around in some kind of little bubble of international territory.

She found the correct office and was subjected to a lecture on how she should have applied for some kind of form before we left on our trip. Then she was charged $10 and was officially readmitted to the U.S.A.

Whew!

Russia was at least a country with which we had diplomatic relations – if often unsteady during those Cold War days. So we both felt lucky that no one seemed to notice that we had also spent some brief time on two separate days in East Berlin, the capital city of the D.D.R. – unrecognized East Germany. The fact that had so upset the consular official on the phone from the American *dacha* in Moscow on Independence Day was apparently unnoticed by the immigration officer in New York.

But remembering the friendly policeman in London in 1957, I was once more aware that in the long run these potentially worrying things have a way of working their way out for the best. Well, so far, anyway.

We couldn't help wondering what officialdom might have made of the facts that during the past few weeks we were shot at and witnessed the war in Vietnam, were held in Moscow by the Russian police, explored and photographed the no-man's land in communist East Berlin, and were recently aiming a big lens from a rooftop at the president of France.

And we had photographs to prove it all – including an excellent color slide of President Charles de Gaulle and the king of Laos (see page 219).

34
Spots on the Rope

ON THE JOB AGAIN at Time-Life Books, I found that except for a few close friends, most of my colleagues were not much interested in our activities and experiences while circling the globe over the previous six weeks. (Strangely enough, many travel writers report the same anomaly. And any comments heard often include the word "gallivanting").

I settled into the job again, and again often found myself partaking in what were popularly called "three-martini lunches." These were really no joke. It was often true that some of the best and most innovative ideas on creating picture essays resulted from a slight degree of midday inebriation.

In the *Light and Vision* book, for example, photographer Ken Kay and I were having trouble illustrating the principle of polarized light. We finally did it by using a machine to twirl a rope, representing a light wave. When the rope was twirled through a pair of parallel bars, they were no longer three-dimensional on the other side of the bars, and just varied in an up and down motion instead of in a spiral.

The only problem was that although it could easily be seen by a pair of eyes, it did not show up in a photograph, which, of course, was only two-dimensional. But after somewhat of an alcoholic lunch, we hit on putting black spots on the rope, and the effect became clear. I credited that at least partly to the martinis in our noon repast.

Throughout the rest of 1966 and 1967, I served again as picture editor on several books in the Science Library, including *Sound and*

Hearing, Ships, Flight, Light and Vision, and *Giant Molecules* (plastics and polymers). On these books, I was officially listed as "picture editor," and this meant that I was generally sending others out into the field instead of going myself.

One exception: For *Sound and Hearing* I flew in an FAA plane briefly to New Mexico to observe a government experiment on the effects of jet planes breaking the sound barrier. While I was there, the experiment was set back considerably because the planes accidentally went supersonic before they were supposed to. The resulting boom set the experiment back considerably, although no one immediately confirmed that assessment.

Moreover, en route our own government FAA plane experienced sudden decompression while we were at a high altitude. With an uncomfortable ear-clapping bang, it dropped all those yellow oxygen masks over our seats – just like in the movies.

And furthermore, Book Division chief researcher Bea Dobie was upset with me later for taking a "free flight." It took some time before I was able to convince her that this was okay since no one on the plane paid anything, simply because it was not a commercial flight.

In due course I was no longer a denizen of Lower Manhattan. Sara and I moved again, this time from our tiny garden apartment on 21st Street to a much more commodious 8th-floor accommodation at 321 West 78th Street, between West End Avenue and Riverside Drive.

And Sara received her New York State registered nurse license and began working for Dr. William J. Sweeney, a gynecologist-obstetrician. This proved to be an especially fortuitous move. (Sweeney was a writer and inventor and later penned a successful autobiography.)

With Dr. Sweeney's help, our daughter, Christina Ann Bone, was born on July 30, 1967, a happy and exciting event that affected our immediate outlook on almost everything. My parents were especially excited when we took her to Bowling Green for Christmas.

But at the office, things began to look black for the future of the Science Library. Those of us working on the series learned that despite the fact that we had several good titles still to be created, they would never come to pass. There were unseen and unfeeling powers at Time-Life – in my mind likely served by Elevator Bank Number

One – who had determined that the series was going to be coming to an end. (Hunter would have called them "Rotarians.")

It was a hard lesson in business practices for many of us younger souls working on the series. Generally speaking, we had a rather naïve and altruistic view of our work. But the facts were now proving that although the Science series was still making money for the company, it was just not making *enough* money. It was soon determined by someone somewhere that it would be more profitable to update and reissue the existing titles than to create new ones.

For a full year, I was assigned to a leading role in developing a new series, known internally as the "*Social* Science Library," for which the first book would be called *The Family*. Although I was complimented on the work, the project was then cancelled entirely. Again the reasons were never made clear to the select few of us who had been pouring sweat and tears into the project.

Then for a time, I was the only Time-Life staffer working on another blue-sky assignment – creating a new TV-related magazine that would be called *Preview*. For that, I was assigned to work with Stephen H. Scheuer, a well-known film and TV historian known for his annual volume called *Movies on TV* containing capsule reviews of old movies. (His brother, James H. Scheuer, was a long-time New York congressman.)

I got along fine with Steve, and I think we came up with a viable project. But in the end, someone somewhere on the mysterious business end of the corporation turned thumbs down on that, too, and so the new *Preview* never saw the light of day. It seemed Elevator Bank Number One had struck again.

Steve himself went on to turn out several successful books about movies and TV, although his main annual publication was eventually eclipsed by Leonard Maltin's similar annual compendium on films on TV.

After that, I was transferred to the *Time-Life Library of America,* which was producing a series of books based on states of the Union. Although I was again a picture (or "project") editor, I found the subject matter not nearly as interesting as my work turning out science books. Similarly other former science reporters found themselves re-assigned to working in the food series (*Foods of the World*) or the culture library (*Great Ages of Man*).

While on the American Library I did shepherd an interesting volume that combined two seemingly diverse states, Alaska and Hawaii, into a single book called *The Frontier States*. Although I did not visit the two states myself during the project, I sent photographers and researchers to them. (Such is often the fate of editors – the need to dispatch others to interesting experiences out in the field. I am sorely reminded again of when I sent researcher Tony Wolff to Paris on board the *S.S. France*.) In any case these two states remained on my bucket list for years until they both became important to me much later in my career. (I did not count the cursory three-day visit on the round-the-world trip.)

The final blow for me was when we learned that, in any case, Time-Life Books would soon be leaving New York for a new headquarters in Alexandria, Virginia, a suburb of Washington, DC. At around the same time, my friend Dave Bridge, who had by then left the Nature Library for a similar job at National Geographic Books, invited me down to Washington to talk to his editor there about another upcoming editorial position. Neither of these options managed to grab my attention, and I was not keen on living in the DC area either.

Beyond all these difficulties, and now that we were parents, and about to be again, Sara and I became much more discouraged by the state of the country and the world in general in 1967. China tested a hydrogen bomb without warning, Israel embarked on the Six-Day War, and the U.S. and U.S.S.R. were at continual loggerheads while trying to come up with a workable nuclear disarmament treaty.

Moreover the racial situation in the South was also depressing, and the country was becoming terribly divided over the morality and uselessness of the Vietnam War. And crime in New York was on the rise.

In 1967, I was still a member of the Overseas Press Club (which I had joined in Brazil), and I read an unusual classified ad in the *OPC Bulletin*. It described somewhat mysteriously an editorial opportunity on a "sunny beach" in Europe. As a result I began a desultory correspondence with guidebook author Temple Fielding.

Temple came from a prominent New York family who lost their shirts during the Great Depression. He was the grandson of Temple Hornaday Fielding, the famous naturalist, author, and father of the

Bronx Zoo. He also claimed he was distantly related to author Henry Fielding.

During World War II, Temple had been an officer in the OSS (precursor to the CIA), taking part in secret operations principally in Yugoslavia. After his discharge he began his annual travel guide operation in post-war Europe and by the time we met him he was known as the premium guidebook author for Americans visiting Europe.

The only thing that provided much joy that year was the birth of our daughter, Christina, on July 30. And now with a child to raise, New York no longer seemed such a safe haven. We were ripe for a major change in our lives.

The nation and world situation began to seem even darker in 1968. Incredibly Martin Luther King Jr. and Robert F. Kennedy were assassinated within two months of each other. (Perhaps the latter hit us more since we had watched RFK make a street-corner speech in Greenwich Village during his senatorial campaign in 1964.) And the country seemed to be being torn apart by controversy over the Vietnam War, racial tensions, and other difficulties. Finally there was the depressing violence and police riot at the Democratic National Convention in Chicago.

Around the same time *The New Yorker* published John McPhee's profile of Temple Fielding, painting an interesting and complex portrait of the travel writer and his operation. Now the possibility of relocating to Europe for the future began to look much more desirable than ever before, and my letters to Fielding and his encouraging replies began to seem much more practical.

The long-established annual 1,500-page *Fielding's Travel Guide to Europe* was losing its position in one emerging part of the market – the young traveler to Europe who was increasingly turning to budget-conscious books like Arthur Frommer's soft-cover *Europe on Five Dollars a Day* and similar publications.

Temple and Nancy Fielding lived on the Spanish island of Mallorca, and consequently his small staff lived there also, although they annually traveled through Western Europe to research tourism facilities – primarily hotels, restaurants, and nightlife – to update his main book, plus another smaller publication devoted to shopping.

When the Fieldings came to New York to consult with their publisher, William Morrow and Company, they invited Sara and me to dinner. They told us they had tried a new paperback version the year before with disappointing results. Now they needed someone to shepherd a more up-beat paperback to less-expensive facilities in Europe, which would be called *Fielding's Super-Economy Europe*. And would I like to move with my family to Mallorca and accept that job?

I would be "senior writer in charge," they said.

The pay would be somewhat less than I was then making at Time-Life. But on the other hand, the cost of living in Spain would also be considerably less than in New York City. And, of course, all traveling expenses while on the job would be taken care of.

I'm not sure if we sealed the deal at that dinner or not. I do remember that Temp warned us that it would be impossible for me to find a decent tuxedo in Mallorca and that he advised me to buy one before leaving New York. (As if the thought had ever occurred to me before!)

So my main job-related expense before moving to this sun-blessed surf-and-sand Mediterranean island would be to buy and tailor a set of formal evening clothes – jacket, trousers, cummerbund, fancy white shirt and a black bow tie.

Of course I sought the advice of others, especially my closest professional friends: Mal Browne, who had won his Pulitzer and consequently was now working for *The New York Times* in South America, Howard Rausch, who had just returned from Moscow, and was also working for the *Times* as a copy editor, and Hunter Thompson, who had finally published his Hells Angels book. He was now working on another while beginning to contribute to *Rolling Stone* magazine. He recently moved to his rural property at Woody Creek, Colorado. This was Owl Farm, which became the base camp for his eccentric activities for the rest of his life.

All three gave us their blessing. And I still have the letter from Hunter, written May 17, 1968. After outlining some of his own recent literary adventures he turned to my news:

> None of this has much to do with my genuinely visceral happiness about your decision to get off to Mallorca and back to the madman's game. But in this case you seem to have some insurance, which is only right in the case of a man who has paid his dues and survived in the total risk league....So it's about time you got a few

dividends from all that bullshit, and in terms of dividends the job with Fielding sounds like pure gold.

Man, $11,000 a year in Spain, with six months of travel and research and a house on Mallorca – I don't see any way you can beat that in this country. The only way to enhance it, I think, would be to write some sort of jangled journalistic log about how it all happened. People like McGarr would buy it in great numbers, because the conventional wisdom these days holds that the sort of life you've been leading is no longer possible.

Only a lunatic, for instance would quit an up-mobile job in NY (*Popular Photography*) and run off to Brazil for a gig with the Rio Chamber of Commerce…and then expect to come back to NY and pick up a job with Life…and then flee again for a fantasy-style job in/on Mallorca. Christ, you have really put the screws to every known theory of how to get by in this world by slowly killing yourself.

You've put the lie to all that, and once you get back in the habit of writing for print, you might get a boot out of writing a very understated Bowling Green to NY to Mallorca saga – with huge emphasis on How to Beat the NY Big Salary-Death-in-Life Syndrome. Shit, you'd sell 50,000 copies in NY alone.

I guess we'll finally see if Hunter was right in his 1968 prediction.

His Majesty Savang Vatthana, King of Laos, and President De Gaulle of France (from story on page 211).
(Photo by Bob Bone)

Sara and Christina beginning the voyage to Mallorca.
(Photo by Bob Bone)

35
A New Adventure

I ACCEPTED A TWO-YEAR contract with Fielding, gave my notice to Time-Life, and we began preparations to ship the family to Mallorca, with the thought that we might spend the rest of our lives living in Europe. But first we had to teach Sara some Spanish. I sent her off to a class, but the results were at first disappointing.

After she came home crying, the teacher called to explain. He said that although his was supposed to be a beginning course in the language, he had never had such a basic beginner before.

Nearly everyone in the U.S. absorbs a certain amount of Spanish perhaps by osmosis. But apparently few New Zealanders of that generation had heard words like *sombrero, mañana, si si,* nor ever conceived of the possibility that an adjective might follow a noun, or that nouns might be designated as masculine or feminine and that modifiers would change accordingly.

I myself was faced with forgetting Portuguese, and I took on the job of demonstrating to my wife at least the basics of Spanish. I remember once trying to explain the word "you" in Spanish was different in singular and plural. Furthermore there were differences between the polite form and the familiar. I told her the singular word for "you" in Spanish was *usted* in the polite form and *tu* in the familiar.

"But when do you use *tu*?" Sara asked.

"Well, you use the familiar form when addressing friends or members of your own family, and, of course when speaking to cats and dogs."

"Cats and dogs!" she exclaimed. "I'm bloody well not speaking Spanish to any cats and dogs!"

She had me there.

And getting a little ahead in the story, let the record show that once Sara was faced with having to speak Spanish in the months and years to come, she came through admirably. In fact there were many who preferred to converse with Sara in bad Spanish than with her comparatively over-educated husband.

We soon discovered that we could ship pretty much all of our worldly goods direct to Palma de Mallorca right along with ourselves. A moving company came to our apartment and picked up everything we decided to take, including furniture and hundreds of my audio tape recordings of old radio shows. Then they built a wooden box around it all forming what was called a "lift van." (Modern industrial shipping containers were still to be invented.)

Next we found a ship scheduled to sail from Manhattan August 30 with a port call in Palma de Mallorca. Our lift van of worldly goods could come right along with us on the same ship, the three-year-old *Raffaello,* one of the last luxury vessels built for the Italian Line.

We made all the arrangements for the four of us – Sara, myself, one-year-old Christina, and the family cat, named Anzie (short for ANZAC) to sail right from home – departing from the same Hudson River docks that I had used two decades before on my initial European adventure, and where I had visited the *Normandy* with my parents in 1939.

But now we were a whole family going to live in the Mediterranean, apparently for the rest of our lives.

Of course not everything was smooth sailing. On the afternoon of August 31, we climbed on board, found our small windowless cabin (A-40), and also discovered that a wildcat strike was going to delay our departure for an unknown period of time – might be 12 hours – might be a week or more.

This proved problematic for Anzie, who had reservations in the ship's kennel up on the Promenade Deck, but who could not be accepted there with the attendant out on strike. Luckily I knew that we had a cat pan and some kitty litter back at our deserted apartment. And luckily, I still happened to have the keys to the place. Luckily again, I managed to find a cab at around midnight to make a quick excursion back to West 78th Street. I asked the driver to wait.

Sara was sure that something awful was in the wind. They would suddenly pull up the gangplank and she would sail away forever with Christina and the cat but leaving me stranded on the shore. I assured her (if not to myself so much) that it was not going to happen.

I returned about an hour later with the required equipment, including some cat food. The next afternoon, the strike was over, the ship sailed, and we booked Anzie in at the kennel, which was up on a First Class deck.

Christina proved to be a popular passenger over the next week on the high seas, as cute as a one-year-old girl could possibly be. When we appeared on an open deck, she had a harness around her waist with Mommy or Daddy at the other end of the leash, so there was no chance of her falling overboard. Thus we would daily make at least one trip up to First Class for a visit with Anzie, a relatively laid back cat. She weathered the trip well despite being surrounded by a few dogs.

When the ship made its only port call en route, on the flower-filled Portuguese island of Madeira, we tied Christina in her stroller and explored our immediate surroundings. A day or two later, we sailed past Gibraltar and through the Pillars of Hercules into the Med. Two days after that we arrived at Palma, the principal port of Mallorca.

One thing we didn't tell Temple and Nancy before our arrival. Sara was pregnant again, and was due to deliver in December. Our next child would be a Spaniard.

36
A Royal Greeting

TEMPLE AND NANCY LAID out the red carpet for us. They showed up at the dock in Palma in their large, chauffeur-driven black-and-white Cadillac convertible that flew two flags, one on each fender. One was the Stars and Stripes; the other was the national flag of Denmark. (Temple was made an honorary citizen when the Danes discovered that his guidebook was bringing hordes of visitors to that country.)

Then we watched the hold open up and a crane raise our lift van from the ship, swing it over, and deposit it on the dock. I don't remember how or who got it from Palma to the village that was to be our home.

But in the flag-bedecked Caddie, Sara and I, plus Christina and Anzie, traveled with the Fieldings to the coastline village of Puerto de Pollensa on the other side of the island, the closest village to the mountain retreat of Formentor, where Temple and Nancy made their home and office.

Members of Spain's oft-feared Guardia Civil, spotting the waving flags, automatically saluted us. Whenever our driver, whom we later learned was Alfonso, the Fielding butler, thought the car might not be noticed on its approach, it was his habit to give a slight beep on the horn in order to bring the Guardia to attention.

In Puerto Pollensa, we initially stayed at an American-style motel called the Motelyn, owned by an American woman named Jackie, and Francisco, her Mallorcan husband. We settled in quickly – except for

Anzie, our New York apartment cat, who stepped gingerly on the grass – a kind of carpet she had never experienced before.

The first few days on the island were eye-openers. For one thing, the indigenous population seldom spoke Spanish among themselves. Their language was Mallorquín. It was a close cousin to Catalan, the tongue used in daily life in Barcelona and the province of Catalonia on the southern coast of mainland Spain. And that, in turn, was virtually the same language as Provençal, which was spoken by many in Provence, the adjoining area in southern France.

Of course Spanish was still the official language of Spain, and every citizen had to be able to speak, read, and write it. But the island population was tolerant of foreigners who struggled with Spanish. After all, it wasn't technically their language. As long as they could figure out what you were saying, you could murder Franco's mother tongue all you wanted to.

One exception was the grocer we often used. When Sara shopped there, he good-naturedly insisted that she use – or learn on the spot – the precise Spanish word for the product. Unlike some other expats, she learned important subtle differences in pronunciation, e.g. *harina* (flour) vs. *arena* (sand).

And at home, Rosita, our housekeeper, usually with a red face, tried to keep Sara from confusing *cajones* (a chest of drawers) and *cojones* – (slang for testicles).

Still, Sara was pretty hip with some of her observations about Spanish culture. We've always laughed about her verbal description of *flamenco* dancing – a way to fight mosquitoes (overhead clapping) and cockroaches (foot stamping) at the same time.

Officially, Spain was under martial law while we lived there. Regional languages were frowned upon by Francisco Franco, who was the ultimate law of the land. No newspapers, magazines, TV, radio, or even street signs were allowed to use anything other than *Castillano* – the pure Castilian Spanish that was spoken by El Caudillo himself, the president for life. Some *madrillenos* (residents of Madrid) are just as arrogant of their native tongue as *parisiennes* are of theirs.

Spoken words were an exception. But we pretty much gave *Mallorquin* a miss. Although when we wanted to ask an attendant to fill our car with gas, we forswore a polite Spanish phrase like *Llena el tanque con gasolina por favor* and choosing instead a single *Mallorquin* word that sounded something like *"Pluff!"*

This prohibition is no longer the case today. If you look at a modern map of Mallorca, many features are now printed in Mallorquín. The same goes for road signs both on Mallorca and throughout Catalonia.

Soon after our arrival, I was interviewed by the local paper, which also used photos of both of us. The long story, which also mentioned Christina and the cat, received a banner headline in Spanish:

MR. ROBERT BONE, CONOCIDO PERIODISTA NORTEAMERICANO AFFIRMA:

Uno de los cometidos principales de un buen periodiosta es descubrir la verdad entre tanta mentira. (One of the cardinal principles of a good news reporter is to discover the truth among all the lies.)

The writer, Jaime Sebastian, also worked part time for Fielding.

One more word on Spanish: Over the years several words and phrases became family words.

"Throw that in the *basura* sweetheart," I would say.

"I think you're kind of *malpuesto,*" Sara might say, if I parked the car badly. (We adopted even more family words after living years later in Hawaii.)

Within a week of our arrival in Spain, we deserted the Motelyn for a nearby 10-room (five bedroom) house with marble floors and a huge picture window of the Bay of Pollensa. The rent was $100 a month, which was less than half what we were paying for our New York apartment. We soon hired a full-time maid/housekeeper and were now off to a good start.

Almost immediately we bought a small car from a departing American at a bargain. It was a *Seat* (pronounced *say-ott*), which was the old Fiat 600, but manufactured in Spain. It was one model up from the tinier Fiat I was so familiar with back in Puerto Rico.

37

On the Job

ONE MAJOR DISAPPOINTMENT with Mallorca was that it was not the tropical location we had expected. True, it seldom snowed. But during the winter the house was not heated, had dozens of air leaks, and was kept livable only by one inefficient fireplace and a couple of butane heaters that we bought to fight the cold air.

Mallorca had a warm-weather reputation – among northern Europeans who, by and large, only visited during less challenging seasons of the year.

Rosita, our housekeeper, was intelligent and *simpatico,* and she quickly became a loyal family friend. And when she married Joaquin and had a baby of her own, there suddenly were two entire families in our house.

Over the next two and one-half years, life was always interesting, although the work was often grueling. Dealing with Temple was easy enough, on the few occasions when we worked side-by-side. My only problem was with Joe, who often made it clear that he was my immediate superior.

Joe Raff and his wife, Judy, had been Temple and Nancy's lieutenants for at least a dozen years before we arrived. (Judy mostly worked with Nancy on a separate European shopping guide.) But there was always some other editor/writer, who usually stayed only a short time before moving on. This time, it was I, and I think I managed to stick it out much longer for perhaps some kind of a record.

While we were there, two other American couples came to work for Fielding and then rather quickly moved on.

Joe was a frequently severe editor when it came to demanding rewrites and strictly adhering to the Fielding literary style, called *Fieldingese*. This was often rather cloying prose – okay maybe for the big guide and that gilt-edged audience, but perhaps not so much for the relatively hip book I was trying to mold. Admittedly it was difficult to avoid some of the same phrases over and over again when reporting about hotels, restaurants, transportation, and other tourist facilities in various European towns and cities.

Fielding guides were often criticized for concentrating so much on the logistics of travel and creature comforts and having almost nothing to say about sightseeing and cultural attractions. I tried to ameliorate that with at least some amount of success in the paperback book. Of course I also contributed from time to time to the main Fielding guidebook, which much more strictly kept to the effusive Fielding style.

One new chapter I researched and initially wrote for the 1971 *SuperEconomy Europe* guide was on Torremolinos, a booming Spanish resort town that was then becoming popular among young travelers. I suppose I may have written a rather too-laconic introduction to the chapter. But by the time Joe and Temp had worked it over, it was turned loose in print like this:

> Madrid, say the wags in Spain, is the nation's mistress whose earnings from Iberia's industrial tenderloins maintain her in elegance.
>
> If this imagery were expanded, then bouncy, bustling, boisterous Torremolinos would be a totally self-sufficient señorita who earns her own false eyelashes, platform sandals, and sweet smell of success.
>
> Although one of her most alluring features is her sunny disposition, she is also—without a doubt—a steamy and sensual lady of the evening.
>
> Her apron rises to a lap of golden sand. Her pineland tresses sought in the romantic Mediterranean breeze. Her costume jewelry, flashy and abundant, is painfully gauche—the selection of an uninhibited country cousin rather than that of a discerning sophisticate.

But even if her rouge is too thick and her laughter a vulgar guffaw, her bathing-suitors and errant knights still clamor to deposit their riches on her ever-ready doorstep.

Her bedlam begins when the jackhammers jump into their all-day rock-and-roll cacophony. It continues almost nonstop until the clarion bands unplug their instruments at dawn's early bedtime.

Here is a curious mélange of incongruities: While her construction birthrate would overtax an architectural Don Juan, don't look now, because that sassy young lassie just happens to be splitting the seams of her mini-bikini.

Clearly, she's not every Lothario's loving cup-lette. But for sun-sand-surf seekers, mix-mirth-merry makers, and swinging swingers with swingless purse strings, she can be a pert and perky pennywise playmate.

Although the guide took that very avuncular position on Torremolinos, the same destination was contrasted with a short and dismissive attitude in the bigger book – *Fielding's Travel Guide to Europe:*

> The streets of Torremolinos and neighboring Málaga now swarm in High Season with non-writing writers, non-painting painters, hippies, dropouts, acid-heads, LSDecadents, and other expatriate nogoodniks of a dozen nationalities. Nearby beaches have become so reminiscent of Easter at the Bronx Zoo monkey house that sea-and-sand buffs in search of peace must now traipse to the outskirts – the more remote, the better.

Sometimes I wondered if I would ever be able to write normal newspaper copy again.

38

Bonfire of the Relatives

OUR SON DAVID WAS BORN in a hospital in Palma on December 20, 1968, with no complications. A month or so later, however, he represented three difficulties for us: (a) we wanted to get him circumcised and (b) we needed to get him an American passport. And before either of those could take place, we also needed (c) to actually register his birth, something that wasn't done automatically in Spain. The doctor doing the registration actually removed his diaper to see that he was a boy, whereupon David peed in the doctor's face.

The Spanish government frowned on the idea of circumcision: ironic as it was, since much of the Mallorcan population had Jewish names. This was a result of the 16th century Spanish Inquisition, during which Jews had to renounce their faith and become Catholic or die.

We eventually did find a physician to do the job, but it was difficult for us to see a six-week-old baby noisily suffer the operation. David became a difficult child in many ways, and we often wondered if he held a deep psychological grudge as a result of this painful event.

In order to get him an American passport, we also had some procedural difficulties. For one thing, at that time a child born abroad of parents where only one of whom was an American citizen was not automatically a full-fledged American citizen. Among the documents we needed, were his Spanish birth certificate and a certificate from another doctor to certify that he was, indeed, a real boy.

These things and perhaps some others I've forgotten had to be taken in person to the American consul in Barcelona on the mainland. When she finally handed over his passport, she warned us that his citizenship could be revoked if he did not spend a certain number of years in the U.S. by the time he was 21 – or something like that. (In later years, David sometimes indicated that he resented what seemed to be his initial status as a sort of second-class American citizen. That problem disappeared when he joined the Navy.)

Not long after David was born, Sara's mother in New Zealand decided she would like to come to Mallorca to meet her new grandchildren. Her only problem was that with a difficult ear situation of some kind, she said she could not fly.

Consequently, she booked passage on a ship, and the only one that seemed to be able to get close to Mallorca was one to Lisbon, Portugal. So we said we'd meet her and bring her back to the island.

By this time, we had bought a brand-new Morris sedan, a relatively commodious vehicle as compared to the Spanish Seat (pronounced *say-ott*, remember?) We left the children with Rosita and took the car ferry from Palma to Valencia on the Spanish mainland and began the overland trip to Lisbon.

When we got to the frontier, however, we were faced with an unexpected impediment.

The captain at the Portuguese border informed us that only I could continue into his country.

"I'm sorry, but your wife cannot pass," he said.

Here again was our oft-felt difficulty arising out of the fact that for several years Sara and I had two different passports.

The man was sympathetic, but apparently firm, explaining that Portugal just didn't happen to have the same type of relationship with New Zealand as it did with the U.S. We would have to turn around and go to the Portuguese consulate in Valencia and apply for a visa there.

Well, there was no way I was going to leave Sara by the side of the road, or leave her mother standing on the dock in Lisbon. So screwing up my courage, I began to address the gentleman in the bad low-class Portuguese I learned in Rio de Janeiro seven years before.

I explained quite truthfully that we were only going to Lisbon to pick up Sara's non-flying, ear-infected mother from the ship tomorrow and that we would immediately return to Spain, most likely at this same border crossing.

"Is there any way you could *dar jeito?*" I asked.

Jeito was almost a magic word in Brazil, but I didn't know if it would have a similar effect in Portugal. Used in this way, there is no direct translation. Vaguely it means to find a way to do something important when there is seemingly no way to do it. It is almost a challenge to someone's politeness and ability to take care of a difficult situation.

The captain expressed surprise and then respectfully accepted the challenge.

"Well, I am authorized to issue *emergency* visas," he said. "But there is a cost to do this."

For a moment, I thought I was going to have to fork over something like 100 bucks – maybe more.

Instead, the fare was the equivalent of about five dollars. And it was all above board, signed, sealed, and with an elaborate official receipt.

It was all downhill from there. We picked up "Mum" Cameron, drove back to Spain, and took the ferry to Mallorca again. And now we had a new story to tell.

Mum stayed for about two months and seemed to enjoy every minute of it. She did make a New Zealand mother's observation about Spanish in a phrase we have remembered often over the years:

"I don't see how these people can ever understand each other with all that jibber-jabber," she said.

In due course my parents and my Uncle Jay and Aunt Donna also came for a visit. My mother got along well with the children and with Temple Fielding, whom she thought was some sort of celebrity. Other people seemed to rub her the wrong way, however, and I think she was uncomfortable not knowing anything of the language.

Of course we had two things that often made every difficult situation seem okay – our two cute little kids who used to hang around the house. (I still miss them a lot at that age.)

One who was never bothered by language or hardly anything else was Christina. When she was about two, she spotted a new and strange creature that was tethered in the garage.

"What's that, Daddy?"

"You know. It's a turkey," I said. "You like turkey. You had some for dinner."

A brief pause to think.

"No! No! Not the kind that walks around!"

39
Back to Work

FOR ABOUT HALF THE YEAR, I was mostly working at long hours into the night on my small portable manual typewriter, trying to conform to the sometimes conflicting instructions from Joe. But I was a veteran of a lot of bosses, beginning with my tank company commander. In the Army, I had learned to "never let the bastards get you down."

Sara was sure that Joe saw me as a potential threat to his own position in the company and was reacting accordingly. Perhaps so, although I tried never to dwell on subjects like that. In any case, in social situations both Joe and Judy were polite and often helpful.

During the rest of the year, I was traveling in Western Europe. The *SuperEconomy Europe* guide covered 27 cities, from Amsterdam to Zurich. Former OSS man Fielding never let himself be tempted to cover any country in the communist bloc – not even relatively independent Yugoslavia, which was beginning to accept international tourists.

Or perhaps *especially* not Yugoslavia, where he said that in the 1940s he worked undercover and managed to earn the wrath of Marshal Tito for some reason. He once hinted to me that he might even be on a death list maintained by the dictator himself. (Tito remained in power until his death in 1980.)

Traveling on the Continent – mostly by plane and train – was always interesting, despite the need to trudge through the corridors and inspect the accommodations of lesser-known and relatively inexpensive hotels, pensions, etc. Every now and then, I would rendezvous with Temp and Nancy. On those occasions, I stayed at large, expensive hotels and ate only in the most posh restaurants with my bosses. This included the Bristol or the Plaza Athénée in Paris and I believe the Hassler in Rome.

On the trips where I might rendezvous with Nancy and Temple, I packed my tuxedo. But on all of them, I never once wore the darn thing.

At least two restaurant experiences with Temple and Nancy stand out in my memory. One was in Rome, the Hostaria dell' Orso, where Nancy pointed out to me that the supporting columns were lined with semi-precious lapis lazuli – the first I ever heard of the stuff.

The other was a particularly dramatic evening that lasted for perhaps six hours at La Tour d'Argent restaurant in Paris, all the while accompanied by the owner, Claude Terrail. The Tour d'Argent was (and still is) located just across the River Seine from the Cathedral of Notre Dame. Temple said the city of Paris could not afford to keep on the floodlights every night on the famous monuments of the city, including Notre Dame. Ergo, the Tour d'Argent paid for four nights of lights, and the city for the other three. (Or maybe it was the other way around.)

In any case, we started our own evening with two hours down in the wine cellar, admiring, tasting, and talking about wines – a few of the more than 400,000 bottles available there. One of our fellow diners by the way was the world sales manager for Mumm champagne. (So I suppose Temp and Nancy forwent their usual bottle of *Dom Pérignon* on this occasion.)

Following that, we ascended to the main room of the restaurant, and to the very best table, surrounded by plate glass that gave an excellent view of the Cathedral of Notre Dame, possibly lit up that night with the lights financed by this very restaurant.

For the main course, I ordered, at Temp's instructions, the Duck, – *le Canard de la Presse* — the house specialty, using the ducks from the establishment's own farm, which perhaps were happily still swimming and quacking early that same morning. With all the extras ordered for us by M. Terrail himself, who sat with us at the table, it was another four hours before we left the establishment.

At some point in the evening, Temp said to me, *sotto voce*, that normally they would never come to La Tour wearing just business suits, but he had explained to the owner that they would do so that evening just for my benefit, since I did not have evening wear.

He had apparently forgotten that he had asked me to buy a tux before I even left New York City, about a year before this event. The thing was at that moment in my suitcase back at the hotel. After that evening, I stopped taking it on research trips. In truth I don't think I wore it until several years later when I began traveling on, and writing about, cruise ships.

The Tour 'd'Argent is often translated to mean "Tower of Silver." Or, of course, the language being what it is, it could instead be translated "Tower of Money," which is what it might cost for a large table of guests like ours. But, of course, it didn't cost that for the Fielding party – not even a *sou*.

The next day, Temp and I also explored his Paris together. We lunched at Maxim's, with no reservation, and he was recognized as soon as we came through the door.

"Good day Monsieur Fielding, your table is waiting," bowed the obsequious maître d'hotel.

On another occasion in Paris, Temp vowed to cure me of my aversion to seafood. Again with no reservation, we went to a special modest-looking favorite on the Left Bank, and he insisted that I have filet of sole. Indeed, it was superb. From then on, I maintained that I was no longer afraid of ordering sole. I always said it was simply that my standards were so high that no other restaurant could meet them.

Sometimes Temp's values were simply embarrassing. On a different trip alone to the Continent I was assigned some research projects in Amsterdam. There, my boss insisted that I must take one evening at a Dutch Indonesian restaurant, a favorite address of his called the Bali, and that I should order the *rijsttafel* – "rice table."

This I was somewhat familiar with. (Sara and I had a favorite, more-modest Indonesian establishment in Palma.) At the Bali, however, the diner is soon surrounded by at least two dozen small dishes, each of which is an Indonesian specialty. At the Bali, by myself, I had a prominent table in view of almost everyone in the place, and I was soon surrounded by a forest of little dishes. Fielding had ordered ahead for me, of course, and I felt almost as if I were on stage with all the waiters hovering over me.

I finished my meal as soon as I could. There was no bill, of course, but I lavishly tipped the waiter and the maitre d' and galloped out of there as fast as the Lone Ranger could shout Hi Ho, Silver.

On most occasions, I did pay for my meals and accommodations, and I did not reveal my connection with the guidebooks. Fielding insisted upon it, since he was often accused of sleeping and eating for free, and he wanted to fight that allegation as often as he could. It was not easy for him as he was almost always recognized any place he went.

The upshot was that I was truly incognito. So I paid, even if he often didn't. But of course I kept accurate records and was immediately recompensed by Temple after I returned home to Mallorca and turned in my expenses.

Although Sara never went with me on research trips, we were occasionally invited to dine with Nancy and Temp at their mountainside home at Formentor called Villa Fielding. They had a household staff of six, counting both husbands and wives. Their cook wasn't always as good as Temp seemed to think she was. One Thanksgiving dinner, we had inedible pumpkin pie since the cook didn't understand that it was supposed to be a dessert dish.

Many of the dinners involved Temple's guests, who were often well-known or accomplished personages of one sort or another. The Bay of Pollensa was large enough to park the 40-some vessels in the Sixth Fleet of the U.S. Navy. On occasions like that, the admiral and other commanding officers would be invited to dinner at Villa Fielding.

From our house, we would see most of the Navy out in the bay, and we would often enviously think of sailors out there having pancakes with maple syrup, hamburgers, or other Yankee goodies that could not be found on Mallorca. (It did, however, have the best peanut butter I had ever tasted.)

Temple was also acquainted with some members of the entertainment world. One evening, we went to dinner at Villa Fielding when the guest of honor was Bert Parks. Probably not a household name today, of course, but during the latter part of the past century Parks was a well-known master of ceremonies, singer, game-show personality, and always the host at the annual Miss America Pageant.

I resisted the urge to ask Bert to sing: "There she is…"

We did develop some good friends outside the Fielding organization. There were few Americans around (Jackie of the Motelyn is the only one I remember). But there were lots of British and other English speakers. We especially liked Dorothy and Alfonso Loeffler who lived nearby and who had two daughters, Yolanda and Natalia who were approximately Christina's age.

Alfonso was in the hotel business. Dorothy (British), was active in lots of island activities (she later took Spanish citizenship). One evening Alfonso brought his brother, Martin, to dinner at our place, and we learned that he was German and had been in the army during World War II. Thinking back to when I was 12 years old and playing war in Pekin, I never would have guessed that I would ever sit down to break bread with a German soldier. After the war, Alfonso's brother had become a priest – and quite an acceptable dinner companion, too.

The Loefflers had a pure Siamese female cat that used to hang out on the beach with various homeless cats. At one point, she gave birth to a coal-black kitten, and we adopted it as a companion to Anzie. Christina named him Blackie. After some time, Blackie disappeared and we later discovered he had had a fatal encounter with a car.

But by this time the Loefflers' ever-fertile and ever-social Siamese had given birth to another male black cat, perhaps a brother or half-brother to ours. Arrangements were made, and suddenly Christina's Blackie re-appeared to again take his rightful his place in our home. Just like Anzie, he was destined to remain for much longer and over some greater mileage than we ever could have anticipated.

40
Fame, If Not Fortune

A FEW MONTHS AFTER we arrived in Mallorca, an editor (Peter Bird Martin) and a correspondent (Gavin Scott) from *Time* magazine arrived on the island, assigned to research a major article on Temple Fielding. The article (and Temp's cartoonish visage) subsequently made *Time*'s cover article on June 6, 1969, where he was identified as "The Supertourist." Far down in the story, I was also named, though Sara was ignored:

> Fielding calls his staff his 'family.' It consists of Temple, his wife Nancy ('My Nancy'), Joe Raff (ex-managing editor of the Rome *Daily American*), Raff's wife Judy, and Robert Bone, formerly of Time Inc.'s Book Division. Each family member has a nickname, which outsiders find rather cloying. Temp is 'Ole Simon,' as in Simon Legree; Nancy is 'Den Mother'; Joe Raff is 'Tio Pepe'); Judy is 'Kid Chocolate'; and Bone, naturally, is 'Billy Bones.'

Time explained our operation further:

> Home is headquarters, and headquarters is home: Villa Fielding, a $400,000 estate in the beach resort of Formentor, a 1-1/2-hour drive across Majorca from Palma, the Spanish island's capital. The staff spends anywhere from two to seven months a year on the road, inspecting new hotels and restaurants, revisiting those already mentioned in the guide. When a trip is in the offing, Villa Fielding becomes a sort of MI6 command post.

A Hallwag highway map of Europe replaces one of the rugs on the living-room floor. On their knees, hunched over it, staffers plot their infiltration routes, circling "soft spots" – places that have been too long unvisited or, according to field reports, are currently undergoing rapid change.

For the record, I don't remember anything like that – much less being called "Billy Bones" (although that was indeed my moniker back at the Buffalo *Courier Express* a decade and a half earlier).

And the article does not mention my chief responsibility, to revamp or create the paperback *SuperEconomy Europe* guide, implemented in response to the popularity of other publications designed for younger travelers, such as Arthur Frommer's *Europe on Five Dollars a Day*.

Temp had a tendency to put down young budget travelers in print with words such as "the Beatlemaniacs." He also had snide words for homosexuals. So I appealed to him on their behalf:

"Temp, these are folks you want to buy the book!"

"Yeah, I guess you're right," he would say. "Let's change it."

I felt this sort of thing was perhaps my best contribution to the operation.

Sara, of course, never got into either the guts or the glamour of the operation. For one thing, she had several medical problems that needed attending to, and which were beyond treatment we could find on the island. She flew several times to London in this connection – on one occasion for a major operation.

Once while I was traveling elsewhere and she was in a London hospital bed, she received mail from Rosita describing how Christina and David were getting along, along with other activities back at Puerto Pollensa. The letters were written in Spanish, of course. Sara could understand spoken Spanish, but was illiterate in the language.

Our Brazilian friend, Darlen, was then living in London. When Darlen visited Sara in the hospital, she would read aloud the Spanish letters from Rosita, and Sara could then enjoy their contents. The kicker was that Darlen, a native Portuguese speaker, could only get a portion of the meaning herself. She had to ask Sara in English just what it was she had been reading to her!

I mentioned that Sara eventually was able to make herself understood in Spanish by speaking it rapidly if badly, perhaps using only infinitives, etc. I remember once when we were conversing with some Mallorcan women, they first listened politely while I struggled mightily but slowly with Spanish, using what I thought was good grammar, paying attention to tenses, gender, etc. They smiled, listened politely, and then finally asked Sara what it was that I was trying to say.

Sara didn't know, of course. She had to ask me in English what I said. So I replied to her in English, and then she put the whole thing in "kitchen Spanish," which was just fine with that audience.

Some customs also took some getting used to. *Leche,* of course, is the Spanish word for milk. And once while Sara was feeding baby David from her breast, the milkman – known as the *lechero* – entered the room, spied the domestic scene and was so taken with it that he immediately came over and stroked the baby's head while voicing compliments on David's handsome appearance.

Sara said later that she was quite taken aback to think that the man she knew as the "lecher" had suddenly become so familiar, especially since she had one breast exposed with David attached to the nipple.

I told her that I thought that as a milkman, he was probably only professionally curious.

Keeping up with the news from the U.S. was a challenge in Mallorca. We had an old black-and-white TV, but it often seemed as if the only thing on was one bullfight after another. And any news was, of course, in rapid classical Spanish. We subscribed to the European edition of *Time* magazine, but delivery was sporadic. And much of what we learned from back home was depressing – notably the National Guard shooting of students at Kent State University in Ohio.

In contrast, however, the moon landing on July 20, 1969 was a real treat for everyone. Mallorcans seemed to be as much interested in the Apollo 11 program as were American expatriates.

As the time for the landing approached, we learned of a British advanced amateur astronomer temporarily living nearby. He had one of those very fat, heavy, and altogether impressive telescopes, and he set it up with a tripod on the shoreline near our house. A small crowd of mostly locals gathered in the evening, and many took a look into the scope before the landing.

The bright moon dramatically filled the screen in the instrument, and with greater detail than any of us had ever seen the moon before. This sophisticated device was focused right on the Sea of Tranquility. Its owner said that he knew he wouldn't be able to see the landing capsule, but still he hoped there might be a small dust cloud or some other tiny indication of the event.

There were two radios somewhere in the crowd – one broadcasting in English (perhaps via the BBC), and another with a Spanish station.

When the capsule finally landed on the moon, as predicted, the telescope's owner couldn't actually see the impact. Still he was excited about it all. And so was the small crowd, which began to applaud with the awesomeness of the feat.

But the thing that struck us the most was that just after the landing, smiling Mallorcans began coming up to shake the hands of Sara and me, congratulating us as Americans and representatives of the country that had made the achievement.

Of course we didn't tell anybody that Sara was really a New Zealander.

One bureaucratic imponderable was that as foreigners, we were required to leave Spain no later than every six months. This was no problem for me since I was often on the job in several European countries. Sara, of course, made several trips to London, usually to visit a doctor.

In addition, the American government required Sara to return to the U.S. at least once every two years to maintain her registered alien status. When that situation came up, we decided to visit our friends Don and Penny Hinkle in New York, and then travel along with them when they made their usual summer visit to a house they had inherited on Martha's Vineyard, Massachusetts.

It was a welcome change from our life in Mallorca, and we were grateful ever after for the diversion.

It was Sara's medical circumstances that ultimately led us to think that remaining in that small village in Mallorca was no longer in the family's best interest. David also had some problems with infantile eczema and other things. Moreover I had a couple of teeth pulled that might have been saved with the availability of more modern dentistry.

I appealed to Temp to allow us to live in a major European city, such as Barcelona, or preferably London. In either location, we could find better medical care for Sara and David. And I could, with frequent short visits to Mallorca accomplish pretty much the same goals on the job as I had been doing.

But he wanted his professional family around him, he said. That was just the way he always worked. I thought perhaps life would have been smoother for us even if we lived in Palma, the capital of Mallorca, but he nixed that idea, too.

By the time I finished my two-year contract in the fall of 1970, I was beginning to think of alternate possibilities to my continuing on the job. Our good friend Howard Rausch, who was now heading up his own technical magazine in Boston, said there were several editorial possibilities in and around that city. He also said that with his large apartment in Cambridge, all of us, including Sara, the kids, and our two cats, could live with him indefinitely until I found a good job.

At the same time, Sara and I also began talking about Hawaii, an American state, of course, and one that would put us in the Pacific, with relatively easy access to and from her family in New Zealand, but a location that would also make it relatively easy for my parents to visit our family, too. And Hawaii was also truly tropical – not cold in the winter like Mallorca.

Finally, I carefully broached the subject directly with Temp, again emphasizing our need for better medical care for both Sara and David. I told him that I thought the Fielding guides could be expanded to include other books on tourist targets in Hawaii and the Pacific. I told him I was confident that with Sara's help and his blessing, I could pull it off.

His answer was emphatic. He said that the Fielding guides had always been firmly associated with Western Europe and he was determined to keep it that way. As effusive as ever, he thanked me for a considerate and well-stated proposal, but he would never make an exception.

I thought at the time that perhaps his publisher, William Morrow and Company, might go for its own exception to that. And much later, I was proven right when I got a contract to create Fielding's Alaska and the Yukon in the late 1980s. (See later.) But while Fielding himself was alive, this was not going to happen.

Anyway, the cat was now out of the bag. Temp now knew I was less than happy, and his attitude toward our family began to change.

He began to think that somehow we were unhappy with him and Nancy personally. And as it became apparent that we were looking for some way out, he felt that we were going to publicly criticize the Fielding operation in general. I tried to assure him that this wasn't the case. Nevertheless, gradually my boss seemed to become somewhat paranoid.

And after all, I had more than lived up to my two-year contract so I did not feel any special obligation beyond that, except to give about two weeks' notice.

Sara and I briefly considered moving to London, a city with which we were both familiar. But she would have to go through the lengthy application for another nursing license. And I would have to fight the foreigner's work permit battle – too much now that we had two little ones to deal with.

I had exchanged some letters with various publication people in Hawaii, including those at the two daily newspapers in Honolulu, but the replies were very non-committal. Sort of "Come say hello if you're town." Still, I thought that I might be able to begin a guidebook operation there, even if it had to be separate from Fielding Publications.

The best bet, by far, was Boston, where Howard had the large apartment and he was willing to put up with Sara and me, along with two kids and two cats. By mail, I had received some vague interest from two newspapers, and a TV station in Boston, although all subject to future interviews.

So Boston it would be. We said some tearful goodbyes, especially to Rosita and the Loefflers, flew first to London for a few days, and then we boarded one of the first Boeing 747 jumbo jets to fly to Boston, Massachusetts.

Part III

1971-2001

41
To Boston
& the Tropics

OUR CHILDREN WERE STILL mostly speaking Spanish to each
other as we flew from London. I think they regarded it as a kid's
language, even though we communicated with them both in English.

It was wonderful to see Howard again, and his large Cambridge
apartment was reasonably comfortable. Boston weather, however,
was not. And then the first thing I had to do was to get a tooth filled,
so I did that with Howard's dentist.

But getting out and about and around the city was difficult. Of
course we were spoiled, I guess. But Boston in February 1971 was
miserable. The air was cold and damp, and the streets seemed filled
with dirty snow and slush. We were ill-equipped physically and
psychologically for these conditions.

The city seemed to have lost the charm that I had remembered
when I was flying up from New York to cavort with Sue a few
summers back. When I came back from the dentist, I broached an
idea to Sara.

"How about if I fly to Hawaii myself and see if I can get a job? If
I can, then you and the kids and the cats can come out to join me?"

Sara's reply was immediate:

"Nothing doing," she said. "If you're going to Hawaii, then we're
all going to Hawaii."

We worked out that we had enough money left to buy round-trip tickets to Honolulu, stay there about a week, and then return to Boston and Howard's bosom once more. I could pick up on those interviews then.

It was okay with Howard. If he was at all overwhelmed by our tribe, he didn't show it. Really, Howard demonstrated again that he must be the most good-natured bachelor in the world. He seemed to love all the excitement and adventure on our behalf.

Actually, we always used to say that Howard was in the habit of collecting "characters," and I guess we fit that definition more than once. I'm sure he enjoyed telling friends about his experiences with us, such as when he hosted Sara and me in Moscow, as much as he enjoyed having us stay again with him.

Anyway, we said goodbye once more, and all six of us (counting two kids and two cats) were off to the airport again, with hearts full of hope.

Ten or twelve hours later, we landed in Honolulu, capital of the state of Hawaii. On final approach, when the air pressure in the plane began to come quickly back to sea level, I suddenly felt something strange in my mouth. My new filling had come out. Was it a bad omen?

We landed at what was known in later years as the "old terminal," and the temperature was 80 degrees outdoors. There were no jetways in those days, and we emerged from the plane at the top of the stairs to see a bright rainbow in the distance. Aha! There was the omen – and a good one, too!

In the days and years to come, we would learn that rainbows are endemic to Hawaii – one of several unofficial symbols of the state, as a matter of fact, and sometimes seen several times in a single day. Scientists can explain it, but we didn't know any of that. It was just taken by us as a special harbinger of good fortune.

We had reservations in an small, inexpensive family-style hotel a block or two from the beach. And from the first "*aloha*," the owner of the place made us feel welcome. We didn't have our cats, though. Anzie and Blackie had been taken off the plane and moved directly to state-mandated quarantine. (We had planned for it.) We explained to Christina and David that we would soon be able to visit their feline friends as often as we liked.

For the first couple of nights, we were serenaded by strange, exotic noises – weird cries of one sort or another that gave us the impression that we had landed in very strange world.

"What's that, Daddy?" asked Christina.

"I don't know," I said. "But now it's time for sleep. We'll find out tomorrow."

We didn't realize that our hotel was only about a block away from the Honolulu Zoo. Some of those inhabitants were non-natives, too. (Sara later said it was the peacocks whose cry sounded like somebody was being murdered.)

We took a couple of days just to get acquainted with our surroundings. We thought Waikiki and the nearby beach were beautiful. But I remember that we wandered into the ABC convenience store on Kalakaua Avenue and Sara suddenly broke into tears. She saw that the price of a dozen eggs was about three times what she thought was normal.

"We can't afford to live here!" she declared.

Later, of course, we found supermarkets outside of the high-rent district, where prices were relatively reasonable.

We also found that being out of the country for nearly three years meant that people's interests, habits, and expressions changed in greater or lesser ways during the interim, and sometimes I felt like a foreigner in my own land. Sara usually adapted much more quickly than I, and she sometimes found my ineptness in picking up new cultural habits amusing.

We both recall that when I was checking out of some kind of store or supermarket, the woman at the cash register asked me: "Paper or plastic?:

"No thanks," I replied. "I'll use cash."

The woman gave me a puzzled look and obviously had no idea what the heck I was talking about. And it was news to me that she was not asking about using a credit card or paper money. She wanted to know whether I wanted to carry my purchases in a paper or plastic bag.

After a few more days of learning our way around the island of Oahu, I put on a suit and tie and decided to visit one of the two newspapers. The *Honolulu Advertiser* was a morning paper. The *Honolulu Star-Bulletin* was delivered in the evenings. I had always liked working on morning papers, and so I sought out the office of "Buck"

Buchwach, the executive editor and the man with whom I had exchanged a couple of non-committal letters about a month or two previously.

After some amicable conversation, Buck asked me if I would come in the following day so we could talk to George Chaplin, the editor. The following morning, I entered Chaplin's corner office, which was almost overflowing with what appeared to be new books. (I didn't know it then, but these were just review copies, and very few if any had actually been read.) There was Chaplin, Buchwach, City Editor Sandy Zalburg, and a couple of other editors – probably John Griffin, editorial page editor, and Gerry Lopez, the slot man who ran the copy desk.

We talked about my experiences on the Buffalo *Courier-Express*, the Middletown *Daily Record*, the *San Juan Star*, *Popular Photography*, *Brazilian Business* Magazine, Time-Life Books, and the Fielding operation in Mallorca. At several of these publications, of course, I had had impressive titles.

I waited for somebody to echo Pat Carbine of *Look*, saying something about it's too bad about my "checkered resume."

Finally, Chaplin spoke:

"Well, unfortunately... uh...

"Unfortunately, we don't have any executive positions available," he said.

My heart leaped forward, but my voice didn't skip a beat.

"Who said anything about an executive position?" I laughed, trying not to show any sign of relief. "I'm a journeyman reporter, and I know what your scale is."

I didn't really know that, but I knew the employees were represented by the Newspaper Guild and were paid a living wage.

Someone laughed and Buchwach spoke again:

"Well, then, why don't you come in tomorrow?"

Everyone laughed again and a couple of the men shook my hand. I went back to the hotel and told Sara we were staying, cashing in the return plane tickets, and that we should start looking at apartments for rent.

I showed up for work the next day wearing a tie and a light blue summer-weight three-piece suit. (I'm not sure that anything like that exists any more.) Sandy Zalburg sat me down in front of a typewriter and gave me an assignment. He said that incredibly, two women on the staff, Ruth Youngblood, who worked on the city side, and Pat Hunter who worked in the Family section, unbeknownst to each other, had both written a series of articles on the same subject — some kind of charity operation, as I recall.

"Do you think you could combine these and wrap them up into something less than five parts?" Sandy said.

It took me two or three hours, but it was really duck soup. I produced the whole package in three parts, and gave the ladies a double byline. Sandy was impressed.

"When you come in tomorrow," just wear short-sleeves," he said. And when you get a chance, why don't you pick up a couple of aloha shirts, too?" he said.

And thus began a new career — one that I thought might last about a year. When someone asked me if I wanted to sign up for the retirement program, I politely said "no" but kept my reasons to myself. First of all, I didn't believe in psychologically tying myself down to an eventual pension. But second, I didn't think I would spend more than about a year or so there before producing some guide books.

I never suspected that I would remain connected to the *Honolulu Advertiser* for the next 13 years. And that we would rely on the Hawaiian Islands in general as a base for scores of world-wide free-lance excursions for a grand total of 38 years. Although we don't live there today, Hawaii will always remain "home" — the place both Sara and I have lived the longest and that had the strongest impression on our lives.

Bone interviews Vice President George Bush in Hawaii.
(Photo by David Yamada)

42

A Reporter
in Paradise

MOST LONG-TIME REPORTERS will agree that working on a daily paper provides enough drama and interesting experiences to last a lifetime. Every day is a new adventure. In my case, I was often offered a "beat" or some other specific responsibility, once even the photo editor job. I would take these occasionally but only on a temporary basis. I really liked being a "GA." a general assignment reporter who could poke his inquisitive nose into any kind of story.

The first week I was on the job, a man walked into the newsroom who was recognized by no one but me. He was Xavier Cugat, the Cuban bandleader famous among other things for leading his Latin-American orchestra often while holding a Mexican Chihuahua in his other hand. He was also the husband of Charo, the "cuchi-cuchi" comedienne who often appeared in his performances.

Among other talents, Cugat was also a professional cartoonist. He sketched a caricature of me while I interviewed him. He also drew a cartoon of himself and his little dog while I watched, and gave me that, too. Unfortunately Charo was not along, and they were divorced the following year.

In the coverage of visiting personages, the paper was similar to my experience in Puerto Rico. Lots of well-known public figures turned up in Honolulu. In the case of politicians, I remember interviewing the first George H. W. Bush, when he was running for vice president, walking along with him while he was on his way to check into his hotel. Others included Senator Barry Goldwater, who was especially friendly and cooperative when I ambushed him when he approached a restaurant.

Various aides and some military men tried to brush me aside, but the Arizona conservative strode right up with his hand outstretched to see what this lone reporter wanted to talk about.

The *Honolulu Advertiser* turned out to have had a long and varied history as "the oldest newspaper west of the Mississippi." Its heritage dated back more than 100 years in the Islands, when the word "advertiser" meant news and not paid announcements. Words by Mark Twain, Robert Louis Stevenson, Jack London and other literary luminaries who visited the Islands had sometimes come to life on its pages.

Now in the 1970s, the two daily papers, the "'Tiser" and the *Star-Bulletin* competed fiercely in their news coverage. By then they had a "joint operating agreement," meaning they both shared the same building (on opposite sides of the structure) and had the same business and advertising departments, the library, the presses, and other facilities but totally separate editorial (news) departments. Unknown to us then, these were to be the final years of this type of arrangement.

As a new reporter in this unique environment, I made plenty of initial boo-boos.

One of my first hard-news assignments was to cover a nighttime prison break at a medium-security installation. I didn't have my own car yet so I rode out with Roy Ito, one of the staff photographers, to Halawa Prison. After conducting interviews with police and other officials, I discovered that Roy had already driven back to the office to develop his pictures, leaving me in darkness and in the middle of nowhere with no phone. There was no way to get my story in.

Finally, I asked one of the policemen who was driving back to town to take me. Apparently they never were allowed to do this, but the officer must have felt sorry for me, so it all worked out okay.

Another *malihini* ("newcomer" in Hawaiian) experience came when I was assigned to meet and briefly interview Hawaii's senior U.S. senator, Daniel Inouye, who was arriving at the airport. I introduced myself and held out my hand. Inouye, instantly shook it – with his *left* hand. No problem really, but I had simply forgotten that the senator was widely known to have lost his right arm while in the Army during World War II.

After all, I was just in from Europe where everybody shakes hands. But I learned later that reporters generally never offered to shake his hand – a mistake, I thought, since the senator handled the situation very well.

But that was not as embarrassing as what happened to Ed Kennedy, another *malihini* staff member on desk duty at the paper. One day Ed was laying out a page that included a photograph of the same distinguished lawmaker. Ed decided the photo looked better flopped, a standard esthetic technique sometimes done to make sure the subject of a photo was looking *into* the page instead of off to the side.

Again, the problem was that unlike most folks, our senior senator was not bilaterally symmetrical. Ergo, the page was published picturing Senator Inouye with the wrong arm missing! We never let Ed live that down for the rest of his career.

Newspaper reporters and editors have good times and bad times, but it is a testament to the character of most that it is usually the fun and funny occurrences that stick in our memories.

City Editor Sanford Zalburg was one of those legendary city editors who ran the newsroom like a first sergeant – condemning his reporters when he thought they deserved it, but often praising them when that was appropriate also.

Sandy was famous for once throwing one writer's multi-page story out the window. Another writer found it out on the street, innocently brought it back to the newsroom, so Sandy threw it out again.

When things were slow, Sandy would call me over and say something like: "You can't do anything useful sitting around the office, Bone. Go over to Ala Moana (a major shopping center), and don't come back 'til you have a story!" No more direction than that.

Sometimes he'd send me out to the Honolulu Zoo with similar instructions. And indeed, I always found something to write about at the zoo. For a time, I almost had an unofficial zoo beat.

There were some mistakes I made only once with Sandy. When he asked me to do a story on some subject, I went up to the library and found a recent clip, either from our paper or the *Star-Bulletin* indicating that a similar story had already been done, and suggesting that he wouldn't want another one.

"Don't you know, Bone, that there's nothing new in the world! Just get out there."

As always, he was right. I came back with an entirely different angle.

Zalburg enjoyed a large amount of independence, but it wasn't without limits. In his book, *Reporter,* Bob Jones recalls that editor Chaplin, a member of the Honolulu Symphony board, among many other organizations, once entered the newsroom in the evening and insisted that Zalburg place a story about the newly hired conductor/music director of the symphony on Page 1, above the fold. Zalburg offered to run it inside, since only a very few readers of the paper would be interested. Chaplin insisted, however, and left the building. Sandy ran the story – on the front page – but below the fold.

There was also an assistant city editor for a time, one of those old-timers who had worked on papers all over the country. Birch Storm had his own set of idiosyncrasies. Sometimes he would type out an assignment, fold it into a paper airplane, and send it flying through the city room to the targeted reporter – or to whichever reporter happened to catch it.

If Birch thought the newsroom was a little too quiet, he was prone to stand up at the city desk and shout into the air:

"Come on! I want to hear those typewriters sing!" he would say. Or something like that.

Newspaper people like me like to believe their business is useful and impartial. That may be mostly true, but there are unfortunate exceptions.

Shortly after joining the paper, my family and I were shopping at Sears, one of the biggest department stores in town. At one point we all stepped onto a down escalator.

David, age three, was wearing a nice pair of bright-yellow rubber boots. About halfway between floors, however, he began to cry. One boot had been caught between the moving stairs and the polished steel side of the device. I used all my reserve strength to try to pull his leg and foot out of the boot before we reached the bottom, but it didn't budge. Sara and Christina (now four) were on the steps just behind us.

When we reached the end of the line, all four of us noisily tumbled over each other on the floor. The mangled boot had finally dislodged from the device and I had David in my arms.

His foot was in one piece, although we later discovered that some of his toes had been broken.

The details escape me now, but I remember talking to a Sears manager about the need for a more easily found emergency stop button and things like that.

Anyway, like most reporters, I knew that personal or family experiences are valid grist for the mill, especially so when there is an important public safety warning aspect. A little research revealed that rubber and stainless steel have just about the highest coefficient of friction of any two substances. And so I wrote up the entire experience as an article for the *Advertiser.*

I soon discovered that there was some consternation being expressed in the executive offices about my little story. Finally, they did decide to run it, but deep inside the paper, with a small headline, no illustration of any kind, and most significantly with the name of the department store where the adventure occurred excised from the text.

At that point in the newspaper's history, Sears was one of the newspaper's biggest and most important advertisers.

In time, David's toes all knitted together satisfactorily. But adventures like this illustrate how journalistic illusions are broken.

One of the first really good things that happened to Sara and me in Honolulu, was that we managed to give up smoking – and the newspaper helped on that score.

We went "cold turkey." I had been a three-pack-a-day man. Sara was considerably less. But we attacked it together. No. 1, we began eating lots of good meals. No. 2, we took part in many activities where smoking was prohibited and other things demanded our attention, like going to the movies. And No. 3, I calculated that our tobacco expense over the period of a year was normally about $500.

That amount was almost exactly the price of a color TV in 1973. So we replaced our little B&W model with a brand-new color version, buying it on a one-year time payment plan so – without smoking – we figured that in effect we got the TV for zero outlay by repurposing the money normally spent for cigarettes.

And the newspaper? Well, City Editor Sandy Zalburg was especially allergic to tobacco smoke. When we were called to the city desk, we reporters tried to remember not to bring along our lit cigarettes, or at least to hold them behind our backs.

Indeed, the quality of my work suffered during the withdrawal period, but Sandy encouraged me greatly by giving me relatively easy assignments, withholding any criticism, even if it was deserved, etc. Sandy would do anything he could to encourage a reporter to quit the tobacco habit in the office.

As a GA reporter, I covered every type of story and soon began to feel that I was really part of the community. Reporters get to know, to at least some degree, various prominent public figures, from the governor on down. (Governor George Ariyoshi somehow never knew my name, but anytime he saw me he always smiled and raised his eyebrows. He knew at least that I was a writer of some kind that he'd met somewhere.)

I knew the current governor of Hawaii, Neil Abercrombie, from the time he was a bearded college-student rabble-rouser. When he interviewed me for nearly a half-hour on his own late-night radio program, I called him "Neil." Now I guess I would have to call him "governor," although we haven't run across each other since we moved from Hawaii and he took office.

But the big thrill for me in the early '70s was that I was getting to know an awesome lot about the 50th state – a million-strong society that was unique in the nation. Although a state since 1959, and a U. S. territory for 61 years before that, it was for me much like a new foreign country with a fascinating history and a unique mixture of certain specific cultures.

Caucasians (*haoles* in the local vernacular) were not the majority of the population – merely the largest single minority. In many respects, Hawaii seemed more Japanese than anything else. And if you mixed in the Chinese, Koreans, Filipinos, etc., it was the Asians who dominated the state. The ethnic Hawaiians were the smallest group of all. And most of them were really of mixed races either with *haoles*, Chinese, Filipinos, or other Asians. It was all new and exciting.

The state also seemed an ideal place for African-Americans to live, too. At that point, they were under-represented in the population, although Wally "Famous" Amos, of the chocolate chip cookies reputation, was a prominent figure in town. When President John F. Kennedy visited the state (a decade before we were in residence), he said something to the effect that Hawaii was what America was striving to be. Locals often described their cultural mix in local terms as a "chop suey" population – one that had learned better than many how to get along with different peoples.

And unbeknownst to me or anyone else living in Hawaii during this period, the future 44th president of the United States was growing up among us in Honolulu, absorbing the attitudes and mannerisms of what was called the "Spirit of Aloha" right along with my own children and all the other youngsters in the state. President Barack ("Barry" in those days) Obama may be nominally from Chicago, but logically enough, the people of Hawaii also like to call him their own.

Newspaper people are often interesting characters, and this led me to make lots of permanent friends among my fellow workers.

Our gossip (three-dot) columnist was a former nightclub co-median named Eddie Sherman, whose comments were often as out of date as they were outrageous. The first time I met him he stretched both his arms straight out wide:

"Hey, Bone! How do you tell an Italian airplane?"

Without waiting for an answer, he said:

"Hair under the wings! Ha Ha!"

At the other end of the spectrum, an interesting staffer was Linda McCrerey, whom I believe was active in the women's movement. She was a good reporter with an especially strong personality.

Once we happened to be atop the newsroom stairs that led to the library and I mentioned something innocuous that I was researching for a story.

On this elevated platform above the sea of writers and editors below, she began to shout, silencing the typewriters and bringing much of the city room to a halt:

"Tits and ass! Tits and ass! That's what you're looking for!" Linda shouted.

"You know what I want to see?" she asked. "More pricks and balls! Pricks and balls! That's what I want."

And she descended the stairs and went about her business, leaving me wondering what in the world I had said to spark the speech. Actually, I think she had been motivated by some of her own thoughts, and that I had just unwittingly unleashed the strong reaction.

The hip generation was represented by Leonard Lueras, whose main job was handling the special youth page in the paper. Eventually the paper's most laid-back reporter quit the job, moved to Bali, and ended up writing about 35 books. He's still there, master of his own *kampong.*

Another favorite reporter memory was forged by my friend Hal Hostetler. Relatively late in life, Hal had become a born-again Christian, which was fine with all of us. But he had a tendency to talk about that from time to time, proselytizing whether he intended to or not. Some said they found that uncomfortable and annoying.

Those who were reserved in their beliefs or, like me, more of the heathen persuasion, were nevertheless loathe to verbally disabuse any person's faith to their face. So Hal sometimes left us feeling rather trapped, helpless, and speechless.

One slow day a few members of the staff were talking casually about our difficulties in losing weight, and sharing ideas to that end. While this conversation was continuing, Hal casually walked into the newsroom while licking an ice cream cone.

He listened to us for a minute and then spoke up.

"You know," he said, between licks. "I lost weight in the easiest way of all."

"Oh yeah? What was that?" someone asked. (Or "bit," perhaps. He really wanted to know some new technique.)

"Well," said Hal, taking another lick. "I just prayed if off!" He then wandered away with his ice cream, leaving us all speechless.

Even now I find it difficult to find fault with Hal, however, because it's possible that he had something there. During this period, also, another reporter, Bruce Benson, was having protracted problems buying or repairing a boat. At the same time, I was having considerable trouble getting a publisher for my first guidebook.

Well, in due course, Bruce finally solved his boat situation, and after considerable difficulties, I found a publisher. And I learned later that Hal had been praying for these outcomes for both of us.

All this sort of thing held no truck with my wife, however, who was a good friend of Hal's wife, Carole.

"I tried to phone Carole today," Sara said on one occasion. "But God answered, so I hung up!"

43
Moving Experiences

IN OUR EARLY YEARS in Honolulu, on the island of Oahu, we found ourselves frequently changing houses – second nature for me, of course, after my many house-moving experiences dating back to my childhood in Pekin, Gary, Bowling Green, New York, and more.

We first had a small, furnished apartment in the Makiki neighborhood of Honolulu. It was on the second floor of a small building, with a balcony (called a *lanai* in Hawaii) about level with the branches of a convenient avocado tree.

Thus, we were set up well for some vegetable protein, but a family cannot live on salad dressing and guacamole alone.

Furthermore, you might say that that tree had its ups and downs for us. First, we had a middle-of-the-night burglary. While we were all sleeping, someone climbed up the tree, entered the apartment, found Sara's wallet, and absconded with it down the tree like Jack on the beanstalk. This meant replacement not only of money and credit cards but of her registered alien "green card." In the morning we found Anzie seemingly terrified (you remember, our New York to Mallorca to Boston to Honolulu calico).

We called the cops, and honestly they actually came to the apartment and dusted for fingerprints! This is was 1971, remember.

I thought that would never have happened in New York at any period in history.

On another occasion, our other cat, the black Mallorcan Siamese named Blackie, decided to scale that same tree and hop over to explore the *lanai* of the apartment just above. We only learned what had happened when the upstairs neighbor complained that someone or something had used their *hibachi* for a litter box.

We sentenced Blackie to jail for that one, and bought a new *hibachi* for the neighbors. The cat remained in custody at a kennel while we searched for another apartment. Anzie, our more well-behaved and usually calm calico, dutifully remained close to home.

The next place we found was a small modest two-bedroom house perched on the side of a hill in a neighborhood called Puunui. It had a wonderful view of Downtown Honolulu framed by a pink *plumeria* (Hawaiian for frangipani) tree. It also came partly furnished because our own worldly goods were still in storage in Mallorca. They were kept there even longer than they might have been by an inconvenient dock strike.

In December 1972, our new position in the middle of the Pacific made it practical and affordable for us all to fly to Sara's family home in New Zealand for Christmas. It was a revelation for Christina, 5, David, 4, and also for Dad, suddenly now a rather old 40.

I had come from a small family – no siblings, no cousins, to speak of – and now even my grandmother and Aunt Dick were long gone. In New Zealand we were suddenly surrounded by a phalanx of relatives, old and young, with our two little Yank nippers making us all the more popular with what seemed to me to be about eleventy-seven *kiwis*.

A kiwi is a flightless bird, native to New Zealand, but New Zealanders themselves also like to call themselves kiwis. Although I had visited briefly on our 1966 world tour, this was probably the first time I really was able to feel a part of this extended family. And Christina and David discovered they had lots of cousins, some of them around their age.

Further, December is the height of summer Down Under, and our enjoyment was accompanied by lots of sunshine and flowers, including the New Zealand "Christmas tree," the bright-blossomed *pohutukawa*, which only blooms at that time of year. Wow! I thought this might be a wonderful place to live some day, surrounded by a lovely country and lots of funny-talking relatives who care about you.

We had to return to Hawaii sooner than I would have preferred, but somehow I knew we would be back again to experience New Zealand in a more meaningful way.

Back in Honolulu, Sara found herself in the same kind of Catch-22 that she had once been in New York – a qualified registered nurse but with no license to work in the state. While waiting for that problem to work itself out, she managed to find an interesting – and eventually useful – job, working in a small travel agency in Downtown Honolulu called "Let's Travel."

These were the days when airline tickets were all written by hand. There was a lot to learn, and Sara picked everything up quickly, at least partly because she was much more well-traveled than either of the other two women in the office.

She began having stories to tell about adventures in the agency, where she met her own interesting cast of characters.

At one point, she had to make arrangements for a charter flight to Seoul, South Korea for many local Korean women, nearly all of whom were named "Kim" (the most common family name in Korea).

"No, I don't want to sit next to that Mrs. Kim. I want to sit next to that other Mrs. Kim!" Sara quoted. She ended up boarding the plane herself just long enough to make sure that all the Kims were arranged and seated to their ultimate satisfaction.

Throughout 1971 and 1972, I felt I had learned enough about Hawaii to begin drafting plans for a travel guidebook to the state. I had begun making some trips to the five main Neighbor Islands (as they are called in Hawaii), and soaking up considerable knowledge about Island history and tourist information on Kauai, Maui, Molokai, Lanai, and the "Big Island" (the Island of Hawaii).

At the same time, I began working on a completely different idea, a plan to create a weekly news magazine – a sort of *Time* just for Hawaii. For financial backing, I turned first to local millionaire Cecil Heftel. The owner of several enterprises, including one of the TV stations in Honolulu, Heftel seemed intrigued with the idea. He also was highly interested in politics.

Indeed, he later became one of Hawaii's two congressional representatives.

When we talked one evening, Heftel began to speak of the project as a way to "Get Fasi!" (meaning Honolulu Mayor Frank Fasi).

I was not a fan of the mayor either, but as an objective newsman, I was not going to use a publication for "getting" anyone.

Fasi was an avowed enemy of the two Honolulu newspapers. However, he was apparently attracted to petite *Advertiser* reporter Janice Wolf enough to put the moves on her.

"Have you got a kiss for an old man?" he asked her on one occasion when they were alone. Janice retreated whereupon he tried to chase her around the mayoral office, and then asked her if she was frigid.

"I just got out of there!" Janice said later.

On another occasion, Janice had to resist the amorous efforts of Canadian Prime Minister Pierre Trudeau. In that instance, she ended up writing a story about it.

Another interested in my weekly magazine idea was fellow *Advertiser* writer David Pellegrin, who had family money that would have been able to bankroll something like that. But Dave ended up quitting the newspaper and buying an existing monthly, *Honolulu Magazine*, which needed some fresh blood and an infusion of cash.

Around the same time, I met Don Eldridge, an executive from Rand McNally & Co., a firm I previously thought only produced maps. But it turned out to have an extensive book operation, too. He was interested in my Hawaii guidebook idea. We exchanged a couple more letters after he returned to Chicago.

Soon after, I received a Rand McNally contract along with a check for $3,000, as an advance against royalties. Hardly believing my sudden luck, I instantly dropped the newsmagazine idea and began turning out guidebook prose – not exactly in the literary style of Temple Fielding, I might add, but using much of the knowledge and techniques I gained during those 2½ years exploring Western Europe for his books. My emphasis, however, was going to be just as much on evaluating and personally commenting on cultural and sightseeing sites as it was on hotels and restaurants, which had been the major points in the Fielding operation.

The contract called for half the book to be finished in six months – by the end of January 1974. I managed to go part-time at the paper, being on the job there just three days a week. For the other four I madly began researching, interviewing, and occasionally flying out to the outer islands in the state. After three months I sent the first portion of the text to the designated editor at Rand McNally.

I kept working on my research, even though I didn't hear anything back from the company for more than a month.

Finally, Sylvia McNair, a highly experienced and well-regarded editor at Rand McNally, telephoned and said she did not like the personal style and critical approach I had taken with my manuscript. She said, "Sadly, it simply is not a Rand McNally kind of book."

I replied quickly that I never was trying to write anything other than a Bob Bone kind of book, and that I had no idea what a Rand McNally style was. Don Eldridge had said nothing about a particular style of writing.

In reply to that, I received a new proposal: I could either (a) revise the book into a less-personal, less-critical style, or (b) cancel the contract, keep the advance and take my project to another publisher.

I chose (b). Since I had come up with Rand-McNally in jig time, surely I could find another publisher as quickly again.

In my letter of explanation to Sylvia, I wrote, in part:

> I do not believe the manuscript has an overall negative tone when compared to today's trends in consumer publications. Although some of my adverse criticism might well be softened, I feel sure that the degree to which I would be willing to do this would be far less than Rand-McNally would desire.
>
> At the same time, I feel that to "depersonalize" the manuscript only erodes my position as its author and authority, and it does not keep clear my role as an expert representative of the traveler's interests.
>
> The style that you found undesirable for Rand McNally's purposes does not come from my newspaper work. Instead, it is strongly influenced by my 2½ years as a researcher and writer for Temple Fielding.
>
> Fielding never hesitated to call a dump a dump, and this has not hurt his sales over the past 25 years. Neither has it harmed Europe's image as a vacation objective.
>
> Hawaii is certainly not a "rip-off." Hawaii is a beautiful oasis, generally populated by warm, genuine people. If it were not, we would not continue to live here. But both Biblical and earthly paradises have their snakes, and Hawaii, too, can claim a number of hucksters and incompetents, even if they are fewer and less venomous than many places on the Mainland.

(That was a bad metaphor, however; Hawaii has no real snakes.)

Your comparison with Florida on the telephone was an unfortunate one. It was a Florida hotel, which once quoted me one rate when we checked in and a higher rate when we checked out. I can't imagine such a thing happening in Hawaii. But the fact that no guide to Florida would warn me about this kind of thing does not mean there should be no guide to Hawaii which points out that the Sheraton-Waikiki often makes up its rooms in the late afternoon.

We love the Islands as much as Don Eldridge does – perhaps even more so since I gave up a career in order that my family and I might live here. Still, we find it no Land of Oz, and we feel that to present it as one would be superficial.

The ease and speed with which I captured my first book contract was not repeated, and I went back to full-time at the paper. About the same time we moved to the Windward side of the island to the small community of Kailua – a 20-minute drive to the newspaper office, but perhaps the most beautiful commute to work of anyplace in the U.S.A.

Meanwhile, Sara's Hawaii nursing license came through. She left the travel agency and began working as the office nurse for a GP at the Windward Medical Center in Kailua. Schools for Christina and David were nearby. Everything would be hunky-dory for our family – if only I didn't harbor this cockamamie idea of writing a critical guidebook.

In the public library I found the names and addresses for scores of book publishers. For all, I sent out my partial manuscript over the next year and a half. I received more than 100 rejections from more than 100 publishers. Some of them were form letters; some were descriptive and complimentary at the same time as they wrote well-reasoned explanations about marketing and distribution problems and why my project was not right for their operation. Many wished me good luck. Believe it or not, I kept them all and have them still.

To many of these publishers, I was calling my proposed book *A Consumer Guide to Hawaii*. But a December 6, 1974 letter from one company inadvertently gave me the ultimate title for the book, and indeed, it was adopted for the whole series of travel books that came after.

That was from the editor at Quadrangle, the New York Times Book Co., in a two-page letter. He first complimented me on my objectives: "I admire very much your effort to write a book that is frank and honest, revealing the blemishes as well as the beauty marks. I think that is the way all guidebooks should be, though I doubt they ever will. But you are bucking against stiff competition...."

Quadrangle's books were then distributed by Harper and Row.

"Since Harper and Row has just published a guidebook of their own on Hawaii, I doubt their salesmen would be enthusiastic about... *a maverick book on Hawaii...*"

That editor's name was Jonathan Segal. But ever after I always imagined his name was *Jonathan Livingston Seagull*. That, of course, was the inspirational book by Richard Bach, one whose lessons in life might be applied to my own aspirations and successes.

Anyway, after Segal's (or Seagull's) letter, I began calling my book *The Maverick Guide to Hawaii*. That title eventually became the theme of an entire series of books.

About a year and a half after my divorce from Rand McNally, and those 100 rejection letters, I received a friendly letter from the president of a book publishing firm in suburban New Orleans, who said he would like to explore the idea with me. This turned out to be an avuncular southern gentleman named Dr. Milburn Calhoun, a family physician who was also president of the Pelican Publishing Company in Gretna, Louisiana.

After some more correspondence, Milburn sent me a contract and a modest advance. Whew!

Left to right, Anzie, Sara, David, and Christina at our hillside
house in Puunui, Honolulu. (Photo by Bob Bone)

44
All Systems Go

UP TO THIS POINT, I had been composing the hard meat of the book – reviewing hotels, restaurants, tourist sites, etc. to demonstrate the critical review portions of the manuscript. But the morning after receiving Milburn's letter, I sat down at my massive old Underwood typewriter and wrote the paragraphs that would introduce the first edition of the *Maverick Guide to Hawaii*. It was a true story:

> One evening not long ago, we were at Honolulu Airport waiting for friends who were coming in on a late flight from the Mainland. We held flower *leis* – the traditional welcoming gift of the Islands – to place over our friends' heads once they stepped off the Wiki-Wiki bus carrying them from the plane to the terminal.
>
> Nearby, an elderly oriental-Hawaiian woman also waited. She told us she was there to meet her cousin who was returning from a vacation in California. She, too, carried a *lei*, and she wore a bright *muumuu*, that long Hawaiian dress which, for more than a century, has enhanced the beauty of every woman who has ever put it on.
>
> Not far away stood two young, attractive, dark-skinned women dressed in *ti*-leaf skirts. Employed by a professional greeting service, they held about two dozen *leis* in their arms. They had been contracted to meet a particular tour group.
>
> After some delay, the first of the buses from the jumbo jet arrived. The tour group soon appeared, and the two hula girls went into their act. The *leis* were dutifully draped over the shoulders of each passenger who was wearing a gummed label of a certain color.

Less than a minute later, the label wearers and the Hawaiian maidens had finished with each other, and they all began to move off – the visiting group toward the baggage area and the young women to a place to change out of their costumes. Other nonaffiliated passengers continued to disembark from the bus.

One mainlander alighted happily, but he immediately let his face fall into an expression of deep disappointment as he watched the two greeter-girls disappear into the night.

"Where's mine?" he asked, at first of no one in particular. Then he spotted our friend, the oriental-Hawaiian. "Don't I get some flowers, too?"

The woman hesitated for only a second. Then she stepped forward and placed the *lei* – the one she had bought for her cousin – around the visitor's neck. She was considerably shorter than the newcomer so he had to stoop.

"*Aloha!*" she greeted him. The man gave her a smiling kiss on the cheek, straightened up wearing his new *lei* – and then joined the crowd in a search for suitcases, blissfully unaware that anything out of the ordinary had happened to him.

"What else could I do?" The woman looked at us helplessly. "He seemed so unhappy!"

That vignette was an illustration of today's Hawaiian contrasts. The once all-pervading Aloha Spirit may have disappeared from the Islands, to be replaced by commercial imitations of its content. Yet the genuine article continues to survive, too, in wonderful and surprising smaller doses.

Again, I was working three days a week at the paper. Part of that time I was on the "Family" section. (Like many newspapers, the *Advertiser* had turned the former women's pages into a features section.)

I interviewed a number of famous visiting experts and personalities. I remember studying hard in advance to understand the concepts before tackling Marshall "the medium is the message" McLuhan. And I managed to find all sorts of strange or interesting people right in Honolulu. Who knew that the governor's chauffeur would turn out to be a *kahuna* (Hawaiian word for shaman)?

Only one of my self-assigned feature stories was nixed – when I interviewed the leader of a sex club that had been operating in the shadows of Kahala, a wealthy section of the city. I thought I had handled the subject as tastefully as could be done. In that case, my immediate boss, Gerry Lopez, took my copy to Buck Buchwach, the executive editor, for an executive decision. Buck said he liked the piece. Nevertheless he killed it without further explanation.

The only other time a story of mine was killed outright was in 1972, when part of the presidential party stayed overnight in Hawaii on the way to the historic meeting of President Nixon and China's Mao Zedong. I was assigned to find some kind of scientific aide staying at the Kahala Hilton Hotel and interview him about his role at the coming talks. I made an appointment by phone and tried to keep it.

As soon as I arrived at the man's room, however, a Secret Service man interrupted, ordered my scientist back inside and escorted me off the property. Following my rule that even a no-story is a story, I wrote one with the lead: "I met a man yesterday I didn't like." But either Buck or George Chaplin killed it.

Gerry Lopez by that time was my immediate boss in the Family section. He was the former copy desk editor ("slot man"), who was given this new, relatively stress-free job until he reached the pensionable age for retirement. We liked each other, though, and with a few exceptions, as noted, he generally let me come up with my own articles to write.

Gerry himself was given to occasionally telling racy stories or reciting doggerel of one kind or another for my amusement.

A favorite:

Take it in your hand, mistress Murphy,
It weighs but a quarter of a pound;
It's got hair on its neck like a turkey,
And it spits when you rub it up and down!

One friend I met through the newspaper was never really employed by the newspaper. Dan Myers was living in Ireland when he began sending short, amusing columns to various papers, including the *Advertiser*. Gerry Lopez liked Dan's writing and bought every one of them and printed them in his section. Then one day Dan and his wife, Gale, showed up in person and said they would like to live in Hawaii for a while. He then became a local columnist.

Dan was always on the lookout for a funny story or clever turn of phrase. For myself and some others, it sometimes became a contest to talk to Dan about everyday experiences. We knew we scored a point or two whenever Dan laughed and pulled out a small notebook from his pocket to jot down a snippet of conversation.

Once Dan made up a small contest, inviting readers to conjugate with adjectives as applied to oneself and others. He gave this example: "I am resolute; you are stubborn; he is a pig-headed fool!" (There were others, but this was probably the best.)

Gerry Lopez liked to "net-fish" and he once confessed to me that he had grown to hate working. But he feared even more the idea of not getting a full pension, so he would stay on until that day. Some time later he became fatally ill while still on the job, and he soon died in the Queen's Hospital. I remember that Janice Wolf and I hugged each other for comfort when we heard the news. And again I vowed that death on the job would never happen to me.

Meanwhile, I came up with several feature articles for the paper that also provided me with research for the guidebook. I once took a tour bus and found that the driver was making up all sorts of stories for the entertainment of the tourists – pointing out a "Hawaiian buffalo," for example, when the bus passed by the zoo. He also pointed out a pandanus tree identifying it as a "pineapple tree."

When that piece appeared in the newspaper, the Hawaii Visitors Bureau began setting up Hawaiian history and culture classes and encouraged the tour companies to send their drivers and guides to take them.

When my guidebook research was nearly completed, the newspaper assigned its most senior feature writer, Mary Cooke, to do a story on my guidebook activities. Mary and a photographer followed me for a few days while I investigated some hotels, restaurants, shows, and other tourist-related interests. The big spread with photos was a welcome shot of publicity for the forthcoming volume – even though the book was not really designed to appeal to locals as much as to visitors and newcomers to the Islands.

Within the limitations of her own job and taking care of the kids, Sara helped me as much as she could. Sometimes we went to restaurants with notebooks in hand. When it was practical, we sometimes sat down at three places in the same evening – for appetizers in one, main course in another, and dessert in yet a third.

I often insisted that Sara order the fish, since I had a general aversion to several types of seafood. Sometimes she protested:

"Hey, I'd like to have a steak now and then, too!"

"Sorry, sweetheart; please order the salmon," I replied.

I always said that the problem was that I had grown up in Pekin, Illinois during World War II, when the only kind of fish that could be obtained was canned tuna. I eventually grew to love tuna, either canned or fresh. A popular tuna in Hawaii was *ahi* (yellowfin). And I could even eat that raw as in thinly sliced *sashimi* for appetizers.

Sometime in the latter part of 1976, I finally turned in all the pages for the guidebook to the publisher. I temporarily regretted my break with Rand-McNally as I drew some rather inexpert maps for use in the book. But David Yamada, one of the *Advertiser* staff photographers took a terrific photo of me for use on the back of the book, and I submitted my own color photo of Waikiki for the front cover. I then completed an index and dedicated the book to my parents and to Temple Fielding.

Sara threw a large "Book End" party, and we invited dozens to the house, concentrating on those who had helped in one way or another.

I went back full-time at the paper again and waited, while suffering from a sort of postpartum depression. Outside of some galley proofs, there was no more correcting and updating – nothing to do but wait.

In March of 1977, I received the first box of a dozen copies of the *Maverick Guide to Hawaii*. I was delighted to see that a few of the volumes were actually produced in hard cover. I forgot that Milburn Calhoun had told me that these were for libraries and other special markets.

I took one of the copies to the office, and my colleagues seemed duly impressed. Advertiser Editor George Chaplin seemed to heft the book, seemingly making his judgment based on how much it weighed. (I had hoped he would ask to borrow it, take it in his office and read a little, but he didn't.)

I thought to myself that if this were the Time-Life Building again, George's office would be on Elevator Bank Number One.

Anyway, this first edition was hardly a pamphlet – about 100,000 words on 436 pages. It was indeed a thrill, and I guessed that my life would change thereafter. It did, but in ways I never would have suspected.

Pelican arranged an autograph session for the maverick at the
ABA in San Francisco. (Photo by Bob Bone)

45

Life as a Published Author

ONE OF THE FIRST INDEPENDENT JUDGES of my literary achievement was a respected reporter for the rival newspaper. *Honolulu Star-Bulletin* writer Pierre Bowman pronounced it a success: "The acid test with a guidebook to your own stomping grounds is whether you'd recommend it to a stranger. The answer with *The Maverick Guide to Hawaii* is an emphatic yes…

"Bone has done a whale of a job with his book," Pierre wrote, giving several examples of insights and other subjects covered in it.

I feared one criticism that, thankfully, did not happen. In a moment of whimsy while writing my chapter on Molokai, I decided to name something that did not have a name – the steep path down the cliff to the former leprosy colony of Kalaupapa. I called it the "Jack London Trail" after one of the many writers who have taken it over the years. Ever since that publication, I have often seen it referred to in print by that name – even in other guidebooks.

My first out-of-town review was by Jackie Peterson, travel editor of *The Sacramento Union*, who was also complimentary. This gave me an idea that I sent on to the publisher, explaining that the best bet was not to send review copies to overloaded book section departments but instead to the newspaper travel editors and to the travel magazines. This technique paid off and I began receiving scores of favorable reviews in columns in newspaper travel sections and a few travel magazines from the U.S. and Canada. In truth, I never saw a bad one.

But for a year or more, bookstores in the eastern U.S., including major cities like New York and Boston, were not stocking the *Maverick*. When queried, these stores reported that their customers seldom went to Hawaii but more often to warm choices in the Caribbean. Then I found out that eastern *travel agents* didn't agree, declaring that Hawaii was indeed a popular destination for many of their clients.

A major breakthrough occurred when *The New York Times* carried a mini review in its Practical Traveler section by Paul Grimes. He called the *Maverick Guide to Hawaii* "a prodigious job," and that phrase usually led the list of quotes in every edition thereafter. *The Times* did a longer favorable review for all my books together a few years later.

By the time the last copy of the Hawaii Maverick book appeared in 2002, it had gone through 21 editions and sold perhaps a half-million copies over 25 years.

But in 1977, that kind of future seemed impossible. I kept my newspaper job, and struggled to increase my new travel author identity. I was up against several well-established guides by Fodor, Frommer and other well-known names. However, no other Hawaii guidebook on the market had been written by someone who was living full-time in the Islands.

Of course I also received some notice on the local scene, too. There was a TV appearance on Betty Smyser's *Conversations* talk show on KHVH-TV. (Betty was often described as Hawaii's answer to Barbara Walters.)

In May of that year, Sara and I were invited to the ABA – the three-day American Booksellers Association trade show – in San Francisco. (It's now known as BookExpo America.) This was exciting. We headquartered ourselves at the publisher's booth, which was decorated with tropical flowers and all sorts of Hawaii paraphernalia. We dressed in Aloha shirts and muumuus and handed out sample packages of Hawaiian macadamia nuts.

Like all authors attending the ABA, I was given an autograph session – a heady experience for me as booksellers and others lined up to get their free signed books from the Maverick himself. And on one of those days, I re-met CBS's Charles Kuralt, who was there to promote one of his 30-some books. I reminded him of the days we took turns using the same radio broadcasting studio in Rio de Janeiro. (By this time Charlie was a household word, stemming from his "On the Road" TV features on CBS.)

I also cadged some free books from other authors who attended the ABA.

There was no time for sightseeing in San Francisco, although of course we looked in on Orah and her mother, Suzie. These two women who meant so much to me 20 years previously in London, were as warm and attractive personalities as ever.

Back home, life as a general assignment newspaper reporter continued as before, although I did begin to investigate the possibility of a second title in the Maverick series. Then the editor of a Los Angeles magazine called *New West* saw a copy of the Hawaii guidebook and gave me an assignment for two articles, one on Molokai and the other on the Big Island of Hawaii, the latter comparing two resort hotels – Kona Village Resort and the Mauna Kea Beach Hotel.

On publication I was proud of the text, which was used almost exactly as I wrote it. I also provided the photographs. But every single caption to these photos was in some way incorrect. From that day on, I resolved to carefully control my photos as much as my prose.

Totally unimpressed with my new community prominence was our landlord who suddenly decided that he wanted to give our house to a relative. He gave us the exact notice that Hawaii's landlord-tenant law required – 30 days. It was a nerve-racking month, of course. But in those 30 days, we managed to find the house at 1053 Lunaai Street that would remain our home for the next 30 years – the remaining time we lived in Hawaii.

If you've read the previous words in this volume, you'll believe it was by far the longest period of time I ever lived at one address anywhere anytime.

Our children, Christina and David were 10 and 9 respectively, and we still had our two cats, Anzie and Blackie, from New York and Mallorca, respectively, plus the runt of a Hawaii-born litter whom Christina had dubbed "Band-Aid." From this point on, we might have been able to keep track of time by a half-dozen or so cat dynasties.

After the three already mentioned – Anzie, Blackie and Band-Aid – there was Mother Hiss (Band-Aid's mom), Mozzie (who looked like a miniature lion), Margaret (a second calico) and Sasha, whom we still have, along with our half-Jack Russell terrier, Keiki. More on Blackie later.

Some people who come to Hawaii for a time soon tire of it. Despite its sunny days, welcoming trade winds, beautiful sur-roundings, and generally accommodating population, they pronounce themselves infected with "rock fever." This is especially true with military personnel and their families, some of whom seem to be uncomfortable with an unfamiliar culture. Thank goodness, we were not infected by this problem.

One thing we loved about Hawaii that year was that many friends we had known in other years and in other countries were beginning to visit us, including, of course, Howard Rausch, who had invested a certain amount of emotional attachment to our family. Somehow that all seemed to mold our past and present together in Hawaii, despite its reputation as the most isolated set of populated islands in the world.

46

A Renewed Interest in Down Under

IN THE LATE-1970S, THINGS BEGAN moving quickly for the Bone family. First, I received a contract to write a second book in what was now going to be a series: another guidebook, this time to Australia.

The newspaper was no problem. In 1978 the *Advertiser* granted me a six-month leave of absence to do our on-site research.

What might have become an impossibly expensive project was ameliorated by a plan by the Australian Tourist Commission to fly Sara and me to the capitals of all six states and two territories of the country and then back home to Hawaii. The Aussies would also arrange for hotel accommodations and several other expenses along the way over a period of two months.

We made a slight alteration in the itinerary in order to drop our two kids off to spend the time with the New Zealand relatives. There they got along with children of similar ages, went to local schools, and learned valuable talents like playing cricket and developing a taste for Marmite – that axle-grease-like stuff all Kiwis love to spread on toast.

At the same time, these young funny-talking Yanks introduced their Down Under cousins to the joys of peanut butter, a substance with which many New Zealanders were not familiar.

Sara and I had our own great experiences in Australian cities and in the Great Outback, too. We climbed Ayer's Rock (well, at least a little of it), scratched the ears of kangaroos and wallabies, cuddled koalas and wombats, recorded howls of the dingo and the laughter of the kookaburra, and collected mountains of notes, menus, audiotapes and photos. We also explored scores of hotels, restaurants, bars and pubs.

Back on Lunaai Street, fellow reporter Ed Kennedy (who cut off the wrong arm by flopping Senator Inouye's photo, remember?) and his wife house-sat our four cats. And, wouldn't you know it, one cat – our Mallorcan half-Siamese Blackie – got a serious and painful urinary tract infection and needed an immediate operation, one costing about $500. (Reminder: This was the same cat that once tried to use a neighbor's hibachi as a toilet.) Ed tried to phone us for instructions, but we were unreachable riding camels or something in the great desert that forms the center of that island-continent.

Like any good reporter, Ed wrote about his current befuddlement in the paper and received considerable mail as a result. A few *Advertiser* readers indeed voted for euthanasia, but by far the preponderance of opinion was that the Bone family would want their cat saved. In the end, and with some help, the Kennedys coughed up the money and crossed their fingers that we would approve and remit.

I'm not so sure we would have gone forward with the surgery. But in the end, we were glad not to have had to make the decision ourselves, and somehow we gradually managed to repay Ed. Indeed Blackie had a lot of personality and quirky traits, and we were glad to have him back.

Among Blackie's endearing habits: surprise jumps onto people's laps (whether family or guests) sometimes while they sat at the dinner table, and sleeping on top of the TV until falling and not waking up until hitting the floor.

Blackie eventually had two separate collisions with passing cars, the second of which he did not survive.

Meanwhile, we were still absorbing experiences and finding friends all over Australia. These included Sally and Ed Kaptein, whom we had known in Greenwich Village, then in London, and at the one-day meeting at the Taj Mahal. And a new friend was Alison Fan, a well-known and knowledgeable TV news personality in Perth, who took an interest in our guidebook work. She and her American husband used to have an annual party to celebrate every Fourth of

July in that attractive west-coast city. We ran across them several times over the years, but have unfortunately now lost contact.

Returning home, I began writing the Australia guide – for the first time on an electric typewriter. And after our experiences there, words seemed to just flow uninhibited from my fingers to the paper:

> Have you been to another planet yet? Or are you even likely to visit one in your lifetime? Most of us probably doubt that we'll live long enough. Or even if we do, surely it will be too expensive for just an average bloke, anyway.
>
> But imagine for a moment what we might find if we did... There are surely many strange animals there, some of which we've never seen or heard of before... Probably some of these creatures won't divide neatly into the great zoological classifications in the textbooks – a mammal (like us) who lays eggs, for example.
>
> The dark of night, spangled of course with an unfamiliar pattern of constellations, obscures the origins of a cacophony of weird cries. Perhaps we'll catch sight of one bizarre bird with twin tall tails. He seems not to possess a voice of his own, but to burst forth instead with the vocal tricks of hundreds of other creatures – even with the realistic noises of nonliving and mechanical objects like lawn mowers and car horns.
>
> Naturally, on this strange planet, there are flowers, plants, and trees that look, act, and smell like nothing else in your previous experience. Grass that cringes when you walk on it, for instance. Trees with elephantine, bottle-shaped trunks that actually do hold water. How about some lovely blossoms that thrive on a protein diet – by trapping and consuming insects.
>
> And the insects themselves... Would you believe flies that capture and devour other flies – even bees – on the wing. What about termites that don't tear down houses, but instead construct some complex condominiums of their own...

I went on and on describing wonder after wonder that are all endemic to Australia – the world's largest island and smallest continent. I couldn't wait to get all this down on paper.

But almost immediately I had to stop since the publisher was again pushing harder for an update on the Hawaii Maverick. I began to suspect this kind of situation was going to repeat itself even more in the future if I were going to write all the Maverick guides.

By the time I finished the Hawaii update, we were out of money. My leave of absence was finished anyway, and so I returned to the paper and again began making a living wage. This means that during my waking hours at home I was going to have to power out the new Australia guidebook, ignoring much of the normal husband/father duties. Sara put up with a lot in those days – especially since she herself was again working for a doctor in private practice.

Somehow I also managed to turn out a few freelance travel articles, too. This included an article on Australia for the *Travel Advisor,* and a Hawaii piece for the January 1979, issue of *Travel and Leisure,* the American Express magazine – my first for such a premium publication. I think that one paid me about a thousand dollars – half of which in effect repaid Ed Kennedy for having the cat cured.

Also in 1979, I began turning out a weekly column for the Advertiser's Travel Section called the "Hawaiian Maverick." Most satisfyingly, these columns were also carried in the *Anchorage Times* in Alaska, which paid me, as I recall, about $100 for each.

47

The Mavericks
Go Down Under

THE *MAVERICK GUIDE TO AUSTRALIA* was published in March, again to universally favorable reviews. And in May, we were again invited by the publisher to the annual ABA convention, this time in Los Angeles.

Sara and I wore cheap imitation Outback Aussie-style hats, with one side brim snapped into the crown, and emblazoned with the book title. This time we received much more attention from book industry attendees, a number of whom were already familiar with our successful Hawaii book. We ran out of guidebooks during the hour-long autograph session.

But the best part was after the convention. Friends in Hawaii put Christina and David on the plane to L.A. and our 12- and 11-year olds proudly flew without accompanying adults to us and on to Disneyland! We also threw other perks in the deal – Universal City, Knott's Berry Farm, and Lion Country Safari. It was our first real family vacation in several years.

A thrill for me, personally, was acceptance as a member of the Society of American Travel Writers later that year. I was familiar with the organization since 1962, during my *Pop Photo* days when travel editor Les Barry was often away at interesting destinations during activities associated with SATW. I have now been an active member for the past 35 years, and still have many close friends in the organization, living in many parts of the U.S. and the world.

A short time later, I went on my first press trip. I was invited by Continental Airlines to join a group that explored tourist areas in both New Zealand and Australia. I returned more enthusiastic than ever about writing another Maverick guide – this time to New Zealand – and I began making inquiries with New Zealand government tourism interests. But this time I was making little progress in seeking financial help.

But everything changed after November 28, 1979.

For two years, Air New Zealand, the national airline, had been making very popular all-day flights from Auckland, the largest city, down to Antarctica for an aerial sightseeing adventure before returning to Auckland.

The flights always carried a well-known Antarctic explorer who pointed out scenic features of the continent that could be appreciated from the air. The plane also did a low-level pass over famous McMurdo Sound so sightseers could get at least a swift view of the international facilities there.

But November 28 was the very last of these adventures since the DC-10 flew briefly into a cloud and then crashed head-on against the slope of 12,000-foot Mount Erebus. All 257 on board immediately perished.

In a country of only about three million inhabitants, it seemed that everybody knew somebody or knew someone who knew somebody who had died in the disaster. Moreover, in the official inquiries afterward, there were attempted cover-ups in the process of assessing the reason for the crash.

Even in far-away Hawaii, Sara and I knew some who died. One man on the plane was a tourism official with whom I had been corresponding in connection with my guidebook plans. Sara knew an Air New Zealand employee who was stationed in Honolulu during her travel agency days.

In short, a secondary outcome of it all was a public relations disaster for the entire country. Soon enough New Zealand began an all-out effort to try to mitigate the consequences as much as possible, especially in regard to international tourism.

The end result for my family was that the New Zealand tourism office decided to fly all four of us round-trip to the country. Further they gave us a rental car to use for as long as we needed to explore and write about the country in preparation for the third book in the Maverick series.

Again, I received a six-month leave of absence from the paper. And again, Christina and David stayed with Sara's sister, Bette, and again they enjoyed all their aunts, uncles, and cousins in Gisborne while their mother and I took two months to explore the vertical country in detail, from Waitangi in the north of the North Island to Dunedin and Stuart Island, in the south of the South Island.

In general, New Zealanders in those days were a little less knowledgeable about the ins and outs of international tourism than were the Australians, a fact that often only made our experiences more endearing and fun.

One day I was being shown around the Captain Cook, then the largest hotel in Wellington, the capital of the country. My guide was the manager of the establishment, and at some point I commented that none of the guest rooms had mixer faucets.

The gentleman confessed that he had no idea what I was talking about.

"You know," I said. "The kind of faucet (or "tap") that takes both the hot water and the cold water, each with its own control but directs the flow out of single pipe. That way the guest can adjust it to a desired temperature."

(Pause.)

"What a marvelous idea!" the man exclaimed. I thought at first he was being sarcastic, or making fun of me – but he wasn't.

New Zealand was hard work, but especially satisfying since we had all of Sara's many relatives to milk for local color. With their help, I made up a list of colorful words and phrases that were in general use in the country.

Many of these, of course, were Maori words that were in common use by all New Zealanders – sometimes twisted to conform to English convention. An example is the Maori word *pakaru*, which means ruined or broken. Taken into New Zealand English, however, it became something like: "Sorry, mate – she's puckerooed!"

Often I would interrupt an animated conversation saying, "Wait – tell me that again!"

I once heard one of Sara's cousins describe a mutual acquaintance:

"I reckon she's as silly as a two-bob watch!"

That one must have been carried over for several years. "Two-bob," of course, as in England, meant two shillings. But New Zealand currency had already been on the decimal (dollars-and-cents) system for several years.

All together, I ultimately devoted six entire pages in the guidebook to New Zealand slang.

48

Low Tech
to High Tech

RETURNING TO THE NEWSPAPER, I found that we reporters, too, were beginning to marvel at new developments in technology when we began writing on electronic keyboards, and seeing our words come up – in white on black – on what seemed to be modest little TV screens called VDTs – video display terminals. Once polished and approved by editors on their own VDTs, our words were sent to mysterious new printers in the back shop and finally appeared on the newspaper pages in the morning.

The most wonderful thing about these devices from my point of view was that I could easily change and edit my words – even check for spelling. Now, I could finally submit clean copy, and I immediately wanted one at home. Especially if I was going to try to keep up with updating old guidebooks while writing new ones. Not to mention continuing to write freelance articles for magazines at the same time.

So sometime during 1981, I had my own word processor. (Hardly anyone called it a computer.) To do this I took out a personal loan from my branch at the Bank of Hawaii. The total was $7000, representing about half for the computer and half for the printer. When I turned on the machine at home, I felt as if I had just secured the key to the universe.

It was called a Xerox 820, using the now-defunct CP/M operating system. And most important, I was the first reporter on the *Honolulu Advertiser* to have my own home computer.

On this wonderful device, I began to create the third book in the series, the *Maverick Guide to New Zealand*:

> New Zealand has always been explorers' country. Made of mountains and valleys thrust up in the remotest part of our planet, it existed for millions of years without feeling the foot of man – or of hardly any animal, for that matter.
>
> Ice ages and glaciers came and went. New ranges and plains were formed by massive movements under the sea. Tectonic plates ground together, and volcanoes erupted again and again in island-building processes that are still going on.
>
> Trees, plants, and flowers drifted on winds and water to this land until they caught hold of rich New Zealand soil. Seeds were also borne by birds blown from their courses on other continents until they reached an isolated haven thousands of miles from their nests.
>
> Some of the species of vegetation that took root in New Zealand have survived to become unique examples of evolutionary change. And many of the winged creatures which contributed to the lushness of the landscape also remained to enjoy the fruits of their new homeland.
>
> Succeeding generations of these birds gradually began to be transformed, too. In the absence of ground predators, some found their wings weakened; finally, having lost the need, they lost the ability to fly. A few grew large and heavy, and one long-necked species called the moa actually developed into a sort of feathered monster...

The 300-plus-page 6x9 book, again with one of my scenic photos on the cover, shipped in April 1981. It almost immediately received excellent notices, even in New Zealand. Writing in the *Library Journal*, published in the U.S., Susan M. Unger reported: "A lively and informative guide to travel in New Zealand... This is the best guide to New Zealand ever seen by this New Zealander."

For the third year in a row, I attended the ABA convention, this time in Atlanta, to promote the new guidebook along with the other two.

Sara took some catch-up courses and was now doing the kind of work she had loved in New Zealand before our marriage. She was now an operating room nurse again, this time in the Kapiolani Hospital in Honolulu.

Back home again, I began to set up an annual routine that looked like it would become a stifling year-in, year-out drudgery: updating the Hawaii guidebook annually along with one of the other two books, either Australia or New Zealand. Together with continuing my reporting job at the newspaper, this began to be almost overwhelming. I had learned to my sorrow that although writing a new book was hard work, though fun, updating a previous volume was pretty much only hard work.

I did begin looking into the possibility of guidebooks to Japan and/or Tahiti, but… but… Something had to give.

On top of that, I was doing more and more freelancing – earning immediate money for travel articles, ranging from $100 on up to a couple thousand.

Then another reporter on the *Advertiser,* Robert Hollis, was also taken by the possibilities of writing with a computer. So together we decided to collaborate on a book. For the *Writers Guide to Personal Computers,* we outlined 11 chapters and 6 appendices.

It was a great idea, and well organized, but too large, too grand in scope, and too slow. It seemed every time Hollis and I completed a new chapter, it was outdated by new introductions in the technology.

More practical if less ambitious was the effort by Hal Glatzer, who for a time had been the Hilo correspondent for the *Advertiser.* Hal quickly got out *Introduction to Word Processing* (Sybex Publishing, 1981) in only 200 pages. Hal's work, too, quickly became outdated. But he had at least managed to grab onto the technical merry-go-round soon enough to get it in print.

In addition, Hollis and I noticed that the Neighbor Island bureaus of the *Advertiser* were sending in their stories to the paper by using something called a "modem." Making a few inquiries, I discovered that by setting up certain parameters on a distant computer, we could do that, too.

By then, we were fortunate to have a managing editor at the *Advertiser* like Mike Middlesworth who allowed us to send numerous test messages into the newspaper's computer system via its telephone port. Mike was a journalist who early on understood the impact that computers were having on the news and publishing business.

Mike had set up the correspondents on the islands of Maui, Kauai, and Hawaii (the Big Island) with Sony portable computers long before it was the custom in other U.S. newspapers. Later, he added stand-alone terminals for the paper's main computer in these offices, replacing the ancient teletype machines that had been used for decades.

Then one time, I covered a late-night meeting that was held near my home in Kailua – on the windward side of the island of Oahu. Instead of taking a half-hour drive back to the office in Honolulu, I simply went home, fired up my Xerox 820, typed the story, then sent the proper codes to the modem, and submitted my text to the city editor in the office. It was a fine test, easily making my deadline, and saving me the drive time to and from the office.

In a word, I was hooked. And I saw the future implication immediately.

The next day I called up Evelyn Kieran, travel editor of the *San Diego Union Tribune*, and asked her if I could send her a travel feature by modem. After some initial confusion, she transferred me to the paper's computer room where I spoke with someone who gave me some numbers to be set in my modem – they were different in some respects from those used by the *Advertiser*, but I could see that they served the same purpose.

Then I sent her a routine travel piece I had been planning to mail. I watched it crawl across my screen. The modem could transmit at approximately voice reading speed, called 300 baud, in the new language of this technology.

Calling Evelyn again, she reported that she found the story in her "queue" of stories, clicked on it, and was immediately able read it. Later she edited the piece, and was able to send it to her own editor who processed it into her travel section.

Things like this are taken for granted today, but in 1981 this was really hot stuff.

But my big breakthrough came a short time later as a direct result of a regional disaster called Hurricane Iwa.

49

Goodbye Western Union & RCA Telex

ON NOVEMBER 25, 1982, I received a phone call from Zeke Wigglesworth, travel editor of the *San Jose Mercury News*.

"Bob, I wondered if you were planning to do a tourism-related story on the impact of the hurricane?"

Hurricane Iwa had hit the Islands the previous day, just grazing Oahu but wreaking considerable havoc on Kauai, cutting communication, closing all hotels and doing millions of dollars in damage to the Garden Island in general.

"Zeke. Glad you called! I've already done a story, and you can have it, too."

"Wonderful. Do you think you could get your story down to the RCA telegraph office sometime before five o'clock?"

"Hey, I can do better than that, Zeke. I can send it to you by modem!"

"By what?"

"I can send it from my computer right now directly into the *Mercury-News* computer system so you can bring it up on your screen."

"Oh. I don't think we can do that. I've heard that the Sports Department has some sort of system, but that's for their own use."

"Zeke – you're right there in the middle of Silicon Valley, and if I can do it anywhere, I can do it for San Jose. (Actually, I wasn't all that sure.) "Do you have somebody hanging around your office called the nerd, the geek, the guru, or maybe just the 'I.T. guy?'"

(Laughing): "Oh yeah."

"Let me speak to him," I said.

Zeke found the computer expert and put him on the phone. He began telling me something about setting start bits, stop bits, modem baud speed, and more codes (all stuff that's now out of date and thankfully forgotten) so that my article would go direct to the travel editor. He finished it all off with the newspaper's dedicated modem telephone number. I asked for his voice line number, too, in case of a problem. But there wasn't any.

Less than 10 minutes later, Zeke called me again and said he was looking at my piece now displayed clearly on his VDT.

From then on, I was off and running. I began calling the computer rooms of several newspapers for which I had been sending hard copy travel articles, for greater or lesser success. These included papers like the *Chicago Tribune*, *The Boston Globe*, and most notably, *The Washington Post*.

"There's a guy on the phone out in Hawaii that wants to send us something by modem!" someone at the *Post* shouted.

"Hey, can you cover sports?" another voice came on the line.

All those papers and a dozen others ended up printing my Kauai hurricane story.

A year later, I visited Travel Editor Morris Rosenberg in his office at *The Washington Post*, and he explained his end of that story.

"I had assigned a regular freelancer to go to Kauai and send me a story on the Hurricane, but I never heard anything more from him.

"But then I turned on my screen in the morning and right there was your story. I didn't know how it got there, but we took a chance and used it immediately."

I continued to freelance over the next several years, with articles in prestigious magazines, including *Travel-Holiday* and *Travel and Leisure*, plus more articles in mainland newspapers. Some, like the *Anchorage Times*, used them as weekly or monthly columns. Somehow I managed to keep my newspaper job and still update the three Maverick guides.

In 1982, my former Time-Life buddy, Dave Bridge, who was still working for National Geographic Publications in Washington, invited me on an expense-paid trip to the nation's capital to talk to him and others in the Special Publications Division about a new magazine the company would soon launch called the *National Geographic Traveler*.

Dave explained that although the division had lots of experience with books, they felt they would like to know more about magazines. I thought they had a pretty good magazine information source in the same corporate structure (the original *National Geographic*), but I didn't say so. I really wanted to go and so did not put up any hindrances to that objective.

I flew in from Honolulu just for the weekend, and the company put me up at the historic Beaux-Arts style Jefferson Hotel across the street from the Society headquarters. I recall wondering what great explorers, adventurers and other prestigious or intrepid folks might have previously stayed in my room.

Dave and I talked about my ideas on travel magazines, and we visited his boss, Robert Breeden. I had exchanged a letter or two with him back in '68 when I ultimately decided to forgo any Washington opportunity to join Temple Fielding in Europe instead.

I returned to Honolulu without any offer of employment. I was ready to consider the editor's job, if it were offered. It wasn't. But sometime later, at Dave's suggestion, I received an invitation to submit a major story for the magazine's first issue.

I heavily researched a new tourism story on the island of Maui. Ultimately, the piece was drastically shortened, but at least it did appear in Volume 1, Number 1 of the *National Geographic Traveler*, and I was paid well for it.

I didn't do another story for that publication until 2007.

Sunday morning in Tahiti. (Photo by Bob Bone)

50

Tahiti, Norway, & "Hang a Right"

I JUGGLED MAVERICK UPDATES, free-lancing assignments, a considerable amount of foreign travel, meetings related to SATW, and my duties at the *Honolulu Advertiser* throughout the first half of the 1980s.

Although I earned good money from my travel articles from several U.S. Mainland newspapers, I provided the same text and photos free to the Sunday Travel Section of the *Honolulu Advertiser*, even though the research and writing were always done during my free time. Understandably, there was still a certain amount of resentment among a few at the paper. And if someone were to call me up at home to check on some fact or other, he didn't always find me readily available.

At this point, Sandy Zalburg had retired, and the city editor was now a former reporter named Gerry Keir. (Not to be confused with Gerry Lopez.)

I continued to take press trips whenever they were offered and could be accommodated in my schedule. Two of the more interesting were by Continental Airlines.

One such was its inaugural flight to Nagoya, Japan, where I devoted my story to learning to play pachinko. This one was later picked up and included in Bruce Northam's collection, *In Search of Adventure: A Wild Travel Anthology*. A total of 100 travel writers were represented in the book. My title was "The Confession of Nagoya Fats."

NAGOYA: Some men spend much of their lives trying to come out ahead at pachinko, the traditional slot machine of Japan. These noisy devices with a sort of vertical pinball face have been installed in colorfully lit pachinko parlors throughout the country. Winnings are supposed to be paid in prizes rather than in cold cash.

Rick Carroll, a reporter friend of mine, and an old hand in Japan, taught me pachinko in Nagoya, sitting down at a machine and deftly shooting some little steelies around the board for a few minutes, paying about three 100-yen coins (about $1 each) for the privilege.

"Here, let me try that," I said as Rick gave up his seat to me and moved on to potentially more fertile mechanisms. For the first time in my life, then, I played pachinko, inserting just one 100-yen coin in the slot and then twisting some kind of a doorknob-like handle.

Suddenly all kinds of whistles and bells seemed to break loose. Lights began to flash. An attendant ran over with a colored flag to place on my machine, gushing something I couldn't understand. With a steady roar, steel balls began to spit and pour from the mouth of the mechanical monster in front of me, and the man had to hook on a special plastic tray to catch them all.

It seemed like it took five minutes for the tray to fill up with everything the machine had to disgorge. With sign language, the attendant motioned that I should carry it – a heavy task – over to a counting machine. In a few seconds, it toted up, I believe, some 3000 pachinko balls.

For these, I was given a group of mysterious small boxes gathered together in a larger cigar box, together with a chocolate bar. Instinctively, the attendant knew I was not going to be satisfied with a new toaster.

"Come," he said. "Get money."

Now he was speaking my language.

He led me outdoors and on a long walk down the street and through an alley to what appeared to be some kind of a small shop. I might have been a worried, except that I was followed by Rick and a few friends who were witnessing these awesome events.

At the store, the woman behind the counter ignored the candy but counted and stashed the boxes, and then handed over 5000 yen in cash (about $40). I calculated later that she might have taken around 1000 yen in commission. Later, back at the hotel, I used my new wealth to buy us all a round of drinks. (We should have gone to a neighborhood bar. It didn't go quite far enough at the Hilton.)

A good journalist, my friend Rick interviewed me as to when I was going to try my luck at pachinko again.

"Never," I told him. "I have retired as a totally undefeated champion." And I still am.

Another inaugural by Continental was a flight to Guam. It was on a reconfigured DC-10, which had set up a sort of lounge between the First Class and Economy areas. (There was no business class.) The lounge had a tiny bar (with popcorn) a banquette and (I kid you not) a small dance floor. A three-piece combo stood over in the corner. Two or three couples could dance at the same time.

Both Economy and First Class were welcome in the bar, as long as it didn't become too crowded.

In 1984, certainly an Orwellian year, I was working just four days a week at the newspaper, a fact that Gerry Keir, then the city editor, did not like. However, my schedule had been approved by Executive Editor Buck Buchwach, so there wasn't much Gerry could do about it. And by switching shifts with other GA reporters, I sometimes was able to have as many as four or five clear days that I used for short trips to the Pacific islands or sometimes even the Far East.

I made an exchange arrangement like that for an extended weekend in September so that I might be included on a special round-trip flight between Honolulu and Tahiti. It was on an airline owned by a South Pacific entrepreneur.

George Wray was a lawyer then living in Pago Pago, American Samoa. He and his clients made so many trips on South Pacific Island Airways (SPIA) that he decided to buy the airline. SPIA usually flew between places like Hawaii, Samoa, Tahiti, and other Pacific islands.

Some regarded SPIA as a rather seat-of-the-pants operation, with occasional financial and logistical problems, some of them related to cultural anomalies of the various islands it served. (Young Samoan flight attendants, for example, could not bring themselves to charge money from older, respected Samoans who ordered alcoholic drinks in flight.) The company was frequently cited by the Federal Aviation Administration for rules infractions.

Earlier that year, SPIA was chartered to fly 150 soldiers from the island nation of Fiji to a United Nations peacekeeping force in Lebanon. Since this was an over-the-pole flight, airlines were required to have some special, more-sophisticated navigation equipment.

The SPIA pilot thought he would not need this sophisticated stuff, and in the latter portion of the flight, the plane suddenly appeared on European radar screens to be headed for a strategically sensitive military installation in the Soviet Union. Earlier that year the Russians had shot down a civilian South Korean airliner resulting in the deaths of scores of civilians. Sensitivities were now heightened in the international community.

A squadron of Norwegian air force planes was scrambled to divert the errant SPIA flight from its path in order to prevent a similar fate. At a subsequent hearing, the SPIA pilot said he believed he didn't need any special equipment for navigation:

"I just figured I would just keep going straight until we came to Norway and then hang a right."

That was apparently too much for the FAA, which suddenly grounded all SPIA flights. This happened on the day that I and three other freelance writers, Leonard Lueras, Roger Coryell, and Scott Stone, were due to fly back to Honolulu after taking notes and enjoying the delights of Tahiti. There was simply no way that I was going to go to work at the *Advertiser* on Monday.

I didn't know the reason for the action at the time, but at least I went into reporter mode to get the Tahiti end of the story, which I felt ought to legitimize or at least ameliorate my Monday no-show. I even interviewed the airline owner's mother who was on our Tahiti flight. Then I made an international call to the newsroom and dictated the essentials of the story to Anne Harpham, another staffer.

Jim Loomis, SPIA's Honolulu public relations representative, made some special arrangements and we were provided tickets on two other air carriers – one to Los Angeles and then after some delay, still another airline from LAX to Honolulu.

City Editor Keir was angry. He did not use the story I dictated to Anne. (*The New York Times* covered the grounding, but the *Honolulu Advertiser* ignored it.) Furthermore, Gerry spoke to my wife, Sara, at home, bawling her out on the phone for my bad behavior.

"Hey, I don't work for you!" Sara said, suggesting that Gerry should save all his invective until I got home.

Tuesday morning, I made sure I was at work on time. I was immediately called into the conference room alone with Gerry. But before he could really let me have all of it, I interrupted and informed him of something I had just learned.

I had made a mistake. The way I had traded days off with another reporter meant that I was actually not due to come back to work on Monday, but on Tuesday – today. If I had not telephoned the *Advertiser* with the story on Saturday, no one would have known anything about my trip to Tahiti.

Gerry was not mollified, however. He continued to express his dissatisfaction with the whole episode:

"We have to know that our reporters are available here when we need them," he said "And not fartin' around in the South Pacific!"

At the end of the conversation, he was still angry, but he said he was not going to make an entry in my personnel file. I knew that under union rules he couldn't do so anyway.

"I'm sorry that you are so unhappy, Gerry," I said. "But I simply don't see this thing in the way that you do."

I went back to work and nothing was said about the incident again. Actually I felt rather sorry for my immediate boss. My own conclusion was that he was getting some pressure in other areas, perhaps from Editor George Chaplin, or News Editor John Strobel, (with whom he occasionally went to battle), and he just felt the need to blow off steam. I had never had any previous run-in with him, and although we were never particularly friendly, we had many friends in common and we held no real animosity toward each other.

Still, the long-term effect on me was to realize that there were new difficulties in a job that I had mostly enjoyed for 13 years. Things had changed, and it was time to leave.

Sara also said that although our finances would be a little more unsure, she agreed that it was probably for the best. On or about December 1, I told Gerry that my last day at the *Honolulu Advertiser* would be December 31 – New Year's Eve. And he said something nice about being sorry to lose me.

But that day was not to be an easy one.

Bob Bone trying out a satellite phone in Antarctica.

51

The Decline & Fall of a Salaried Employee

THE EVENING SHIFT FOR REPORTERS on the *Advertiser* was from 1:15 to 9:45, and somehow I thought that maybe I might not have to work quite as late as that on my last day. New Year's Eve is usually a pretty quiet time as far as significant news goes.

But apparently Night City Editor Tom Brislin didn't see it that way, and there was something for me to do seemingly every second. I think I ground out several obituaries, if nothing else. When I came back to the office after dinner at about 7 p.m., he said there was a community association meeting out at Laie, about an hour's drive away along the North Shore, at which an important controversy was going to be aired.

It was a running story I was already familiar with, and I was sure that this was not the case, and I told him so. Nevertheless, Tom still wanted coverage.

So I called up an officer in the group and received an answer something like: "Are you kidding? It's New Year's Eve. We're not going to do much more than take roll call."

Again Tom wouldn't budge. He ordered me out of the office and out to Laie. By then it was beginning to rain. So I went.

I couldn't help resenting it. After all, by then I was a successful writer in my own right, with my travel articles being carried in many newspapers and magazines throughout the country while maintaining three guidebooks in annual production, and with lots of people in Hawaii and around the nation seeking my attention for one thing or another.

The thing to do was to shrug my shoulders and remember that a prophet in his own land is without honor. And all that stuff.

Although I also couldn't help conjuring up the old Army phrase about the anticipated joy in "getting out of this chicken-shit outfit."

It was pouring when I got to Laie, and the meeting went just as promised. It was over in about 10 minutes with no action being taken on the anticipated controversy. Instead, it would be taken up sometime later in the new year.

I scribbled a four-paragraph story in my notebook and found a very wet outdoor pay phone. I called in a short story outlining the situation and explaining that the fireworks did not materialize because of the holiday. The rain was soaking my clothes and washing my words right off the notebook as I spoke.

Tom thanked me and wished me Happy New Year. I drove straight home, my 13-year career at the *Honolulu Advertiser* at an end.

The morning of January 1, 1985, I picked up my copy of the paper at home. There was not a line based on my last assignment. And that was as it should be. Nothing times nothing still equaled nothing.

So again, there was a denouement to a significant event: The pigeon-drop scheme in Paris, the air-pressure drop on Trans-Continental Airlines, the sniper incident in Vietnam, the delayed departure and embassy snub in Moscow, and Sara's re-entry denial in New York.

But just like my stolen passport adventure in London, everything had worked out okay in the end. Just as my grandmother always said: "Everything always works out for the best."

I should point out that Tom Brislin's diligence served him well in subsequent years. He became one of the most respected journalists and college professors in Hawaii. I bear him no ill will, of course. I just love telling the story.

52

Free at Last,
Free at Last

IT'S HARD TO BELIEVE that the Orwellian year of 1984 would be my last year as an employee of any kind. At age 51, I was now embarking on about 20 years more of exciting world-travel journalism from an ideal base of operations in Hawaii.

The *Honolulu Advertiser* continued to print my travel pieces, except that now they paid me for them, although not nearly as much as some other clients. While still in harness at the paper I had provided them free. One piece I particularly enjoyed writing in those days was based on my trip to Guam, an island I judged perhaps the least desirable destination for American tourists in the Pacific. It was also carried by the *Chicago Tribune* and a few other papers.

Guam, beaten to a pulp in WW II, had lots of small problems and two big problems in the 1980s. One was the creature called the brown tree snake, whose ubiquitous presence once even crossed electric wires and shorted out a large section of the island's power. Another was the fact that violent annual typhoons regularly scoured the island of anything not welded to the ground. Its massive utility poles were made of cement. Many architecturally uninspired houses consisted of single-story concrete walls with unsightly metal rebar rods sticking up on top where a second story might be connected at some future time.

The most artistically attractive building was the airport terminal.

In its quest for tourist dollars, Guam once put up a statue representing Quipuha, the chief who greeted the Spanish when they colonized Guam in the 17th Century. The only problem was that the local residents in those days, certainly including Quipuha, ran around totally naked – except for a hat to ward off the merciless sun.

Otherwise no one knows what Quipuha looked like. But the statue that was created depicts him wearing a sort of American Indian-style loincloth. And no hat.

Another statue was more interesting. It is of Pope John Paul II, who once visited Guam. In order not to insult any of the residents living in neighborhoods surrounding the statue, it was erected on a clock base so it rotated once every 12 hours, thus allowing the pope to face everyone at least twice a day.

I met a woman archeologist resident in Guam who also found it interesting.

"We call him our rotopope," she said smiling.

I took a dim view of Guam's quest for cheap tourism in the 1980s, which then catered largely to Japanese who enjoyed playing with guns and live ammunition, the kind of thing that was strictly prohibited in Japan.

This resulted in a plethora of shooting galleries on the island. I recall one where the Japanese visitors dressed up in American cowboy gear, sat on a sort of stagecoach set, and fired at targets that were depictions of feathered American Indians. (One can only hope that this no longer exists today in the 21st Century.)

I also noted that the restaurant in the Guam Hilton had two different menus – one for local residents with prices significantly lower than for out-of-towners. This came to light when a Honolulu businessman I knew sat down to eat with a Guam associate. He told me he then discovered they were given the two different bills of fare.

I don't know if my story had any effect on these things. I was told that the *Guam Daily News* in an editorial was critical of my evaluation. I had a more direct report from Baba White, aka "Baba Kea," a successful designer of hotel employee uniforms, and the mother of my daughter's boyfriend in Honolulu. Baba later visited the manager of the Guam Hilton on business.

"Do you know anything about a writer named 'Bone?'" he asked.

Cruising became a new addition to my professional activities in the late 1980s. Both Sara and I had traveled from time to time over the years on shipboard, but those previous trips were "line voyages" – designed for transportation from one place to another. This is how the name "liner" became attached to passenger ships. My 1957 trip to Europe, Sara's trips from New Zealand to Canada, and our family relocation from New York to Mallorca were all line voyages.

But cruising was now becoming heavily marketed to those who wanted an adventure on the water and short visits to exotic ports. These were either round trips or structured so that cruisers received a round-trip experience, in a package priced with the necessary air flights to/from the appropriate ports. Thus modern cruise ships are no longer "liners," although they are often described as such. And "passengers" these days are more accurately described as cruisers.

Of importance to Sara and me was that certain of these cruises were being offered to me, as a travel writer, either free or with only minimal cost. But in addition, the writer's spouse or companion was welcome to come along for the ship portion, too, as long as they occupied the same cabin and paid any necessary air fare to and from the points of embarkation and disembarkation. In this way it was often an improvement over the usual press trip, where a guest was generally not allowed.

Over the past 20 years, I have covered somewhere between 50 and 60 cruises, and Sara has come along on a good number of them. She doesn't write, but her keen powers of observation have genuinely been helpful to me.

Not counting those line voyages, the first cruise that we took, along with some other press, was a 1986 Australia-New Zealand adventure aboard a ship from the Royal Viking Line. This was ideal since the experience also helped our ongoing research for revisions in the Australia and New Zealand guidebooks.

Except for the small press contingent, the cruise clientele consisted predominately of senior citizens. And the ship seemed under the impression that the passengers' main objective was to relive the past. There was lots of music on board, canned and live, but I gradually realized that Royal Viking did not allow popular songs written after 1945.

The *Royal Viking Star* sailed from Sydney, a wonderful scenic harbor. From there it went to Melbourne, where we once again were able to visit Sally and Ed Kaptein, erstwhile friends from New York, London, and the Taj Mahal. After that, we crossed the Tasman Sea to make several calls at ports in New Zealand, including a day exploring the waters of Milford Sound, one of the most attractive fjords of the country. The cruise concluded in Auckland, which was certainly handy for us, both for gathering book updating information and seeing our New Zealand family members again before flying back to Honolulu.

The only slightly sour note on that cruise was that one writer in the group, a young bachelor, was chastised for beginning a shipboard romance with a nubile Swedish lass, a member of the crew, even attending a party in the crew discotheque. (The first we knew there was such a thing.) Of course there were no candidates for canoodling among the geriatric paying passengers. But there were many attractive young people among the staff.

Less than a year later, we had a different and discomforting experience on the Atlantic. This was not the usual press trip, but the 1986 national convention of the Society of American Travel Writers (SATW) held on board the *Queen Elizabeth 2*, while sailing from New York to Southampton. This was to be the ship's last crossing before a major refurbishment, when its engines would be switched from coal to diesel oil. Quite a big deal.

A day out of New York, the weather turned ugly. For the rest of the trip we were buffeted with near-hurricane-force winds and heavy seas. On top of everything else, the stabilizers on one side of the ship became inoperative. This meant that while the ship would still roll, it rolled more on one side than the other, an unsettling and sometimes frightening experience.

The author James Michener, then about 80, was at our table in the dining room. He was quite frail and walking with a cane. Now the rest of us felt as unsteady as he, and it was difficult for anyone to make headway on the rolling decks. Dishes broke, wine and caviar spilled, hot liquids were no longer served, and in the staterooms many passengers put their mattresses on the floor to keep from rolling out of bed.

This technique was not always helpful. Janet Fullwood, travel editor of *The Sacramento Bee*, was struck on the head by her telephone during the night. Others, like Sheila Donnelly, queen of Hawaii public relations professionals, never left their cabins for the rest of the trip.

Mercifully, Sara and I did not get seasick. But on one evening we recall making our way up to the dance floor where we found that we tended to fall into the bar on one roll and then into the band on the other.

Rita Ariyoshi, a Hawaii-based writer-photographer, was in the ladies' room when two ship's officers' wives came in. They didn't see Rita in the stall while they discussed some inside information gained from their husbands. They said that on many of the more severe rolls, the propellers were coming out of the water, opening a danger of burning out the bearings on the drive shafts. That kind of failure would have made the large ship uncontrollable – totally at the mercy of the wind and giant waves.

Somehow the ship did make it to Southampton. There was to have been a welcoming party, but those folks had all given up and left the area long before we pulled into port almost a day late. The next day we all left for Ireland for the concluding part of our convention.

Sara had an Irish cousin, a retired ship's captain, and we paid him a short visit near Dublin. Not surprisingly, he was aware of our recent sea saga, and it was his opinion that the QE2 and all who sailed in her were very, very lucky.

My only significant memory of the Irish portion of the trip was the day when many of us showed up for an opportunity to kiss the Blarney Stone at Blarney Castle, perhaps to express appreciation for our survival. I don't know if you have had that experience, but at that time it too was a harrowing process. After climbing to the top of an ancient, crumbling tower the stone kissers had to lie on their backs, in a precarious position at a great height above the ground in order to be able to smooch the storied stone. It seemed to some like taking their lives in their lips.

I asked my friend Jane Ockershausan, a no-nonsense travel writer from Pittsburgh, if she had climbed the tower to take part in the athletic ritual.

"Are you kidding?" she asked, her feet planted firmly on the ground. "I *blew* it a kiss!"

I thought that was a good idea.

The mayor's proud achievement: mice wine. (Photo by Bob Bone)

53

From Peripatetic
to Gallivanting

WHEN I THINK OF THE FINAL 15 YEARS of the 20th Century, and the first five of the 21st, I remember heavy amounts of traveling and writing. In 1985 we sent Christina to college in New York and David off to the Navy at around the same time.

Encompassed by this period, from 1992 through 1994, were my duties as Chairman of the Western Chapter of the Society of American Travel Writers, the largest chapter in SATW. I turned down an invitation for a trip to Bali when it conflicted with that responsibility. (I had been to Bali and Indonesia on an earlier occasion – but I really wanted to go back!)

In retribution, I subjected the chapter members to a brief performance on the ukulele.

These were the years when various enterprises seemed to fall over themselves trying to capture me to come see and write about the world's wonders. I never promised a thing in return, but usually I found plenty of worthy material to cover in stories and photos.

By and large, newspapers and magazines like upbeat travel stories; the market for genuine criticism or a negative article runs from slim to none. When I ran across a badly run tourist operation, I usually just declined to write about it.

Only one cruise operation ever fell into that category. We loved our experiences in Antarctica in February of 2003, but the company that took us there was woefully substandard. I think they're now out of business.

Unlike other cruise destinations, Antarctica still can be dangerous. If something goes wrong, help might be a long way – and a long time – away. Luckily, we had no serious problems, but a recent article in the *Christian Science Monitor* warned about floating ice, unpredictable weather, and outdated nautical charts for any company offering cruises to the southern continent.

While I was employed by the newspaper, I had been forbidden to write for any other publication in Hawaii. We got around that a bit by letting *Honolulu Magazine* print various excerpts from the *Maverick Guide to Hawaii*. But now that I was no longer in harness, I was free to do what I wanted.

So after I left the paper I turned out a few travel stories for *Honolulu Magazine* – usually travel to Samoa, Tonga, the Cook Islands, and other Pacific destinations. Selling stories to American newspapers was fairly easy in those days. (I remember there was one year in the '80s where I was in at least one U.S. mainland newspaper on all 52 Sundays.) My main outlet was the *Chicago Tribune,* where I lasted through about six consecutive travel editors. The Trib often called me asking for some Hawaii copy.

There were several trips to Europe, including a terrific adventure in Poland, and others to Central and South America. On one Maupintour excursion to Peru and Bolivia, I was the only writer along. It was a good tour, if it weren't for my fellow travelers, many of whom complained that the mean ol' lady escort kept them moving too much – not enough time to take naps, etc.

If that woman hadn't cracked the whip to get us up early to catch an early-morning train out of Cuzco, for example, we'd have gone to Machu Picchu without seeing a thing. She knew when the fog would come in. But several of the paying customers were going to write to Maupintour later to complain. I eventually wrote and told the company how great she was and how juvenile many of my companions had acted.

The story was a hard sell, however. That "negative" thing again. I believe only one paper bought it – the *St. Petersburg Times.*

On another trip I had a stopover in New York and decided to take a nostalgic look at my old stomping grounds in Greenwich

Village. Entering a subway entrance afterwards, I got mugged. The guy said he had a gun in his coat and I decided to believe him.

I held my wallet firmly with two hands while opening it to make the money, about $50, easily visible and grabable. He took it all, and then I remonstrated:

"I will have no way to get home," I said.

He looked at me and gave me one dollar back before running away. That was then the cost of a subway token.

At that time, my old Puerto Rico and Greenwich Village compatriot Ted Klemens was writing a three-dot column in *The New York Daily News,* and he made an item out of it – something about the inherent kindness of the average New York crook, as I recall.

A press trip to Kyushu provided some special moments. Compared to crowded buildings in other areas in Japan, this warm southern island is almost rural. Sometimes you would see a cow with a large Japanese language character painted on its hide – a humane method of branding.

At an ancient health spa in Kyushu, I laid down on my back, fully naked, into a depression in the black sand or lava. Then two rather elderly women tried to cover my entire body by shoveling more hot black sand on my well-rounded stomach. First of all, it tickled and then I couldn't stop laughing, which caused the sand to fall off my shaking belly. The women laughed too and finally gave up trying to bury my uncooperative torso.

On another occasion in Japan a small group of us sat cross-legged on the floor in a semi-circle surrounding a Japanese woman who began some sort of rather serious tea ceremony in front of us. At one point she bowed, and directly in front of her writer Richard Carroll, often the most enthusiastic participant in any activity, unexpectedly decided to bow also. The resultant bicultural clunk when their foreheads met still cracks me up when I think of it.

NB: "Richard Carroll" should not be confused with "Rick Carroll," who was a colleague and who appears elsewhere in this tome. Two different people – both interesting – but not related.

While my newspaper successes were legion, my main goals were the big national magazines. It seemed that *National Geographic Traveler* would have nothing more to do with me after that article in the inaugural issue, until I finally scored with a short piece on driving around the Big Island of Hawaii. I made several sales to *Travel &*

Leisure (the American Express magazine) and especially *Travel* Magazine. I also sold three cover stories to *Diversion*, the travel magazine that is marketed to medical doctors. I made many sales to airline in-flights, too.

Travel-Holiday once gave me an assignment based on a terrific two-week press excursion in Malaysia. It began in what we called "KL" – Kuala Lumpur – then continued all the way up the east coast and finally over to Penang, with its rusty remnants of British nineteenth-century colonial days.

I always thought of (and often wrote about) Penang as the Singapore or Hong Kong outpost that didn't make it. I remember its many paint-peeling former British mansions surrounded by large weed-covered gardens.

In the famous "snake temple" there, I got up close and personal with snakes known elsewhere as the Wagler's pit viper. Scores were hanging around inside the building, all supposedly kept docile by some kind of constant smoke in the air. For a photo, I even held one of these sleepy creatures that supposedly had been de-venomed – although I'm not all that sure it was.

A few years later I visited Penang again during a stopover while traveling on a luxury train between Bangkok and Singapore. I was always intrigued with the venerable E&O (Eastern & Oriental) Hotel, which was apparently unchanged since the days that Somerset Maugham visited. (Recently, I've seen photos indicating that it has apparently been gussied up similarly to the overdone Victoriana now layered on at the Raffles Hotel in Singapore.)

After President Nixon's 1972 visit opened up China for Americans, that country was soon available for travel writers too.

First, Sara and I were on a short airline inaugural to Taiwan and Hong Kong. While at the latter, we discovered there we could buy an all-day tour into mainland China (called Communist China in those days). It consisted of a quick hydrofoil ride to the Portuguese enclave of Macao and then a tour bus trip into the mainland as far as Cuiheng, which had been the childhood home of Dr. Sun Yat-sen. This wartime Chinese patriot was revered in both China and Taiwan. He also had spent some quality time in Hawaii. Thus I had a local angle for the *Advertiser*.

On the way, the bus stopped at a small village where the guide said the mayor was especially proud of his "mice wine." I thought he was having a little trouble with pronunciation.

"You mean 'rice wine,'" I corrected him gently, knowing that Chinese sometimes have trouble with English consonants.

The guide found the mayor and he held up the bottle saying that any of us could taste a sample if we wanted.

I don't recall that anyone did. But I took a close-up photo as he held the bottle. At least half of the container was indeed filled with the tiny babies or perhaps embryos of bleached mice, their tiny eyes closed forever while enclosed in the transparent lime-colored beverage.

The *Honolulu Advertiser* used the photo in black-and-white. The Chicago *Tribune* used it larger and in full color.

The story got good play with headlines such as "How to visit three Chinas in four days" (meaning Taiwan, Hong Kong, and mainland China.)

A short time later, I was on a one-week airline press tour in Singapore, when our escort suddenly announced that he had received a special invitation, and those who wanted could extend for another week in China, beginning in the topographically interesting Guilin area. This featured an area then practically unknown by foreign travelers. In my article in *Honolulu Magazine,* I called it the "Land of the Gum Drop Mountains." It sold again later to *Recommend,* a magazine directed to travel agents.

From time to time, other Chinese opportunities were especially welcome. Except for the food, only a small portion of which I could manage, China afforded some great experiences.

In 1997, I was invited to take part in a cruise on the Yangtze River, in which there was considerable interest because the new Three Gorges Dam was just beginning to be constructed. The world's largest hydroelectric project was to control the annual flooding of the river and to provide cheap electrical power and would take 10 years to complete. This was controversial even in China, since the Yangtze would be raised at least 300 feet. It required the evacuation of one entire city and many other areas, and several cultural treasures would also be inundated.

The cruise began in Chongqing and finished in Shanghai. At one port call along the river, Shashi, we visited the Jingzhou museum. There we saw the perfectly preserved body of a 2000-year-old man in a bleach-colored liquid. It's a long story, but he didn't look much different from the bodies in the mice wine.

The cruise resulted in good copy and good photos, and a chance to see some more areas of the country not available on the routine Beijing – Great Wall excursions then being run for Americans. (The story sold seven times. One version, as printed in the Spokane *Spokesman-Review*, is still on my web site.)

I've always regretted not being invited to take the same cruise again on the Yangtze River now that it is flowing at its new height. Those who have, however, say it is still a worthwhile experience.

By 1988, I had completed arrangements with my Louisiana publisher to have others update future editions of my three Maverick guidebooks, while I continued to collect royalties. By this time, I was traveling often and churning out travel articles on destinations all over the Pacific. However I did the update myself again for what turned out to be the very last edition of the *Maverick Guide to Hawaii*. It was published in 2002. With that, all three of my Mavericks were taken out of print, all casualties of the Internet.

At some point, I began corresponding with Eunice Riedel, whom I had known as Temple Fielding's last editor at William Morrow & Company in New York. Together we came up with the idea for me to do a guidebook to Alaska under the Fielding imprint. The only person who might have objected to that was Temple himself, who had always wanted his name to be associated with Europe alone. But he had died a few years before.

I always wanted to have my name on a Fielding guide. I began some reading and soon realized that the area logically should be expanded to include not just Alaska but the adjacent Yukon Territory of Canada. It shared a historical bond and mutual cultural identity with Alaska dating at least from the Gold Rush days in 1898. After I made a couple of quick scouting trips to the far north, William Morrow & Company offered a $10,000 advance against royalties to do a book called *Fielding's Alaska and the Yukon*. That seemed like a lot of money in the 1980s.

Traveling to the important, yet often remote, destinations over this vast area was going to be a challenge. I was going to need a lot of help from Sara, who quit her hospital nursing job so she could come along on the main research trip – a road-trip experience in June, July, and August of 1988. Basically, we agreed that she would do most of the driving (Kiwis tend to be car nuts anyway), and I would handle the maps, take pictures, collect literature, and write notes.

We leased a large Oldsmobile station wagon in Washington State and started our drive north connecting with the Yellowhead Highway through British Columbia to Prince Rupert, where we could drive our car onto the Alaska Ferry. Prince Rupert turned out to be a surprisingly interesting town, and we ultimately created a separate chapter for it, even though it was neither in Alaska nor the Yukon Territory.

We then took the Alaska Ferry to traditional tourist stops in Southeast Alaska, the "panhandle" portion of the state, rolling our car off and on the ferry at ports such as Wrangle, Petersburg, Ketchikan, Sitka, and the capital at Juneau. With the Olds we could easily explore scenery and tourist facilities in these islands and other land-locked areas not connected to the continent. And we often picnicked with food carried in the back of the commodious car.

At Skagway, we left the ferry system to continue on land routes hitting the towns on the Alaska Peninsula, then Anchorage, Denali National Park, Fairbanks, then taking a tour bus clear up to Prudhou Bay (where independent driving was then prohibited), and flying to no-road places like Nome, Kotzebue, Katmai National Park and the Pribilof Islands in the Bering Strait. We also drove on the Alaska Peninsula to Seward and Homer, the end of the road.

From Fairbanks we drove the summer-only Top of the World Highway into the Yukon Territory to Dawson City and Whitehorse, and continued down the Alaskan Highway south into the U.S. mainland again. I also made a couple of flying trips from Hawaii in the winter time, even checking out the skiing possibilities at Alyeska near Anchorage and another ski area near Juneau.

Back home, for the first time I wrote the entire book on my latest computer, with Microsoft Windows. (The machine itself was built by Sara's brother, Ian Cameron.) It seemed almost a magical convenience at the time. (It was considerably easier than today with my then relatively young, unbent fingers.)

And in the process of all this activity, Sara and I discovered that we liked the wild world of Alaska so much that we seriously considered moving there. We finally changed our minds – not so much because of the challenging climate but more because of the relatively short periods of daylight in the winter.

Nevertheless, for several years after our big trip, we often took the opportunity of returning to Alaska, including going on at least three cruises. We also dodged a bear or two in a time or two. (Anyone who spends any time in Alaska simply *must* come back with at least one bear-encounter story.) I also sold several Alaska stories to newspapers and magazines.

The book itself was a success for the company but a money-loser for us. We did have excellent reviews, with one exception – sort of. That was from *Alaska* magazine, which seemed to believe that no one from "Outside" could really understand and appreciate the complexities of the Far North. In a list of several Alaska guidebooks in print that year, they gave us a grudging first-place ack-nowledgement as "the best of a bad lot."

Over the years, I have often run across those who wonder how someone from somewhere else can presume to understand and explain their own particular domain. I can only repeat what other travel writers have said.

"The patient may change, but the operation remains the same."

As for the disappointing financial rewards, we couldn't have done it without that 10 grand advance. But later we calculated that it cost us more than $15,000 in expenses.

At about the same time the book went to press, William Morrow & Company sold the Fielding imprint to an independent entrepreneur who apparently was not interested in continuing the Alaska/Yukon book. Thus, our little labor of love received no promotional activities at all, and unlike all our other books, there was no updated edition.

And this time no one asked us to the ABA convention of 1990.

On top of that, our contract had been negotiated by a literary agent for the first time. She overlooked the fact that instead of the 15% royalties for books sold in the U.S., the amount was only about 3% for foreign sales.

And wouldn't you know, the book sold very well in Canada. Sniff!

Nevertheless, Sara and I had a wonderful time doing the research. We had some breathtaking visual experiences, discovered some terrific wild life, met some great people, and the on-the-road portion of the work – hard as it was – turned out to be one of the most satisfying experiences of our lives while discovering America's "last frontier." I tried to reflect some of that in the introduction to the book. In part:

> To many of us, the romantic notion of the frontier disappeared soon after the mid-1800s, when the Spanish were driven out of California and the Indians began to move to reservations. Horace Greeley told us to go west, and so we did. There we met up with the Pacific Ocean, built Disneyland, and that was that.
>
> No one told us to go north. In fact, lots of folks cautioned against it. Yet, in the latter half of the nineteenth century while many weren't looking, the American frontier took a sharp right turn. A few with the gumption to live on the cutting edge of society followed. Most did not.
>
> There was one big exciting difference with this new frontier – somehow it never quite came to an end. Although a few good roads were built and Hershey bars followed apace, Alaska remains a place where moose are a definite traffic hazard and bears have discovered they love chocolate as much as does any backpacker.
>
> You will find out for yourself that in many ways the last frontier is still there today. It's no secret to the sourdoughs who live, work, and play in or near the wilderness areas of Alaska and northern Canada. ... It is still waiting to be discovered by millions of us *cheechakos* who have a special appreciation for unbridled nature and a robust past...

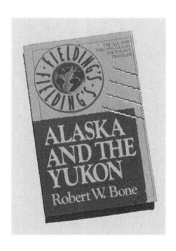

1991: A total eclipse of the sun in Hawaii, as seen from on-board
a cruise ship. (Photo by Bob Bone)

54
Heavenly Days

FOR A TIME, I MANAGED to hold onto the Time-Life stringership for Hawaii, even though I was no longer working at the *Advertiser*. I had that mantle when I received the invitation to experience a natural phenomenon – the total eclipse of the sun in Hawaii on July 11, 1991 from on board a cruise ship.

Actually, this involved two old ships, the *Independence* and the *Constitution*, which were operated by American Hawaii Cruises. In the press contingent, this turned out to be quite a party. An old *Advertiser* pal, Rick Carroll, was covering it for United Press International, my old outfit from the late '50s. In the 1990s, however, UPI was no longer a conventional wire service, concentrating on various kinds of feature stories. Several other writers and other friends were also on board.

Although we didn't know it then, American-Hawaii's days were numbered, too. Its two aging ships were originally launched in the 1950s, and they were only kept in service because as American-built (not foreign-built) passenger vessels, they were legally allowed to travel from one American port to another without stopping at a foreign port en route. This made them ideally suited for the multi-island Hawaii cruise. (I had already traveled several times on AH's regular interisland cruises prior to the eclipse one.)

Time magazine virtually ignored my resulting eclipse coverage, which was not surprising. (Too bad it didn't happen on the East Coast.) However in time I wrote other stories in other years based on the experience. This included the following in the travel section of the *Miami Herald,* which diligently covered Latin American tourism. It was printed in advance of another solar eclipse, which would take place in the Caribbean later that year.

Part of my solar story:

Now we're not talking about a namby-pamby "partial" eclipse. Seeing a partial is like drinking half a beer, or going out on a heavy date and sneaking only a pleasant goodnight kiss.

A total eclipse of the sun is the ultimate, the zenith, the apex of this kind of experience. No one who has ever seen one can really tell you what it's like. Some have described it as akin to dying and being born again.

Of course the basic facts sound mundane. The path of the moon places it in front of the sun for a few minutes. During that time, you can safely look at the sky with or without binoculars to see a black orb surrounded by the sun's corona – a ring of fire with occasional licks of orange and red flame.

(At times other than during the period of totality or in areas where only a partial eclipse is visible, you must view the event through special dark filters in order to protect your eyes. Residents of southern Florida will see only a partial eclipse this time.)

All who witness a total eclipse seem to feel it in a deeper part of their soul. It's frightening, it's beautiful, it's totally awe-inspiring as it shakes a part of the psyche far removed from our logical frontal lobes. You can feel some of the fear that folks in ancient times must have felt – those who were not armed with the scientific information that we have today…

Part of the tantalizing nature of a total eclipse is that being in the right place at the right time does not always ensure that you will have the complete experience. Clouds and other variations in local weather patterns can drift across the sky at just the wrong moment.

Hundreds were disappointed in 1991 when crowds of scientists and others gathered on the Big Island of Hawaii – directly in the path of totality – but saw nothing more than a temporary dimming of their surroundings while a mischievous cloud hovered overhead. Others, perhaps only a mile away, were treated to the whole enchilada.

The fortunate few talked of birds beginning to roost, and of stars appearing. Many gasped as a dark velvet glove seemed suddenly to be cast over the entire world – a glove that seemed for a moment to wear a gleaming diamond ring.

My own experience that day was fortuitous. I was aboard one of two cruise ships then operated by American Hawaii Cruises. As the hour of totality approached, their captains were also worried about clouds gathering in the area. But using their radar, the ships were able to navigate to a clear portion of the sky

I saw the menacing shadow approach us across the water at breakneck speed and then suddenly we were captured in a sort of deep twilight, seemingly held in the shadow's grasp as all on the deck gasped or shouted. I was so taken by the enormity of the experience that in three minutes I only managed to take one decipherable photograph. It showed the other ship, its lights suddenly visible while our own passengers on two decks were silhouetted against a gray sky with the mysterious black but shining orb above.

But no photograph, and perhaps no verbal depiction of the event, could do justice to the experience itself. Later many of us spoke to those who had been positioned at various points on land to see the "partial" eclipse. They had found it "interesting." But none reported the same heart-stopping, almost religious experience of those of us who had a clear, unobstructed view in the path of totality.

My article concluded with some notes about the location of future solar eclipses including: "Residents of the continental United States will be able to view a total solar eclipse perhaps without leaving home in August 2017."

That sounded like a long way off in the 1990s. Now I'm looking forward to it – totally. (I'll be 84, with any luck.)

For the rest of the century, and a few years more, life was rewarding, both at home and on the road. After returning from our Alaska adventure, Sara began working in the operating room of Shriners Hospital for Children in Honolulu, which she continued doing for the next 20 years.

The mission of that wonderful institution was to scour the Pacific islands and other areas to find children badly in need of orthopedic medicine. Many of them had afflictions, some as simple as club feet that would have been caught and fixed at earlier ages if they had been living in the U.S.A. and other more-developed countries. Some had one leg shorter than the other, which could now be gradually corrected through controlled artificial breaks and the application of an Ilizarov bone-growth device.

We have been grandparents since 1989 and foster parents since 1998. After he came to live with us at age nine, our foster son was diagnosed with Asperger's Syndrome, which challenged us to see that he had a good education and that he was no longer bullied by his peers. With a lot of our effort and valuable help by knowledgeable contemporaries, everything eventually came out just fine. Both our grandson Harley, and our former foster son Robert, are now young adults and continue to live and work in Hawaii.

The Internet came along in the mid 90s, and like other writers, especially travel writers, I saw it as possibly a wonderful new way for us to broadcast our stories and photos.

And for a while, it was. In those years I briefly had a column on America On Line, and AOL happily bought my stories and photos resulting from trips to all parts of the world. I was especially proud of my "Elephant Walk in Zimbabwe," where I got to know a particular family of elephants living in Mana Pools National Park.

The matriarch, whom rangers had named Agatha, even flapped her ears and false-charged us once. It was just a brief warning to get out of the way while she led the rest of her family for a swim in the Zambezi River. (Some of these old stories are still on my website, robertbone.com, which I first built in 1996, and which is still alive nearly two decades later.)

Speaking of Africa, I jumped at the chance to visit South Africa, once apartheid was finally eliminated there. This was an incredible trip, conducted by Peggy Bendel of DCI (Development Counsellors International) in New York. Most press trips I have taken consist of around six to a dozen participants. Peggy managed to wrangle no less than 50 journalists, which even included a couple of TV news crews. My subsequent story and photos were carried in at least a dozen newspapers.

A few years later I was included on two more great trips with DCI, one to Argyle and Mull in Scotland, the other to Tasmania. Both resulted in good, salable stories.

When I think of the 1990s, however, besides the solar eclipse, I remember Hawaii's second major storm, Hurricane Iniki, which struck on September 11, 1992. It was the most powerful hurricane to strike the Islands in recorded history.

Just like Hurricane Iwa 10 years earlier, the storm again ravaged the island of Kauai, leaving the other islands pretty much alone. I was on Oahu in Honolulu, and reports from Kauai were at first sketchy and sporadic since normal communications were destroyed. The airport was damaged and no planes would be landing or taking off for days. That evening, however, I received a phone call from Tony Bartlett, Honolulu correspondent for *Travel Weekly*, a news-magazine for travel agents.

"Come on Bone!" he said. "I've got a ride to Kauai for us tonight on the Navatek!"

The Navatek is an unusual type of twin-hull vessel that normally was used for dinner cruises out of Honolulu. The owner had called the local radio stations and announced that his boat would take as many relief supplies as it could and would leave at midnight for the battered island 100 miles away. It would then evacuate tourists and refugees and bring them back to Honolulu.

Throughout the rest of the evening many Honolulu grocery stores and private individuals brought to the dock whatever they thought Kauai residents might immediately need. It was a totally unscientific and amateur operation, taken before any official relief efforts could get organized and underway.

I called the *Chicago Tribune* and got the go-ahead for a news story but was given a strict deadline for the next afternoon. When we sailed from Honolulu, surprisingly the only news people on board were Tony and I, plus one two-man TV crew from San Francisco. Not even the two Honolulu papers, the *Advertiser* or the *Star-Bulletin*, managed to get any reporter or photographer on board before we cast off. (Although the *Advertiser's* resident Kauai correspondent, Jan TenBruggencate, was on-scene.)

We tried to sleep on the bare deck among all the groceries and medical and hardware supplies but it was hopeless. We got to the battered island at first light and found so much waterfront destruction it was all the Navatek captain could do to tie up to a dock. The nearby road was so littered with downed power lines and other debris that the only vehicle waiting there was a rugged Hawaii National Guard Humvee.

In time, however, the supplies were unloaded and it was announced that any person on board the boat could go ashore. But due to some health restrictions they would not be allowed to re-board and return to Honolulu. The San Francisco TV crew left, to experience whatever adventures might await them. Tony and I did not, realizing that on an island with no electricity there would be no way to get a story out for some time.

Then we picked up about 400 passengers, nearly all of whom were visitors to the island. Most of these tourists had been staying at one of the luxury hotels badly hit by the storm. There was no air service and this boat was the only way they were going to leave and get out of the way of local residents trying to recover from the storm.

On the way back to Honolulu, we started interviewing the tourist refugees about their travails. All had stories to tell about having to flush their toilets with buckets of sea water in the dark, etc.

In my case, aware of my assignment, I was often asking, "Who here is from Chicago?"

The upshot however was that the boat didn't make it back to Honolulu in time for me to make my *Chicago Tribune* deadline. Nevertheless, once we docked I did manage to get my story off to some other newspapers, notably the *San Diego Union Tribune*.

It came out the following day with lots of quotes from people who lived in Chicago.

An early digital camera captured Bob Bone on a Mexican ATV.

55
Technology
on the Half Shell

IN EARLY 1994, THE INTERNET as we know it today was still
around the corner. Hardly anyone had seen anything that might have
been called a website.

Digital cameras were still to come, but digitized color
photographs – at least those that could be converted from slides –
were hot stuff, and I was working with them on my computer.
Nevertheless I still was not able to service my clients with illustrations
in the same way as I was with words.

But with the help of the *Miami Herald*, I made a technical
breakthrough. Practical aspects of the accomplishment were heralded
soon after in an article in the *Cole Papers,* a newsletter that covered the
technology of newspaper publishing. The April 1994 edition was
headlined "Freelancers need to learn to join the digital photo
revolution."

Cutting out most of the geek speak, it read in part:

> For freelance travel writer Robert Bone, sending his first color
> photograph from his home office in Hawaii to the *Miami Herald*
> was *déjà vu* all over again.
>
> Back in the early 1980s, Bone was the first journalist in the
> Hawaiian Islands to transmit freelance news and travel stories
> electronically from his Xerox 820 (remember when 64 kilobytes of
> RAM was the standard?) to mainland publications.

Like all pioneers, Bone faced enormous difficulties at first. Often, editors – to whom he had repeatedly shipped copy from the RCA Telex office in Honolulu – hadn't a clue as to how to receive a freelance story electronically. The usual drill was to find a key person at the newspaper who understood modems, transmission parameters and story headers. Then Bone and he would painstakingly figure out how to get a story to pop up on the target editor's VDT. (Video Display Terminal.)

"It was an educational challenge for everyone at first," Bone recalled. "Eventually we worked through the problems." Today, Bone is a master self-syndicator. He routinely transmits travel stories via modem to as many as 40 U.S. and Canadian newspapers. Many travel editors have come to rely on Bone for quick turnarounds on Hawaiian topics. If only his picture turnarounds could be as quick.

Now Bone is tackling the same kinds of challenges he faced in 1984 as he again blazes a trail by sending his first color images electronically from his personal computer in Oahu.

"It seems like history is repeating itself," said the 61-year-old author, former newspaper reporter and magazine editor who turned to full-time freelancing more than a decade ago. "When I call up editors today and offer to send a picture into their system, they'll sometimes say, 'You can do that?'"

Bone has mastered the technology with little help....

"The main purpose of the whole thing has been to support my writing," said Bone, author of four guidebooks (on Hawaii, Australia, New Zealand and Alaska). "The idea is to sell my travel stories, and pictures help sell a story. That can only increase my income potential."

The day will come, too, when his library of thousands of photos taken in Hawaii, across the Pacific and in Asia is digitized and available online. Such an electronic stock photo operation "has the potential to really help my business," he said....

So far, Bone has transmitted one photo successfully to the *Miami Herald*. It illustrated a story that developed from a Mediterranean cruise he and his daughter Christina took last year. (An attempt to transmit to the *Chicago Tribune* was unsuccessful.)

The Herald sale developed through a classic situation faced by freelancers every day: Travel Editor Jay Clarke needed a photo within hours to illustrate the story Bone had submitted two weeks earlier. Without an illustration, Clarke told Bone, the story could not be published...

"It came across perfectly the first time," recalled Bone. "It was then that I realized I had mastered the process. I was very happy."

Indeed, all that was terrific while it lasted. But just around the corner the wide acceptance of the Internet would rapidly turn much of this into just a quaint tale of technology in an earlier time.

And that same Internet was going to make everyone a writer and photographer, and ultimately suck the profits from thousands of talented individuals. Moreover it would contribute to the slow destruction of several newspapers in the U.S. and Canada. Many that survived reduced the size of their travel sections, or eliminated them entirely.

During the period of the *Cole Papers* article, I was already into digital photography – in a crude way. I was taking my favorite travel slides to a Kodak photo counter at a nearby mall and having them turned into digitals and burned on a CD-ROM disk. Afterward I could edit them on the computer, improving contrast, color balance, etc., and perhaps even taking a more drastic step such as removing annoying elements like utility wires which sometimes ruined the look of my potentially prize-winning creations.

One day in the late 1990s, I conducted an experiment. I took one of the first webcams around and pointed it toward Blackie, and somehow captured a still impression of my cat stretched out on the rug. The photo was crude, but recognizable. Wow – a photo made without film!

Soon after, I began looking at a new invention being offered at the local Computerland – the digital camera. After much research, I swallowed hard and shelled out 600 hard-earned bucks to buy a nicely designed Epson PhotoPC 800, a modest 2.1-megapixel digital camera after somehow convincing Sara that it just might pay for itself some day.

After a mad rehearsal of sequentially shooting and dizzily deleting (impossible with a film camera, of course), I carried the new possession with me to the February 2000 meeting of the Western Chapter of the Society of American Travel Writers taking place at Cabo San Lucas on the Baja Peninsula in Mexico.

I was the only writer or photographer at the meeting who had such a device – one which some of my professional colleagues took to be some kind of an expensive toy, and not a serious tool for a true professional. But the resulting photos were sharp, clear and bright, and they remain so still today.

As part of that meeting, I learned to drive an ATV on a sandy beach. At one point, I handed my Epson to a colleague, asking him to grab a shot of me with my helmet, bandana, and other paraphernalia while astride my vehicle.

Using my portable computer with its slow, built-in modem, back in my hotel room that same day, I hooked it up to the telephone and sent that photo to the computers of my wife in Honolulu and to my daughter in New York.

As soon as I returned to Hawaii, I wrote a letter to a public relations representative for Nikon, asking him to lend me one of their more sophisticated – and even more expensive – digital Nikon Coolpix 950s to take with me on an upcoming research trip to Australia. They agreed, sent it, and off I went.

The resulting story – "How to Travel with a Digital Camera" – using photos from both those trips was soon carried in the travel section of several newspapers. It subsequently won a prize after it was printed in Denver's *Rocky Mountain News*.

I thought Nikon should have offered to let me keep the camera after all the publicity I gave it, including photos of the unusual wasp-waist camera itself. They offered only a $100 discount to buy it, which I accepted.

And even with both those cameras, the articles pretty much paid for them. I gave the Epson to my son, and that trusty Nikon still serves as a backup to the more modern digital cameras I use today.

Almost as soon as I began using digital cameras, the Kodak CD scanning service I was using went out of business. I still have those disks, however, and occasionally I have sold a photo from them. My thousands of pre-1990s slides? Well, some more well-known professional photographers have digitized their entire massive collections. In my case, I have done that to a few. Other slides I may end up giving to some kind of institution.

56

Keep On Keepin' On

HERE'S AN UNSOLVED MYSTERY: Also in 2000, an Italian film-maker named Silvana Zancolo gathered a small group of actors together and produced a motion picture. The title was "Bob Bone, Turista e Clandestino."

Before you ask, I plead guilty to being a tourist sometimes, but never a spy. I have no idea what that was all about, and I had nothing to do with it. It is simply an intriguing coincidence. Ditto for my father, another Bob Bone, and whose Italian language abilities when he was alive were not much better than mine.

I would have liked to have seen the film, though – if only to see if the eponymous *clandestino* also had a gap between his front teeth.

In the '80s and '90s, I almost perfected the art of resales. That is, I attempted to find travel stories that never – or almost never – go out of date. One story like that was the "Waterfalls of Hawaii." Indeed, I think it has been used in about a dozen different publications – maybe more.

What could go wrong? It's not even seasonable, since folks visit Hawaii's waterfalls winter or summer. Actually, I did have to update it at some point. One of the featured falls managed to kill some people during a flash flood. Since it looked as if it might happen again, the state government closed the park and the trail leading to it.

Another story that sold every spring was "Summer in Hawaii." It was a good angle since Hawaii's summers with its cooling trade winds are, by and large, more gentle than many mainland summers. It sold over and over again in Canada, in lots of small newspapers – some of which still haven't gotten around to paying me for it. The story was accompanied by my photos of Hawaiian tropical flowers.

But the granddaddy of this type was my article on Olympia, Greece, the location of the original ancient games. You would think that would sell every four years, but you'd be wrong. It sold every *two* years for quite some time. On winter Olympics years, I merely changed the lead paragraph saying something about the fact that Ancient Greeks competed in the nude, and that they would not have thought very highly of winter sports as a result.

The Olympia experience was also an example of getting more stories out of a cruise than just the cruise itself. And as time moves on, cruises seem to be the answer for more story material. I now welcome the occasional ocean-going opportunity when one sails my way. I've had some especially enjoyable cruises on Crystal, Holland-America, Royal Caribbean, Norwegian, Princess, and others. Some smaller vessels were also excellent, notably those run by Windstar and Voyages to Antiquity.

Unfortunately, many American travelers limit their cruise choices to Alaska, the Caribbean, and the Mediterranean. Some of the most rewarding experiences are now in the Pacific and Asia. Three Sara and I will never forget were a Norwegian coastal sailing with Celebrity, a long Pacific Islands cruise (Hawaii to New Zealand) with Crystal and an Asian coastal experience with (despite the name) Royal Caribbean. The latter went from Hong Kong to Singapore via Bangkok and other exotic ports. All provided me with sales of articles and/or photography.

At the end of the latter cruise, we managed to stay a few days extra in Singapore, which provided me with both newspaper and magazine article sales.

After more than two decades of self-syndication, the opportunities for my kind of operation began to dwindle in the Internet age. For a time I also worked with the small New York headquartered Travel Arts Syndicate run by Terese Kreuzer. I really liked the way she handled my copy, but there were other difficulties that made that impractical, too.

One way or another, I've hit just about all the places in the world I've wanted to hit, and had generally good experiences in all.

Probably the most luxurious press trip in my career took place in 2001. Sheila Donnelly, Hawaii's premier travel PR professional, then had the publicity contract for the Oberoi Hotel chain in India. Sheila made up a blue-ribbon list of a half-dozen well-known travel writers – plus me.

The more prestigious attendees included Rudy Maxa, who then had a regular National Public Radio program (*The Savvy Traveler*) and several TV presentations, Keith Bellows, head honcho of *National Geographic Traveler*, Anthony Dias Blue, the famous LA radio-TV wine guy, and Sheila's new husband, no less a literary heavyweight than Paul Theroux, author of an amazing number of highly regarded if egocentric books. There were perhaps a couple of other intellectual highrollers whose names I have forgotten. I felt terribly honored to be included in the group.

As indicated earlier, Sara and I had made a brief visit to India in 1968, our sensitive feelings assaulted by its poverty. But this trip would show me the better half of India while staying in the top-drawer Oberoi resorts at all stops along the way.

We traveled on several different conveyances, including buses, rickshaws, jeeps, private town cars, elephants, and even the Oberoi family private airplane. We saw the best of Delhi, Agra, Jaipur, and Shimla and lots in between, with occasional showers of rose petals, and private dance performances.

We had some dramatic and unscheduled experiences, too. When our bus was blocked by a farmers' demonstration in the countryside, Rudy Maxa pleased the protesters by interviewing and recording some of them explaining their problems. Still our bus could not pass.

Then the owner of the hotel chain, Biki Oberoi, sent a squadron of town cars to rescue us on the other side of the blockade. We made our way across the barricade on foot to board the cars, although our luggage had to stay behind with the bus for the time being. That evening we went to a reception and dinner at the Oberoi family hilltop mansion, every one of us wearing the white Indian Kurta pajamas that had been provided us for the occasion.

From what I had read, I was fully prepared not to like Paul Theroux. I had known Sheila before he did, and those of us in Hawaii who admired her knew that as smart as she was, she had had some romantic disappointments. We feared the marriage would be a disaster.

But my thoughts about Paul changed when I got terribly sick to my stomach – not from Biki Oberoi's hotel kitchens, of course, but from something I ate when we visited a private home. Somehow I also felt ashamed, worried about holding up the group, etc. But it was Paul who put me at ease:

"Don't worry," he said gently. "Until you've been sick, you haven't been to India."

Paul was a gentleman but not a wuss. At some point, he acquired an unusual souvenir – a kind of a flute apparently made from a human femur. Like Hunter Thompson's "human skin lamp," it was something I would not have chosen. And then there was my childhood aversion to flutes in general.

Nevertheless, Paul's kind comment helped me immensely. (He was obviously an Elevator Bank Number Two guy.) And I'm glad to say that Sheila and Paul remain happily married to this day.

Further, my India articles and photos also sold to several publications.

And again, Grandma – Just as you said – everything came out for the best in the end.

EPILOGUE

THE *HONOLULU ADVERTISER* SURVIVED another 25 years after I said goodbye to it in 1984. But like so many good dailies in the new century, it ultimately folded. It lives on in name only as part of its one-time rival, now called the *Star-Advertiser*, which now has no meaningful competition.

During the years we lived in Hawaii, we often saw old friends who passed through the Islands. Howard Rausch came twice, and we managed to visit him at his new home in Boston, too. He died in 2005 of a melanoma. Malcolm Browne never made it while we were there, but we saw him and his wife Le Lieu again early in the new century on a New York visit. Mal died in 2012 of Parkinson's.

Don and Penny Hinkle arrived a couple of times to look after kids and cats while Sara and I were working some far away destinations. And we managed to attend the New Jersey wedding of one of their daughters in between adventures in Ecuador and Turkey. Orah and the twins came by on their way to live in Saipan. Suzie (Susé) Moyal visited too, on a separate trip.

Many others with whom I had had long talks and soul connecting sessions in the past breezed in and out with the trade winds, all pleasant diversions without our relating on the deeper levels we often enjoyed in the past. Then when high school and blister-rust camp buddy Dick Clark and his family sat on our couch in Lunaai Street, our tabby cat, named Cueball, jumped up on Dick's lap and quietly but effectively farted.

As awful as that was, it was also funnily reminiscent of 1951 when five young guys crammed into a ten-year-old Chevy Club Coupe for a 5000-mile trip to the west. Once again, our groans were mixed with laughter.

As for Hunter, his letters became less frequent over the years. Instead, I would receive the occasional phone call, always sometime after midnight. Drunk, stoned, or sober, he was almost always easy to talk with.

I think, too, that he was happy to speak with someone from a time when he was a very different person – someone who was not awed by his eccentric public persona.

We met in person one last time. He came to cover the Honolulu Marathon for ESPN.com in December 2001, showing up with Sean Penn, with whom he was talking about a movie based on one of his books. We met up in Waikiki, and – no surprise, I guess – he looked terrible. I asked him if he realized that he rocked back and forth when he sat down, and he didn't answer me.

We took some photos. Hunter raised his hand, I think in an attempt to make the Hawaiian "shaka" sign. Instead, he seemed to confuse it with Star Trek's "Live Long and Prosper" gesture – and he didn't get that quite right, either.

Three years later, his pains were apparently too much. HST was dead by his own hand. In a tribute on my website, I recalled some words by Boris Pasternak, whose grave we visited in Russia:

"The writer is the Faust of modern society, the only surviving individualist in a mass age. To his orthodox contemporaries, he seems a semi-madman."

-30-

P.S. Many of the articles and photographs mentioned in this memoir and more may be found on two websites, robertbone.com and travelpieces.com, and my latest email address is given there, too. In 2008, after living nearly 38 years in Hawaii, Sara and I sold our house in Kailua and moved to the Bay Area of San Francisco. Like many senior citizens, we have been operating at a more halting pace lately. However, we did traverse the Aegean on the water and on the web in 2012. And in 2013, I sold and then wrote a daily blog on a rewarding cruise around the tip of South America. We're not done yet.

Hunter Thompson, Bob Bone, and Sean Penn in Honolulu.

INDEX

NOTE: Page numbers in **bold** refer to photographs or illustrations.

Dear Reader:

I hope you enjoyed reading these stories of rocks and roses garnered during my long career, along with my words of appreciation of others whose lives touched mine over some eight decades. I had fun writing these accounts. It was less fun pruning them down to a practical number to include in a single volume.

You will find more about the subjects covered in *Fire Bone!* if you follow the leads in the personal web sites I've had for several years, robertbone.com and travelpieces.com. I have also posted several photographs directly related to this book, some of which were not included in these pages.

Thousands of readers and travelers familiar with the Maverick guidebooks that I began while working with the Pelican Publishing Company wrote me with comments and suggestions over several years. I received other reactions forwarded to me from the newspapers and magazines that carried my articles. I really miss reading those letters, and I hope this volume generates some more today. My current email address can be found on robertbone.com.

Also, if this book has struck you favorably, I would especially appreciate it if you would write a few sentences on the *Fire Bone!* page on Amazon. You can easily find it by going to my author page at https://www.amazon.com/author/robertbone, scroll down and click on the *Fire Bone!* title.

Aloha

Bob Bone